Art and Archaeology of Challuabamba, Ecuador

Art and Archaeology of Challuabamba, Ecuador

By Terence Grieder

Professor Emeritus, History of Art, The University of Texas at Austin

with

James D. Farmer

Chair, Dept. of Art History, Virginia Commonwealth University, Richmond

David V. Hill

Archaeological consultant, Denver, Colorado

Peter W. Stahl

Professor of Anthropology, SUNY, Binghamton

Douglas H. Ubelaker

Curator of Physical Anthropology, Smithsonian Institution, Washington, D.C.

UNIVERSITY OF TEXAS PRESS ⬩ AUSTIN

Copyright © 2009 by the University of Texas Press
All rights reserved
Printed in the United States of America
First edition, 2009

Requests for permission to reproduce material from
this work should be sent to:
    Permissions
    University of Texas Press
    P.O. Box 7819
    Austin, TX 78713-7819
    www.utexas.edu/utpress/about/bpermission.html

∞ The paper used in this book meets the minimum requirements
of ANSI/NISO Z39.48-1992 (R1997) (Permanence of Paper).

Library of Congress Cataloging-in-Publication Data

Grieder, Terence.
  Art and archaeology of Challuabamba, Ecuador / by Terence
Grieder ; with James D. Farmer . . . [et al.]. — 1st ed.
       p.   cm.
  Includes bibliographical references and index.
  ISBN 978-0-292-71892-0 (cloth : alk. paper)
1. Challuabamba Site (Ecuador). 2. Cañari Indians—Ecuador—
Cuenca—Antiquities. 3. Indian pottery—Ecuador—Cuenca.
4. Effigy pottery—Ecuador—Cuenca. 5. Pottery figures—
Ecuador—Cuenca. 6. Indian seals (Numismatics)—Ecuador—
Cuenca. 7. Excavations (Archaeology)—Ecuador—Cuenca.
8. Cuenca (Ecuador)—Antiquities. I. Title.
  F3722.1.C2G75 2008
  986.6'24—dc22
                                        2008039552

CONTENTS

This book reports the results of excavations at Challuabamba, in Ecuador, during the years 1995–2000. It brings together studies by a group of specialists working independently and cooperatively to present a view of this ancient site. When someone looking at the pictures asked why all the pottery was broken, I realized that an explanation was needed. Most of the pots were broken in use or crushed in burials long ago. Restoration of ancient pottery is a time-consuming project for specialists. Our project promised to leave every artifact with the Ecuadorian National Institute of Cultural Patrimony, taking with us only our notes, drawings, and photographs. Our photographs show pots which have been washed and given a minimum restoration with water-soluble glue, to give observers the basic idea. For museum display they will need to be disassembled and rebuilt by experts with adequate time and techniques for that work.

The principal funding for the Challuabamba project came from re-search funds of the David Bruton Jr. Professorship in the History of Art at the University of Texas at Austin, augmented by substantial gifts from Dana DeBeauvoir and an anonymous donor. The zoo-archaeological study by Peter Stahl was supported by the National Science Foundation (BCS-0130588). The Instituto Nacional de Patrimonio Cultural del Ecuador authorized these studies each year from 1995 to 2000. Dra. Mónica Bolaños expedited that process, under the supervision of Ldo. Carlos Guerrero B., the national director. The regional director in Cuenca, Srta. Mónica Zabala D., supervised our work and archaeologist Byron Camino participated in the work as inspector for the institute. Archaeologist Antonio Carrillo represented the institute and made a valuable contribution to the work.

The 1995 excavation was made on the property of Francisco Chimbo, who permitted the work and took an interest in it. In the following years (1996–2000), the excavations were made on the neighboring property of the Jaramillo family through the kind permission of Juan Pablo Jaramillo.

In 1995 the Texas group consisted of Senja Foster and Elizabeth Jenkins, graduate students at the University of Texas, Dagmar Grieder, and the project director (Terence Grieder), with a faithful local crew of Teresa Balarezo and members of her family, who continued in the following years. In 1996 the participating Texas students were Bradford Jones, Yvonne Rocha, and Mark Brignole. Manuel Guayas also joined the crew. In 1997 James Farmer joined us, bringing students Maria Naula and Julie White from Virginia Commonwealth University; and in 1998 Bradford Jones, Terence Grieder, and Antonio Carrillo supervised the work. Laboratory analysis occupied a larger share of the time each year.

In 1999 the GPR-magnetometer survey was conducted by Mark Willis and Joe Brandon. Cuts 4 and 5 were based on that survey.

Terence Grieder owes special thanks to Steven Wille, Carlos Vintimilla, Doña Costanza di Capua, and Lic. Mariella García de Parra, the director of the Center of Archaeological and Anthropological Studies at the Escuela Superior Politécnica del Litoral (ESPOL) in Guayaquil. Karen Stothert was very helpful in facilitating our analyses at her archaeological laboratory in Cautivo, Ecuador. As project organizer, Terence Grieder appreciates the dedicated work of his colleagues in the production of this report.

James Farmer gratefully acknowledges support from the University Grant-in-Aid Program for Faculty, Virginia Commonwealth University.

Peter Stahl thanks Antonio Carrillo, José Luis Espinoza, Ross Jamieson, Michael Muse, and Mariana Sanchez for their help in Ecuador and Felix Acuto and Josh Trapani in the United States. AMS radiocarbon dates of the excavated bone material were generated by the University of Arizona National Science Foundation (NSF)–Arizona Accelerator Mass Spectrometry Laboratory with the help of Greg Hodgins. Many thanks to John Lundberg of the National Academy of Sciences in Philadelphia for confirming the catfish identifications and to the staff of various departments in the American Museum of Natural History, specifically Linda Ford (Herpetology); Rad Arrindell, Barbara Brown, and Scott Schaefer (Ichthyology); Ross MacPhee, Jean Spence, and Rob Voss (Mammalogy); Peter Capainolo and Shannon Kenney (Ornithology); and Gene Gaffney (Paleontology).

Introduction to the Project

Today Challuabamba (*chī-wa-bamba*) is a developing suburb of Cuenca, the principal city in the southern highlands of Ecuador (Figure 1.1). The old farmsteads that once composed the village are being replaced by large suburban houses, and even the Pan-American Highway along the north bank is being superseded by a new four-lane divided highway on the south bank. The bridge over the Tomebamba River, just seven kilometers downstream from the site of our excavations, is a vital link in a wide network of roads leading north to Riobamba and Quito, west to the coastal plain and Guayaquil, and south to Cuenca and beyond to Peru or eastward to the Amazon basin. This is not an invention of modern transportation systems but follows what must have been ancient trails along an array of rivers and streams that join to drive a gorge through the eastern foothills of the Andes on their way to the Amazon. Challuabamba sits near the junction of these ancient trails.

Challuabamba has been known as an archaeological site for nearly a century since Max Uhle's work there in the 1920s. In an interview in 1962 with a Quito newspaper the archaeologist Edward Lanning described the site in these words: "From a professional point of view, Challuabamba is the most fantastic site in the world, since the ceramics one encounters there in unbelievable quantities are extremely fine" (*El Comercio*, September 1, 1962; my translation). My interest in Challuabamba was stimulated by the results of my previous studies in the highlands of northern Peru. At the preceramic site of La Galgada, occupied c. 2800–1800 BC, we had found carved stone bowls, textiles which revealed the progression from looped and twined to heddle loom construction, and the first traces of pottery about 2000 BC (Grieder et al. 1988:185). At Pashash, in the same province, we had unearthed very fine Recuay style pottery and jewelry of gilt arsenic bronze, dated between AD 300 and 600. While both La Galgada and Pashash had large stone buildings in styles unknown in Ecuador, the pottery and textiles showed techniques developed ear-

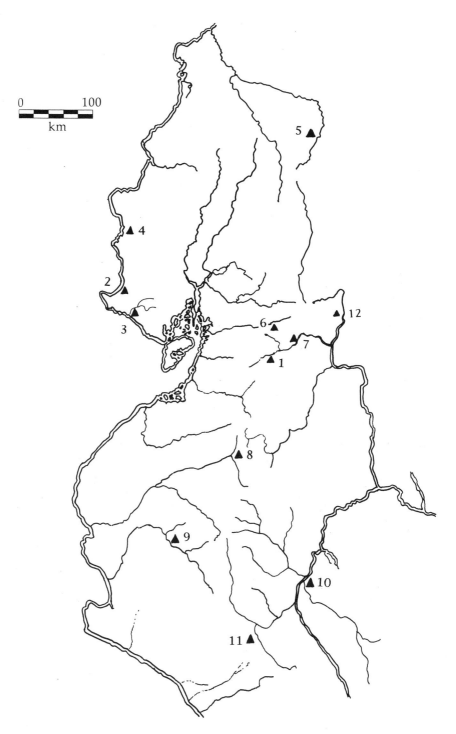

Figure 1.1. Ecuador and northern Peru, with the locations of archaeological sites and modern cities mentioned in the text: *1*, Challuabamba; *2*, Valdivia; *3*, Real Alto; *4*, Machalilla; *5*, Cotocollao; *6*, Cerro Narrío; *7*, Pirincay; *8*, Catamayo; *9*, Cerro Ñañañique; *10*, Bagua; *11*, Pacopampa; *12*, Macas.

lier in the Valdivia culture of coastal Ecuador (Marcos 1979). Challuabamba, in the Ecuadorian highlands on the eastern slope of the Andean cordillera, looked like the ideal location to search for links in the chain that led to La Galgada and Pashash. In 1995, with research funds from the University of Texas, I undertook a series of small excavations along the banks of the Tomebamba River on the site of Challuabamba (Figure 1.2). (Those place-names, given after the Inca conquest of the 1480s, are in the Quechua language: *tome* or *tumi* [axe], *challua* [fish], and *bamba* [field].)

The area along the river is in the cool, rainy highlands, at about 2,300 m (7,545 ft) above sea level at Challuabamba. Flowing east from lakes near the crest of the Andes, the Tomebamba River joins a group of highland streams to form a major Amazon tributary, and its waters eventually reach the Atlantic Ocean, some 3,400 km (roughly 2,100 miles) to the east.

Figure 1.2. The Tomebamba River at the Challuabamba site in the drought year 1995.

Inhabitants of the Tomebamba Valley can reach the Pacific Ocean much more easily, crossing a low pass toward the southwest and following the Jubones River about 130 km down the steep Andean escarpment to the shores of the Gulf of Guayaquil. Although only 300 km south of the equator, the surrounding regions provide almost all the varieties of natural environments, from sandy desert to tropical rain forest, from ocean beach to frigid tundra.

A visitor looking for ruins at Challuabamba will be disappointed, for there are few signs on the surface of ancient life, only grassy meadows, old farmsteads, a modern highway, and the beginnings of suburban development. Nevertheless, the valley has been the site of a series of important archaeological studies.

Previous Studies

While the archaeology of Ecuador's coastal lowlands has been intensively investigated during the last fifty years, the southern highlands are still in a relatively early stage of exploration. Max Uhle (1922b:108) was the first to write of the archaeological resources of Azuay Province, including "the unexpected discovery of great treasures," followed by "a period of frantic search of the whole region" between 1856 and 1899. The result was the destruction of the ancient tombs and "everything they contained, only the gold being saved" (see also Salazar 1995:143–155). Uhle's work at Challuabamba remains the most important account of the site. Uhle (1922a:206), long familiar with Peruvian sites, was inspired by his reading of H. J. Spinden's study of the Maya and believed that he had found a civilization founded by the Maya in the interior of Ecuador. While the Maya connection has not found acceptance (Collier and Murra 1943:90), Uhle's definition of a "Chaullabamba [sic] civilization" occupying nearly all the Ecuadorian highlands south of 2 degrees south latitude (the Río Chanchan) and parts of the western lowlands has remained influential. In this report we return to the correct spelling (according to the Ecuadorian Instituto Geográfico Militar) of the site name to distinguish it from the archaeological materials gathered under the rubric "Chaullabamba civilization," which are still mostly hard to assign a specific location or period.

The exploratory studies made by Max Uhle are fundamental to the work that followed, though the diffusionist theory that inspired Uhle has been proven wrong. Donald Collier and John Murra (1943), at the end of their studies at Cerro Narrío (about 20 km north of Challuabamba), made a survey of collections and archaeology of the Cuenca area. The close relationships among the ancient peoples of those neighboring areas have always been clear, and Wendell Bennett's (1946) excavations along the Tomebamba River carried on the work of Collier and Murra. The ceramic typologies established by Collier and Murra and Bennett have served as models for later investigators.

Several archaeologists have studied Formative sites in the area in recent years, and studies in other nearby districts offer comparative data (Figure 1.3). Elizabeth Carmichael, Warwick Bray, and John Erickson (1979) found some material closely related to Challuabamba in the Jubones Valley, and Carmichael (1981) obtained radiocarbon dates from Challuabamba as part of that larger study focused on the Jubones River. Mathilde Temme (1999) has made extensive studies of Putushío, near the headwaters of the Jubones, in the highlands south of Challuabamba, while Jorge Arellano (1994, 1997) has studied early settlements with ceramics at Loma Pucara in the Cebadas Valley, to the north between Cuenca and Riobamba. Pirincay, 20 km downriver from Challuabamba, has been excavated by Norman Hammond and Karen Olsen Bruhns (1987), by Bruhns (1989, 2003), and by Bruhns et al. (1990, 1994) (and see Miller and Gill 1990). With a long sequence of building, ceramics, and craft specialization, Pirincay shows important connections both with the Pacific lowlands and with the Upano River Valley in the Oriente (eastern lowlands), mainly during the first and second millennia BC. Dominique Gomis (1989, 1999) has published studies of Challuabamba ceramics, and her work is also presented in Anne-Marie Hocquenghem et al. (1993). Her analysis, based on different criteria, provides a useful check on our work and seems to represent the same early period in the history of the site. Her early period is referred to by Michael Tellenbach (1998:305) as "Apangora [sic]" (Abangora), the creek that enters the river on the Vasquez property about 500 m east of our excavations, where traces of excavation remain. Jaime Idrovo Urigüen (1992, 1999) refers to Gomis's work at the site and proposes a larger picture of Formative developments in the region. References to these studies are made throughout this report. The Challuabamba ceramic collections are particularly closely related to those from Pirincay and Cerro Narrío.

When we map out the locations of previously published studies in the Tomebamba/Paute River system it becomes evident that these valleys have been an important focus of archaeological interest during the twentieth century. It is clear that we are still far from a complete picture of that society and its history. Its region may have extended from Cerro Narrío in the north to at least the Jubones Valley

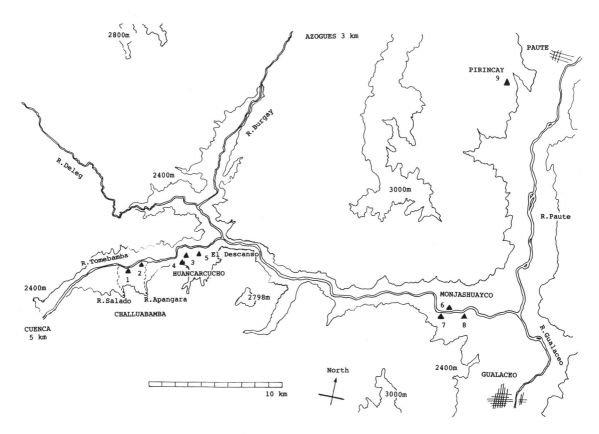

Figure 1.3. Archaeological sites in the Tomebamba-Paute River area: *1, 2,* Challuabamba; *3, 4, 5,* Huancarcuchu; *6,* Monjashuayco; *7,* El Carmen Alto; *8,* El Carmen Bajo; *9,* Pirincay.

in the south. It may have been united by a common language, as it was by Cañari in Inca times, as well as by ceramic and other artifact styles. In this study we can present only an account of the remains recovered at Challuabamba, but wider comparisons are offered to suggest the range of cultural interaction.

The Present Study

For as far as human records and memories go back, the autochthonous population of the provinces of Azuay and Cañar has been the Cañari people. They dominated most of the territories of the modern provinces of Cañar, Azuay, and Loja and the northern coastal region of El Oro before AD 1400 and only lost the parts of Loja south of the Jubones River to their sometime allies the Jívaro (or Shuar) in the 1400s. In the hierarchy of Cañari chiefs, the chief ruling at Tomebamba was considered paramount; when the Inca Empire conquered the region in the 1480s, it became an important city and received its Quechua name. Emperor Huayna Capac (reigned 1493–1524) was reported (by Betanzos 1996 [1557]:121, 182) to have been born at Tomebamba, on the site now occupied by the city of Cuenca, which he endowed with monuments and sacred sites that established its rank as equivalent to that of Cuzco. Fiercely independent, the Cañari welcomed the Spanish invasion and joined Francisco Pizarro's forces against the Inca. After the fall of the Inca Empire in 1533 the region became part of the Spanish colonies. An early Spanish document describes fishing as an important occupation in the Tomebamba Valley (Murra 1963:799), and the inhabitants of Challuabamba (Fish Field) are supposed to have paid their taxes in fish from the river.

After discussing contacts and similarities between Formative Peru and Ecuador, Richard Burger (2003:481) concluded that "despite these similarities and linkages, the world of the Ecuadorian Formative appears to have been profoundly different from that of the Central Andes in terms of its economic organization, its sociopolitical structure, and ideological frameworks that made life comprehensible and meaningful." Different attitudes about their social group, leadership, and the possibilities open to them as individuals are evident in the patterns of habitation and production in Ecuador compared with their contemporaries in Peru. The Challuabamba project was conceived as a way to explore the Ecuadorian version of Formative life and art.

Excavation is the only way to obtain specimens of ancient art in their original cultural context. Too often we are dependent on the excavations of treasure-hunters who have no interest in the artifacts beyond their market value and provide no useful information about the provenience of their finds. The Challuabamba excavations were undertaken to contribute to filling a gap in the art-historical record of the north Andean highlands. The resulting sample consists of over 63,000 potsherds and about a dozen nearly complete ceramic specimens, another dozen stone carvings, traces of building foundations and wall materials, evidence of seven burials, and a very large collection of animal bones. Based on the stratigraphy and other contextual evidence we can put much of the sample into a temporal sequence, assign it approximate dates, and show its technical and design relationships to other sites. While we have a little evidence of social rank, we are not in a position to speculate about social organization in general. But the material provides a good record of technical, design, and expressive achievements during a crucial period in the history of the region.

It was not only research in Ecuador that focused archaeological interest on that country, for Peruvian preceramic and Initial Period sites have long yielded materials with Ecuadorian connections: *Spondylus* shell in preceramic levels, unquestionably imported from Ecuador, followed by early loom weaving, evidently practiced earlier in Ecuador (Marcos 1979), and ceramics, probably inspired by Valdivia pottery in Ecuador made centuries earlier (Grieder et al. 1988:1, 16, 189–190, 197).

A general picture of cultural development in South America has been forming since about 1950. One of the important advances was the making of ceramics. As in the case of the other major technical achievements of Pre-Columbian South America in textiles and metallurgy, ceramic products were valued for both utilitarian and expressive purposes. With our present knowledge we can make some generalizations about the sequence of those technical advances: looped and twined textiles invented by preceramic societies, ceramics spreading through the tropical lowlands before 4000 BC and down the Peruvian coast and into the Andean highlands by about 2000 BC, and the earliest experiments with metalwork, which seem to have occurred about 1500 BC (Burger 1992:127).

Although Challuabamba's climate is too damp for the survival of textiles and our excavations show no signs of metalwork, introduction of ceramics from sources on the Ecuadorian coast and relationships with other early pottery-making sites are manifest in the excavated materials. On the basis of this general picture we can hypothesize that much of the material in our excavations was produced during the second millennium before the modern era.

The present study emphasizes art and the development of the Formative culture that fostered it. Two radiocarbon assays of wood carbon that we collected at Challuabamba gave dates in the range 2300–1700 BC (calibrated), which encouraged us to continue our search there for early participants in the developmental surge implied by its name, Formative Culture.

The Excavations

In June 1995, having obtained the approval of the Ecuadorian National Institute of Cultural Patrimony in Quito and Cuenca and accompanied by the Ecuadorian archaeologist Antonio Carrillo, our small crew began some preliminary examination of the south bank of the Tomebamba between two small tributary streams, the Salado and the Abangora. The area consisted of pleasant meadows and woods, with some modest houses of local farmers interspersed with a few fine new houses of the emerging suburbs. The site is bordered on the north by the river and on the south by hills, with a huge construction project at the base of the hills, where a highway and water treatment facilities for the city of Cuenca are being built. The only hint of ancient construction was lines of river boulders visible in the upper levels of the riverbanks; in places potsherds were eroding from the bank, testifying to an ancient occupation. In my notes I identified the common pottery type as Cerro Narrío Red-on-Buff, a Formative type named at the site about 20 km north that had been studied by Collier and Murra (1943). This, we concluded, was part of ancient Challuabamba. In the following days, accompanied by Antonio Carrillo as the local representative of the national archaeological administration, I made an agreement with the landowner, Francisco Chimbo, to make small excavations into the river terrace on his land.

The project's first year was designed to obtain a stratigraphic profile to sterile soil and gather some information about the lines of stones eroding from the upper levels. The 1996 field season moved upriver about 100 m to the Jaramillo property, through the courtesy of Juan Pablo Jaramillo. Two excavations were laid out at the edge of the terrace, designated Cuts 2 and 3 (Figure 1.4). In subsequent years the upper levels between Cuts 2 and 3 were expanded to reveal the

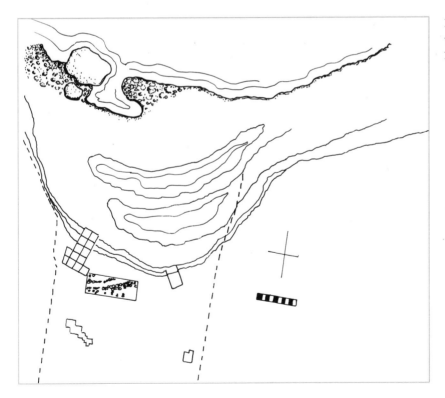

Figure 1.4. The locations of our excavations, 1996–2000.

late walls. Cuts 4 and 5, made in 2000 following magnetometer and ground-penetrating radar (GPR) mapping in 1999, were exposures intended to examine late floor and wall patterns. The excavations reassured us of the integrity of the deposits, which showed no evidence of having been subjected to looting or prolonged flooding. Although erosion had occurred at the edge of the terrace, and perhaps between some stratigraphic levels, the main body of the terrace was intact, with horizontal strata and no interruptions in the sequence of cultural deposits.

Cut 1 is shown in plan and section (Figure 1.5). The location was selected on the basis of a line of river boulders appearing near the surface of the terrace and a fairly deep vertical terrace wall showing numerous potsherds. The eroded bank was cut to reveal the strata in a 3 m wide vertical profile to establish the depth of cultural deposits (1.6 m) and an exposure 1.5 × 5 m was laid out parallel to the edge of the terrace 1 m south of the profile.

Figure 1.5. Plan and section of Cut 1.

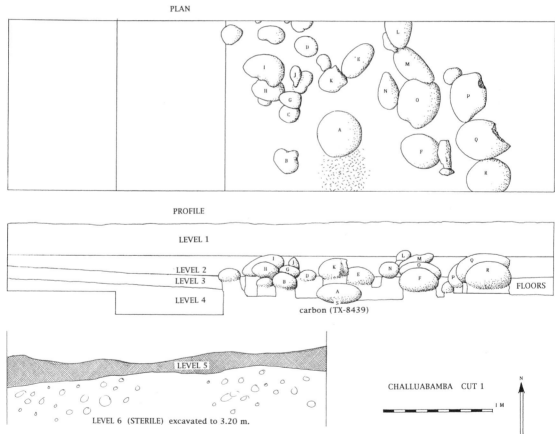

Art and Archaeology of Challuabamba, Ecuador

Cut 2 was a 3-m square at the north edge of the terrace, excavated in 1996–1997 (Figures 1.6 and 1.7). Five cultural levels are defined (the sixth is sterile base). The upper level contains several fragments of modern glass along with abundant ceramic, lithic, and bone debris. The later of two layers of river cobbles occurs at about 50 cm. A layer of smaller cobbles lies at about 70 cm. The larger upper layer is associated with four shallow pit burials (Burials 1–5) with offerings. While the upper layer seems associated with the burials, neither layer shows a definable building pattern. Level 3 has two layers of ash and charcoal, and in Level 4 we encountered the only good post-mold in our excavations (about 37 cm deep), with no trace of the post but with a large Red-on-Cream potsherd lying in the bottom. Level 5 shows some ancient excavation, with the very light soil of Level 5 resting on top of a layer of dark Level 4 material.

Cut 3 is shown in a plan, a section, and a view. Located about 20 m west of Cut 2, it is the largest area and the deepest of our excavations. Figure 1.8 shows a plan of the excavation and a synthetic section from the north (the river side) into the trench, with the south

Figure 1.6. The north profile of Cut 2 (1996).

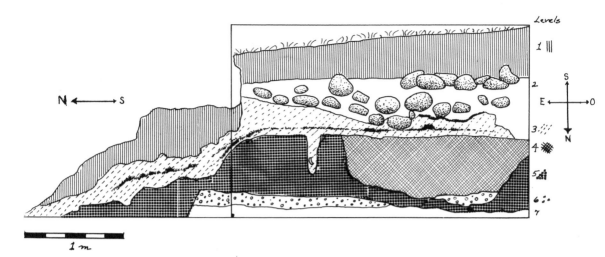

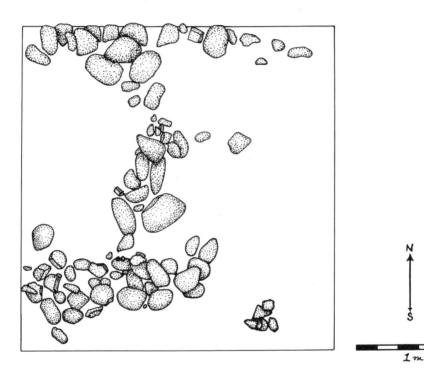

Figure 1.7. Plan and profile of Cut 2.

wall of Sector G in the center, the east wall of the trench on the left, and the west wall on the right. Each sector is 2 × 2 m. The depth of the cultural deposit is 2.1 m in seven natural strata in the trench (Sectors A–J) (Figure 1.9). The remaining area of Cut 3 (Figure 1.4) was excavated only to the base of Level 2 to reveal the pattern of the stones.

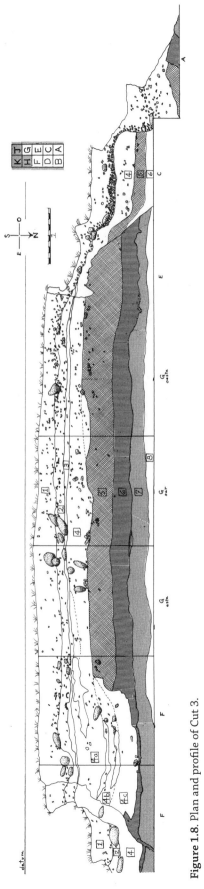

Figure 1.8. Plan and profile of Cut 3.

Figure 1.9. Photograph of Cut 3 trench: Sector F on the left and E on the right. Numbers indicate levels.

Level 1 in Sector L contained a bed of bone debris about 1 m square near the surface, with the remains of a butchered deer. The bones had all been cooked or burned and broken into small fragments, except for a larger piece of antler. The materials suggest a small group feast, with an unusually fine bridge-spout bottle (Figure 4.16) broken in the debris. Levels 3 and 4 of Sectors E and G contained small fragments of bone and fine potsherds that were interpreted as evidence of disturbed burials; and in Sector H at the base of Level 4 and in the surface of Level 5 were two intact burials (Burials 6 and 7) with offerings. In Sector F there are signs of ancient excavation in Level 4 into Levels 5 and 6.

An area about 8.5 × 19 m was exposed to the base of Level 2 to trace the large stone walls (Figure 1.14). The parallel lines of river boulders are about 2 m apart, running northeast-southwest. The eastern end of the southern wall appears to be a massive revetment for a low platform. These late constructions are discussed below.

Cuts 4 and 5 were excavated in 2000 following magnetometer and ground-penetrating radar mapping of the meadow area in 1999, which suggested stone constructions in those areas. The small stone lines in the center of Figure 1.11 may have lined a stockade wall or perhaps a small canal. A later large-stone wall is at the left (Figure 1.10).

Cut 5 was also in response to the magnetometer/GPR study and showed traces of two levels of walls and a series of fragmentary floors, the deepest at 60 cm, with traces of small stone lines. Traces of burning show on the mud floor under the east wall. On top of the small stones are a line of larger river boulders at about 50 cm depth. They appear to be part of a structure of which two pieces of floor remain: one with numerous traces of burning and carbon deposit, the other packed brown adobe (Figures 1.12 and 1.13).

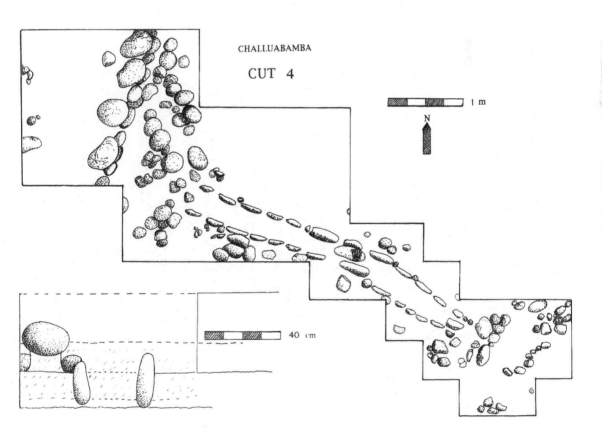

CHALLUABAMBA

CUT 4

1 m

N

40 cm

Figure 1.10. Plan and section of Cut 4.

Figure 1.11. View of Cut 4 looking east, showing stone walls.

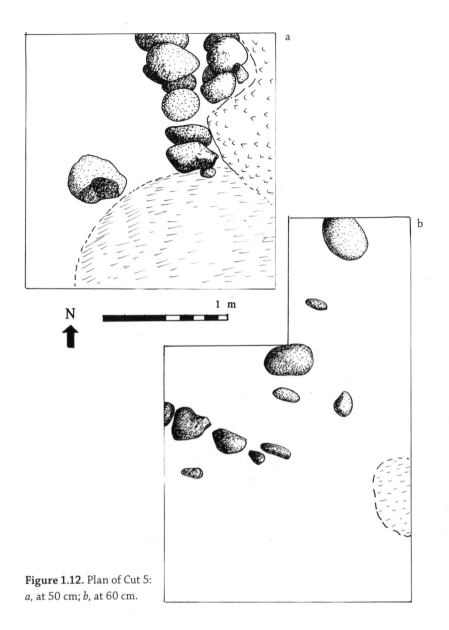

Figure 1.12. Plan of Cut 5:
a, at 50 cm; *b*, at 60 cm.

N

1 m

Figure 1.13. Section of Cut 5.

Stone Used in Building

The most obvious traces of ancient occupation on the site are the clusters of waterworn boulders from the river evident in the eroded face of the upper terrace of the riverbank. The largest on average measure about 50 cm in their longest dimension. Their appearance in lines high above the riverbed is an indication that they were carried there by human beings. While boulders were moved by periods of strong current, the patterns of stones seen in the riverbed have nothing in common with those above the riverbank. Excavation reveals that lines of stones are found only in the upper half of the deposit and can be separated into an earlier style using smaller stones averaging 30 to 40 cm in their longest dimension and a later style using larger boulders (Figures 1.14 and 1.15). Both periods of building are apparent in the photograph of Cut 4 (Figures 1.10 and 1.11), with parallel lines of small stones in the deeper area (about 60 cm) and a row of larger boulders stacked across the near corner, representing the latest period.

Max Uhle (1922b:207–208; my translation) refers to "foundations, formed generally of river stones, which still show the outlines of their ancient buildings," which he saw in Challuabamba, Huancar-

Figure 1.14. Cut 3: stone walls in Levels 1 and 2 (in areas L, K, J, I, etc.).

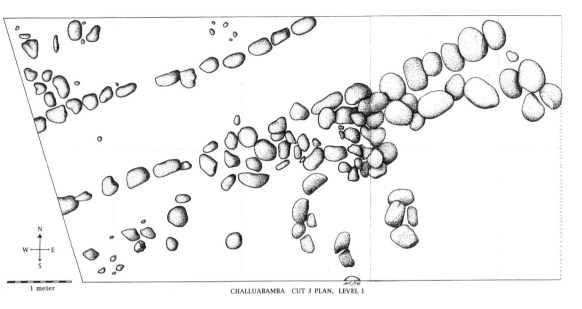

CHALLUABAMBA   CUT 3 PLAN, LEVEL 1

1 meter

Figure 1.15. Plan of the late-period walls.

cuchu, and Carmen, all sites that could be considered part of what we might call "greater Challuabamba." Gomis reported (in Idrovo Urigüen 1999:119) house foundations in Challuabamba made of river boulders in circular and rectangular patterns. These alignments had a long tradition behind them. The earliest examples currently known are in the upper Zaña Valley, in northern Peru, where stone-framed earth platforms bearing cane and daub domestic structures date from the period 6000–4000 BC (Dillehay, Netherly, and Rossen 1989).

Although no platforms are known to survive intact, there is good evidence for a sequence of building practices. Earliest to appear are chunks of dried mud bearing the imprints of posts and cords which indicate the erection of walls of *bajareque* (wattle and daub) (Figure 1.16).

Found in the lower parts of Level 4 of Cut 3, the chunks of mud show that the walls were substantial and solid, with a smooth layer of about 3 cm of mud on the surface and a total wall thickness of more than 10 cm. The smaller stones that appear in Levels 2, 3, and 4 seem to have been used along the base of *bajareque* walls. They were superseded by the large stone alignments, which appear to have supported earthen platforms for buildings. Small areas of packed clay floors survive in all the excavations, presumably interior floors which had some protection from the weather and erosion.

Figure 1.16. Mud plaster (*bajareque*), Cut 3.J Level 4. Note cord marks and shape of wooden post.

The development from house floors at the same level as the exterior earth surface, separated from the ground outside only by a stockade wall with small stones set along its base, to a floor set on an earth platform about 20 or 30 cm thick supported by a double or triple range of large stones along its margins, with the stockade wall heavily plastered with mud, seems to have occurred during Level 2. Such a raised floor would have been drier than the earlier floors that were level with the ground outside, and the plastered walls would have provided shelter from wind and rain.

The patterns of stone, especially in Cuts 2, 4 (Figure 1.11), and 5, suggest continual building, demolition, reuse, and rebuilding, with stones being thrown aside as walls were taken down then often recovered and reused at the edge of floors or bases of walls or buried in fill as a new platform was leveled. The riverbanks seem to have been favored places for building (more so than even a short distance back from the river), for cultural deposits are deeper nearer the river and the evidence of rebuilding is greater.

The building remains found by Jean Guffroy (1987: Plates 15, 16) at La Vega, Catamayo, south of Azuay on the headwaters of the Chira River system, are the most similar to the Challuabamba remains and particularly to the later lines of large stones, the principal difference being the source of the stones: a quarry at La Vega and the riverbed at Challuabamba. At Cotocollao, in contrast, many postholes were found but no rock alignments (Villalba 1988:41–59). The single good posthole identified at Challuabamba and the numerous pieces of mud plaster with post-molds suggest that the walls there were similar to the *quincha* (*bajareque*) walls that Guffroy (1994: Figure 22) shows for Cerro Ñañañique, on the upper Piura River in northern Peru, although those later constructions were not based on stone revetments.

Radiocarbon Dating

We have tested ten specimens, selected because they seemed likely to provide secure points in the stratigraphic sequence. To reach the closest approximation of a calendar date requires the use of the calibrated calculation, given here in the 68% calibration. They are given in order from earlier to more recent. The first five, TX numbers (University of Texas and University of Washington laboratories), are radiocarbon tests on burnt wood; the second five, AA numbers (University of Arizona), are accelerated mass spectrometry (AMS) dates on animal bones selected from the storage collection.

The AMS dates were taken from specimens of animal bones selected by Peter Stahl from Cut 3, Sector G, and submitted to the University of Arizona laboratory. They give dates that confirm the integrity of the stratigraphy but run about four hundred years later than the wood carbon series (Tables 1.1 and 1.2).

The AMS dates correlate most closely with four dates obtained by a team from the British Museum led by Elizabeth Carmichael. Although the samples were assigned to the Challuabamba site, the details of the excavations and information on the samples have not been published. The calibrated dates range between about 1100 BC and 950 BC (Carmichael 1981:176). While the TX series suggests a sequence of about 800 years, the AA series suggests about 350 years. This discrepancy is not unusual. For example, among the 55 radiocarbon tests reported by Marcelo Villalba O. (1988: Figure 136, pp. 242–243) for the site of Cotocollao, the thirteen tests on human bone all fall between 805 and 450 BC (uncalibrated), while the wood carbon samples date between 1545 and about 545 BC.

Table 1.1. Radiocarbon Dates on Wood Charcoal

Laboratory #	Age (Radiocarbon Years before Present)	Calibrated (68%) Years	Excavation Location
TX-9241	3530±72 BP	2334–1744 BC	Cut 3.H Level 4
TX-8439	3950±200 BP	2334–1709 BC	Cut 1 Level 4
TX-9027	3200±60 BP	1510–1390 BC	Cut 3.B Levels 1–3
TX-9026	3160±50 BP	1470–1370 BC	Cut 3.A Levels 1–3
TX-9025	3130±60 BP	1460–1340 BC	Cut 2 Level 3

Table 1.2. Accelerated Mass Spectrometry Dates on Bone

Laboratory #	Age (Radiocarbon Years before Present)	Years	Excavation Location
AA55501	2947±49 BP	cal. 1260–1230 BC	Cut 3.G Level 5
AA55500	2972±47 BP	cal. 1300–1110 BC	Cut 3.G Level 4
AA55499	2768±49 BP	cal. 980–950 BC	Cut 3.G Level 3
AA55498	2734±49 BP	cal. 920–825 BC	Cut 3.G Level 2
AA55497	2704±49 BP	cal. 900–815 BC	Cut 3.G Level 1

Austin Long and his colleagues (1989:231) of the Arizona laboratory discuss methods for obtaining reliable AMS radiocarbon dates from bone, noting that "bone dates often elicit undisguised skepticism and rebuke." Their analysis of the problem applies particularly to Challuabamba:

> Fresh bone containing protein (mostly collagen) and inorganic minerals (primarily apatite), when exposed to moist oxidizing conditions will begin to change in response to its environment. The protein will, with the help of water and micro-organisms, oxidize and degrade to smaller, more soluble molecules. Water flowing through the system will help remove both organic and inorganic components of the bone, leaving a porous, high-surface area structure. This inorganic structure can adsorb organic matter produced in the soil, which would most likely be younger than the bone and have a different ^{14}C content.

This comment comes from the Arizona laboratory that tested the Challuabamba bones. Since the prevailing system of dating to which Challuabamba must be compared derives almost entirely from dates based on wood carbon, it seems most reasonable to make our comparisons on the basis of that system.

A series of excavations by natural levels cannot be expected to show a similar series of levels, since each location will almost certainly have its particular history. The two oldest (and nearly identical) dates both come from Level 4 (the top of that level in Cut 1 and the bottom of the level in Cut 3), which suggests that those deposits represent the same period. Those two dates (calibrated) imply that Level 4 in both locations was deposited around 2000 BC.

The midpoints of the other three calibrated dates (1450, 1425, 1400), all associated with Levels 3 and 2, suggest that those levels were deposited around 1400 BC. All three of those dates are based on wood carbon collected in two excavations about 25 m apart, with some common stratigraphy. All five of our excavations have stone revetments in the upper levels, which can all be dated in the period 1400–1200 BC, judging by these three radiocarbon dates. A diagram of the comparative stratigraphic levels of the excavations with the locations of the carbon samples makes the general chronological picture somewhat clearer (Figure 1.17). Returning to Cut 1, if Level 4 was deposited in the early 1700s BC and the stone revetments were built in the 1200s BC, the 25 cm of Level 3 would represent about 500 years—surely an indication that considerable material had been eroded in ancient times. It is also clear that erosion from the surface has removed all deposits later than about 500 BC, with the black clay

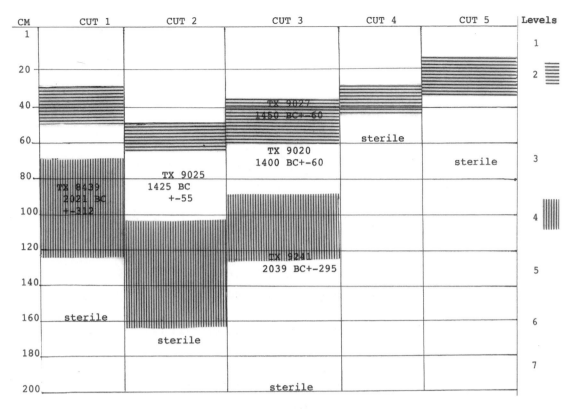

Figure 1.17. Comparative stratigraphy with radiocarbon dates. Levels 1, 3, 5, 6, and 7 are unmarked. Level 2 has horizontal shading; Level 4 has vertical shading. Dates are the midpoints of 68% calibrated dates.

of Level 1, containing a mixture of ancient potsherds and modern glass, having been laid down in modern floods. It is significant that there is no evidence of flooding below the surface level; all the earlier levels have friable soil containing little clay but much undisturbed cultural material.

Bibliography

Arellano, Jorge

1994   Loma Pucara: A Formative Site in the Cebadas Valley, Ecuador. *Research and Exploration* (Washington, D.C., National Geographic Society) 10(1):118–120.

1997   Loma Pucara: Un asentimiento de Formativo Tardío en el valle de Cebadas, sierra central del Ecuador. *Fronteras de Investigación* 1(1):78–100.

Bennett, Wendell C.

1946   Excavations in the Cuenca Region, Ecuador. Yale University Publications in Anthropology, No. 35. New Haven: Yale University Press.

Betanzos, Juan de

1996 *Narrative of the Incas.* Translated and edited by Roland Hamilton and
[1557] Dana Buchanan. Austin: University of Texas Press.

Bruhns, Karen Olsen

1989 Intercambio entre la costa y la sierra en el Formativo Tardío: nuevas
evidencias del Azuay. In *Relaciones interculturales en el área ecuatorial del
Pacífico durante la época precolombina,* ed. J.-F. Bouchard and M. Guinea,
57–74. British Archaeological Reports, International Series 503. Oxford: BAR.

2003 Social and Cultural Development in the Ecuadorian Highlands and
Eastern Lowlands during the Formative. In *Archaeology of Formative
Ecuador,* ed. by J. S. Raymond and R. L. Burger, 125–174. Washington,
D.C.: Dumbarton Oaks.

Bruhns, Karen Olsen, James H. Burton, and George R. Miller

1990 Excavations at Pirincay in the Paute Valley of Southern Ecuador,
1985–1988. *Antiquity* 64:221–233.

Bruhns, Karen Olsen, James H. Burton, and Arthur Rostoker

1994 La cerámica incisa en franjas rojas: evidencia de intercambio entre la
sierra y el oriente en el Formativo Tardío del Ecuador. In *Tecnología y
organización de la producción de cerámica prehispánica en los Andes,* ed.
Izumi Shimada, 53–66. Lima: Pontificia Universidad Católica del Perú,
Fondo Editorial.

Burger, Richard L.

1992 *Chavín and the Origins of Andean Civilization.* New York: Thames and
Hudson.

2003 Conclusions: Cultures of the Ecuadorian Formative in Their Andean
Context. In *Archaeology of Formative Ecuador,* ed. J. S. Raymond and
R. L. Burger, 465–486. Washington, D.C.: Dumbarton Oaks.

Carmichael, Elizabeth

1981 Datación mediante el carbono 14 de muestras de carbón de sitios de
cerámica fina provenientes del altiplano del Ecuador. *Revista de Antropología* (Cuenca, Núcleo del Azuay de la Casa de la Cultura Ecuatoriana)
7 (November).

Carmichael, Elizabeth, Warwick Bray, and John Erickson

1979 Informe preliminar de las investigaciones arqueológicas en el área de
Minas, Río Jubones, Ecuador. *Revista de Antropología* (Cuenca, Núcleo
del Azuay de la Casa de la Cultura Ecuatoriana) 6 (July): 130–144.

Collier, Donald, and John Murra

1943 *Survey and Excavations in Southern Ecuador.* Anthropology Series 62.
Chicago: Field Museum of Natural History.

Dillehay, Tom D., Patricia J. Netherly, and Jack Rossen

1989 Middle Preceramic Public and Residential Sites on the Forested Slope of
the Western Andes, Northern Peru. *American Antiquity* 54(4):733–759.

Gomis, Dominique

1989 La alferería de Chaullabamba. *Catedral Salvaje* (supplement to *El Mercu-
rio*) 24:4–5 (11 June).

1999 La cerámica Formativa Tardía de la sierra austral del Ecuador. In

Formativo sudamericano: una revaluación, ed. P. Ledergerber-Crespo, 139–159. Quito: Abya-Yala.

Grieder, Terence, Alberto Bueno Mendoza, C. Earle Smith, Jr., and Robert M. Malina

1988   *La Galgada, Peru.* Austin: University of Texas Press.

Guffroy, Jean

1987   *Loja préhispanique.* Paris: Éditions Recherche sur les Civilisations.

1994   *Cerro Ñañañique: un établissement monumental de la période formative, en limite de désert (Haut Piura, Pérou).* Paris: Orstom.

Hammond, Norman, and Karen Olsen Bruhns

1987   The Paute Valley Project in Ecuador, 1984. *Antiquity* 61:50–56.

Hocquenghem, Anne-Marie, Jaime Idrovo, Peter Kaulicke, and Dominque Gomis

1993   Bases del intercambio entre las sociedades norperuanas y surecuatorianas: una zona de transición entre 1500 A.C. y 600 D.C. *Bulletin de l'Institut Français d'Études Andines* 22(2):443–466.

Idrovo Urigüen, Jaime

1992   *El Formativo ecuatoriano.* Cuenca: Museo del Banco Central de Ecuador.

1999   El Formativo en la Sierra Ecuatoriana. In *Formativo sudamericano: una revaluación,* ed. P. Ledergerber, 114–123. Quito: Abya-Yala.

Lanning, Edward P.

1962   Quotation in *El Comercio,* Quito, September 1.

Long, Austin, A. T. Wilson, R. D. Ernst, B. H. Gore, and P. E. Hare

1989   AMS Radiocarbon Dating of Bones at Arizona. *Radiocarbon* 31(3):231–238.

Marcos, Jorge G.

1979   Woven Textiles in a Late Valdivia Context (Ecuador). In *The Junius Bird Pre-Columbian Textile Conference,* ed. A. P. Rowe, E. P. Benson, and A.-L. Schaffer, 18–26. Washington, D.C.: Textile Museum and Dumbarton Oaks.

Miller, George R., and Anne L. Gill

1990   Zooarchaeology at Pirincay: A Formative Period Site in Highland Ecuador. *Journal of Field Archaeology* 17:49–68.

Murra, John

1963   The Cañari. In *Handbook of South American Indians,* ed. Julian Haynes Steward, vol. 2, 799–800. New York: Cooper Square Publishers.

Salazar, Ernesto

1995   *Entre mitos y fábulas: el Ecuador aborigen.* Quito: Corporación Editora Nacional.

Tellenbach, Michael

1998   Acerca de las investigaciones de Max Uhle sobre las culturas tempranas de Surecuador. *Indiana* 15:269–353.

Temme, Mathilde

1999   El Formativo en Putushío, Sierra Sur del Ecuador. In *Formativo sudamericano: una revaluación,* ed. P. Ledergerber-Crespo, 124–138. Quito: Abya-Yala.

Uhle, Max

1922a *Influencias mayas en el Alto Ecuador.* Boletín de la Academia Nacional de Historia 4, Nos. 10–12. Quito: Tipografía y Encuadernación Salesianas.

1922b *Sepulturas ricas de oro en la Provincia del Azuay.* Boletín de la Academia Nacional de Historia 4, No. 9. Quito: Imprenta de la Universidad Central.

Villalba O., Marcelo

1988 *Cotocollao: una aldea Formativa del valle de Quito.* Quito: Museos del Banco Central del Ecuador.

Pottery Wares and Forms

Ceramics have been one of the primary subjects of archaeological study in the Andean region from their Formative origin to the late spread of imperial styles. Through analysis of the geological sources of their constituent clays they can inform us of their region of origin, as David Hill tells us in his analysis of the petrology of some sherds from Challuabamba and the Chorrera region. From the technical knowledge exhibited by potters' products we may be able to discover where they learned the craft and what their cultural connections were. The ultimate origins of ancient pottery in the Americas are still uncertain, but before 5000 BC (Roosevelt 1995) ceramics were known in the tropical lowlands of South America and were spreading slowly into the Andean region and along the Pacific coast.

Pottery Wares

By the second millennium BC the forefront of Andean technical experimentation focused on the pyrotechnologies, ceramics, and metallurgy. While ceramics already had a long history, potters at Challuabamba and some of its contemporary centers were experimenting with new ways of firing their clays, slips, and paint. At that time metallurgy was taking its first steps at places such as Putushío (Temme 1999:134–135), about 80 km south of Challuabamba, where gold was being cast, and Waywaka, far south in Andahuaylas in the highlands of Peru, where gold was being hammered into thin foil (Burger 1992:127).

At Challuabamba the material was clay: experiments focused on the composition of the clay, methods of forming it and applying decoration, and especially ways of firing it. Pottery was by far the richest artifact sample, with 63,758 potsherds (including 8 complete vessels) recorded. The largest fraction of that total came from Cut 3, which produced 57,308 sherds, of which 10,254 were rims. Virtually the entire body of material was produced locally, with only a few probable imports. The local character is evident in the volcanic origin of the material, which obviated the addition of tempering to the clay and produced the thin-walled, hard surfaces that distinguish its pottery.

Ceramics has a rich vocabulary, but one that emerges from common language and requires definition for scientific purposes. Pottery collections are first divided into *types* or *wares*. Definition of types in Anna Shepard's (1965:306–320) sense is still premature for our region, and "ware" is a step toward more precise definition.

Four wares are defined at Challuabamba by their surface colors, which were produced primarily by the method of firing and secondarily by a standardized paint color (Figure 2.1). The wares are Red-on-Cream, Red-and-Black, Burnished Black/Gray, and Matte Orange. The clay bodies of Red-on-Cream and Red-and-Black wares show no significant differences, all firing to a cream, light brown, buff, or light orange surface and a brown wall interior in a moderate open (i.e., oxidizing) firing. The Red-on-Cream was given at a minimum a red rim and often extensive decoration with red-orange slip-paint that was fired with the body.

The Red-and-Black ware had the same oxidizing firing, emerging from the fire with a cream or buff body decorated with areas of red slip-paint. The areas to be left cream or red were covered, probably with a liquid clay, and the pot was then exposed to a smoky fire to deposit carbon. The final steps were washing off the unfired clay masking the red and cream areas and in some cases burnishing the black areas.

While the basic firing for the first two wares was in an oxidizing fire (with access to oxygen), Burnished Black was fired in a reducing fire in a sealed kiln, like that used to make charcoal, to make a black body with a black surface. In the later phases (after about 1350 BC), when lighter colors were preferred, some oxygen was supplied toward the end of the firing to produce a gray core and surface.

Reduction firing has such a long history in South America that we have tended to take it for granted and underestimated its significance. Perhaps its earliest appearance is about 4000 BC at San Jacinto I in northwestern Colombia, where pottery was "fired in reduced conditions (possibly in earth ovens)" (Oyuela-Caycedo 1995:139). Kilns similar to earth-ovens were common (fifty-seven excavated examples) at Batán Grande in Peru's Lambayeque Province beginning about 1850 BC (Shimada et al. 1994). Valdivia potters achieved "a shiny black surface" (Lathrap et al. 1975:34) as early as Phase 3 (2800–2400 BC), which required smudging or a reduction firing. Re-

Figure 2.1. *Top* (all from 3.H Level 4): Red-on-Cream: domed bottle, flared bowl, and bottle. *Top row, front center:* Burnished Black effigy vase (3.H Level 4). *Bottom:* Red-and-Black jar with red interior (3.G Level 5); Red-on-Cream jar with fire-clouded base (3.H Level 4). Photograph by Bradford Jones.

duction-fired blackwares remained one of the basic wares in the succeeding Machalilla and Chorrera periods.

Experimentation with firing was common throughout this early period. Lanning (1963:154) describes the basic ware, Thin Red, in the Paita style, made on the Pacific coast near the mouth of the Chira River (which is the Catamayo in southern Ecuador) as red on the exterior and gray or brown on the interior. "Apparently," he writes, "these pots were fired in a mouth-down position in a more-or-less reducing atmosphere, but were exposed to air briefly during the cooling period, to produce a reddening of the exterior surface." The combination of red and black appears on Valdivia 5 (2250–2100 BC) carinated bowls, where the exterior wall bears "a red slip that contrasts with the deliberate, dense black smudging applied to the rest of the surface" (Lathrap et al. 1975:29). That is a good description of Challuabamba's Red-and-Black ware, which participated in this widespread style.

More recently reduction-fired fine wares have been found paired with majority oxidized wares at a large group of northern Andean Formative sites. The blackwares seem to have had special social and ritual significance (Guffroy 1994:421). Challuabamba was part of that group of sites, the Red-on-Cream being the majority ware and Burnished Black the special minority ware.

The fourth ware, Matte Orange, is so rare—just six sherds recorded—as to be statistically negligible. It appears only in the latest phase of our Challuabamba sequence and was used for a few very special items: Cylinder Seal No. 14 (Figure 2.2) and a bottle rim. It was at first considered a probable import, but reconsideration suggests that it is part of the consistent local interest in surface color and texture. It was produced by a very controlled oxidizing fire to produce an even orange body color without fire-clouding. The result was intended from the start, since the examples show no use of slip, burnishing, or textured decoration, the color and texture apparently being considered unimprovable. Despite its rarity, it was evidently considered an important part of the local ceramic style.

Figure 2.2. Cylinder Seal No. 14, Matte Orange ware.

The best comparative data we have on the popularity of the three common wares come from the adjoining Sectors G, H, and J in Cut 3, about 26 m³ of cultural deposits (Table 2.1). The sherd counts from the other cuts tend to confirm the picture provided by Cut 3 (Table 2.2).

Taken as a whole, the 4,894 rim sherds in this sample show Red-on-Cream ware at 84.6%, Red-and-Black ware at 5.6%, and reduction-fired Burnished Black/Gray at 9.6%. These figures underreport Red-and-Black, because in Cuts 1 and 2 all the oxidized wares were lumped together as part of Red-on-Cream. The percentages in Cut 3 give an accurate picture of the early importance of Red-and-Black relative to Burnished Black and the increasing production of reduction-fired black and gray pottery in the later (3 to 1) levels.

The higher numbers for reduced wares in Cut 3 may be another indication that this area was a focus of ceremonial activities, and particularly burials, throughout the later years of the occupation. Cut 4, located just 15 m from Cut 3, had the highest overall percentage of reduced wares among the other excavations. That area of Cuts 3 and 4 shows several other signs of special status during the period represented by Levels 4 to 1, such as small stone sculptures and an

Table 2.1. Rim Sherds by Wares in Levels of Cut 3

Level	Red-on-Cream	Red-and-Black	Burnished Black/Gray	Total Rim Sherds per Level
1	972 (83%)	78 (6.6%)	122 (10.4%)	1,172
2	768 (79%)	23 (2%)	176 (18%)	967
3	238 (85%)	11 (4%)	31 (11%)	280
4	584 (77%)	106 (14%)	65 (9%)	755
5	133 (70%)	50 (26%)	7 (4%)	190
6	1 (trace)	0	0	1
7	0	0	1 (trace)	1
TOTALS	2,696 (80%)	268 (8%)	402 (12%)	3,366

Table 2.2. Rim Sherds by Wares in Cuts 1, 2, 4, and 5

Cut and Level	Total Rims	Oxidized Red-on-Cream Rims (%)	Red-and-Black Rims (%)	Burnished Black/Gray Rims (%)	Matte Orange Rims (%)
Cut 1					
1 (0–30 cm)	327	309 (94.5)	0*	17 (5.2)	1 (trace)
2, 3 (30–60 cm)	153	143 (94)	0*	9 (6)	1 (trace)
4, 5 (60–130 cm)	22	20 (91)	1 (4.5)	1 (4.5)	0
Cut 2					
1 (0–50 cm)	522	515 (99)	*	7 (0.1)	0
2, 3 (50–110 cm)	64	60 (94)	*	4 (6)	0
Cut 4.A					
0–25 cm	263	246 (93.5)	1 (trace)	16 (6)	0
25–58 cm	141	123 (87)	0	16 (11)	2 (1.4)
Cut 5					
50–60 cm	36	29 (81)	6 (16.7)	1 (2.8)	0
TOTALS	1,528	1,445 (94.6)	8 (0.5)	71 (4.6)	4 (trace)

* Red-and-Black was not separated from Red-on-Cream in Cut 1 Levels 1 and 2 and in Cut 2.

elaborate burial offering, which tend to reinforce the interpretation of reduced wares as a mark of status.

Nevertheless, Burnished Blackwares are present throughout the sequence. The sample from the 50–60 cm level of Cut 5 is a good example. The single rim sherd of that ware was part of the spout of a bottle, but that level also produced seven Burnished Black body sherds that appear to be part of the same vessel. They show part of the slightly flattened base of a bottle and five sherds from the globular body. The same level yielded a body sherd from a Burnished Black carinated bowl or basin and a cut-out circle 1.7 cm in diameter with a black "mirror finish" on one side but unsmoothed edges. Those body sherds suggest that the percentage of Burnished Black vessels may have been a little higher than the rim sherd figure indicates. But that relatively early deposit also tells us that Red-and-Black ware was more common than Burnished Black, as it was also in early levels of Cut 3.

The Significance of Color

In our time artifacts and their attributes have become so numerous that they have tended to lose significance and value. We have many more things (dishes, chairs, cars, etc.) than earlier people would have imagined possible, with an unlimited choice of color and design. The result is that we simply do not have the time or energy to pay attention to all those things. Earlier people saw more meaning in the things they owned or used simply because they were rarer and more valuable.

The predominance of red, black, and cream-to-buff on Challuabamba pottery is partly explained by the relative ease with which those pigments can be obtained or those colors achieved in the firing. Availability partly accounts for their predominance in accounts of modern body painting in tropical South America (Turner 1969:70; Wilbert 1972:20–21). But observers agree that there is widespread consensus about the significance of these basic colors. Johannes Wilbert describes the Yanoama's understanding of red and black as signifying, respectively, "life and happiness" and "death, warfare, and mourning." Red, black, and white are the colors most directly associated with states of life, with all the psychic and emotional power that implies. Technically, white and black are not colors but the presence or absence of light, which helps explain their psychic and emotional power.

Colors can be used for classification (assigning them to directions, teams, political groups, etc.). Such assignments are arbitrary and can be changed without changing the meaning; the blue classification can be changed to yellow with a simple command, but red cannot be made to express sadness by merely saying so. "It is known that strong brightness, high saturation, and hues corresponding to vibrations of long wave length produce excitement. A bright, pure red is more active than a subdued grayish blue" (Arnheim 1954:326–327). Red, which has the longest wave length in the visible spectrum, produces a bodily response. Rudolf Arnheim (1954:327) notes that "Feré found that muscular power and blood circulation are increased by colored light 'in the sequence from blue—least, through green, yellow, orange, and red.'" That helps explain the finding of Robert Barton and Russell Hill (2005) that in the Athens Olympic games the individual or team wearing red had an advantage over those wearing other colors, most clearly when the opponents were considered very evenly matched, in which cases red won 60% of the contests.

In her discussion of the expressive use of color, Mary Helms (1987:72–74) maintained that black "is one of the most widely recognized symbolic colors in native America. Black and blue-black rank with orange-reds and with yellow-whites as basic color categories conveying associations of supernatural power and energy." Black has associations with "the night; riches, merchants and travel; warfare and the control of power; priests, sacred communication, and access to esoteric knowledge and wisdom. . . . Perhaps equally or even more important than color was the high polish" which reflected light, which was in itself a spiritual presence, as Helms said. The assignment of special spiritual and elite values to black and shiny surfaces in many regions and periods in Pre-Columbian America is an indication that those values were most likely assigned especially to the Burnished Blackwares at Challuabamba and perhaps to a lesser degree to the orange, red, and "yellow-white" wares, which were much more numerous there.

In 1598 Don Diego Collín, the powerful chief of the native community of Panzaleo in northern Ecuador, stated in his will: "declaro que tengo unos queros negros para bever mando que los aya y herede Andres Maynaguano mi nieto" (I declare that I have some black cups for drinking I will that they be had and inherited by Andres Maynaguano, my grandson) (Caillavet 1983:16; my translation), which suggests that fine blackware vessels, among numerous other serving vessels, were possessions appropriate to chiefly rank. While black pottery was known in Valdivia before its appearance at Challuabamba, the emergence, through Red-and-Black, of black pottery as a distinct type may be one of the manifestations of the gradual emergence of chiefly power. The offerings of pottery in Challuabamba burials suggest that sets of serving vessels as a chiefly attribute may long precede the sixteenth-century example from Panzaleo.

Pottery Forms

The three common wares were associated with certain vessel forms throughout the history of the site: the Burnished Black mostly with fancy low bowls and basins and a few bottles, the Red-and-Black with more utilitarian jars and serving bowls. Red-on-Cream appears in the large jars, some bowls and bottles, and the widest range of forms, including some ceremonial forms (Figure 2.3).

Challuabamba's pottery is unusually varied in form, but it is possible to define a set of basic vessel forms. Figures 2.4 to 2.12 show the development of nine pottery forms and the general range of their variations, with the rim diameters of the examples given in the captions. These forms include 99.6% of the total rim sample and are defined by general form, assigning function only in the most general terms. The forms are listed in Table 2.3 in the order of the total number of sherds (not vessels) assignable to each form. The definition of each numbered form exclusively by the rim means that some forms, such as Form 1, include a variety of vessel types, volumes, and uses.

These numbers probably exaggerate the dominance of the jar forms (1, 2, 4) since the jars are notable for their thin walls and would have broken easily and left a larger number of sherds per vessel than the smaller forms. Form 5, on the other hand, may be underrepresented, since its walls were usually thicker than in other forms. The general increase in the number of sherds in higher levels does seem to indicate much greater production and use of pottery in this location in the later periods.

Facing page

Figure 2.3. Three wares in four phases. *Right side (1–29):* Red-on-Cream; *center (30–48):* Red-and-Black; *left side (49–67):* Burnished Black or Gray. Phases I–IV marked on left side. Red-on-Cream and Red-and-Black colors are represented by hatching for red, crosshatching for black, and no marking for cream or unslipped. Burnished Black is unmarked, since the surface is solid black or gray reduced color. Phase I is at the bottom. Sources: *1–3:* Cut 3.J Level 5; *4, 5, 7, 31–37, 49:* 3.G Level 5; *30:* 3.A Level 5; *6, 8–12, 38–42, 50, 56:* 3.H Level 4; *51, 52, 54, 55, 57:* 3.G Level 4; *53:* 3.J Level 4; *43:* 3.F Level 3; *63:* Cut 2 Level 2; *64:* 3.E Level 2; *62:* 3.F Level 2; *13, 14, 16–18, 20, 21, 59–61:* 3.G Level 2; *15, 19, 44:* 3.H Level 2; *58:* 3.J Level 2; *29:* Cut 2 Level 1; *23:* 3.A Level 1; *25, 26, 65:* 3.F Level 1; *22, 24, 28:* 3.G Level 1; *27, 45–48:* 3.J Level 1; *67:* 3.L Level 1; *66:* X-1, surface outside excavations.

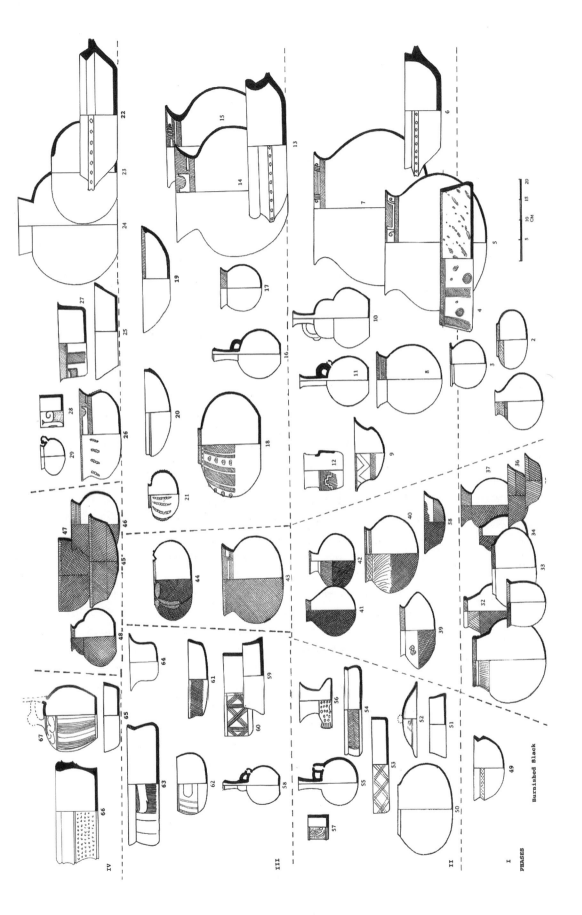

Burnished Black

PHASES

Table 2.3. Pottery Forms (Defined by Rims): Number of Rim Sherds per Stratigraphic Level in Cut 3

Form	Level							Total
	7	6	5	4	3	2	1	
1. jar, everted low neck	0	29	89	561	73	1,487	2,085	4,324
2. jar, high flared neck	0	8	48	228	38	683	1,329	2,334
3. flared bowl, round base	4	10	26	62	21	374	937	1,434
4. jar, low vertical rim	9	3	20	103	4	226	590	955
5. bowl, vertical wall, flat base	2	4	2	65	15	266	317	671
6. carinated bowl or basin	6	1	11	13	12	27	140	210
7. bowl, round base, incurve	0	1	1	8	6	36	146	198
8. plate, wide rim	0	0	0	1	0	20	88	109
9. bottle, single spout	0	1	2	5	0	2	10	20
Totals	21	57	199	1,046	169	3,121	5,642	10,255

It should be noted that the vessel bases are globular, rounded, or flat. Bennett (1946:25) mentions that "[b]oth annular and flat bases are represented [at Huancarcuchu], as well as a rare footed base," but our collections include only traces of three annular bases, all from Cut 3 (C Level 1; J Level 1; and G Level 2) and one black nubbin-foot (Cut 3.J Level 2). Those base types may have been imports or very late developments of the period in our excavations.

The nine defined vessel forms are shown in Figures 2.4 to 2.12, with a group of reconstructed vessel forms followed by a series of sherds. The forms are defined by a few specific traits, but variations of the basic form appear throughout the sequence. The cut and level for each sherd or reconstruction is given in the caption, which may aid in envisioning the development over time. Form 1, a globular jar with a low neck and everted rim, and Form 2, which differs in having a longer neck and usually a larger capacity, are the common large containers (Figures 2.4 and 2.5). Form 3 is an open bowl with flared walls and a rounded base (Figure 2.6). This appears to be the common serving vessel for food or drink. Its form remains consistent throughout the sequence, with a slight tendency to become wider and shallower in later levels. Form 4 (Figure 2.7) is usually a smaller jar with a low vertical rim, which was the most common in Level 7 and remained popular throughout the sequence. The average rim

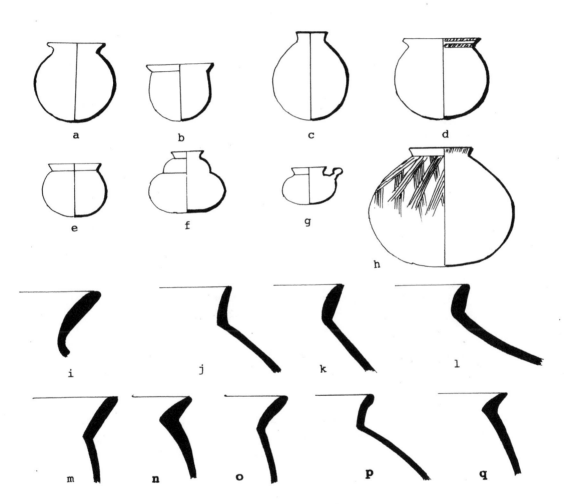

Figure 2.4. Form 1: globular jar with a low neck and everted rim. *Reconstructed forms: a,* 3.J Level 5; *b,* 3.G level 5; *c,* 3.H Level 4; *d,* 3.H Level 3; *e,* 3.G Level 2; *f,* 3.J Level 1; *g,* 2 Level 1; *h,* 3.G Level 1. *Sherd profiles: i,* 3.J Level 5; *j,* 3.G Level 4 (rim diam. 5.5 cm); *k,* 3.J Level 4 (16 cm); *l,* 3.G Level 4 (12 cm); *m,* 3.I Level 2 (20 cm); *n,* 3.J Level 1 (22 cm); *o,* 3.J Level 1 (20 cm); *p,* 2 Level 1 (7 cm); *q,* 3.G Level 1 (18 cm). Average rim diameter 15 cm. The common form is that shown in *a, d,* and *e; f* and *g* are elaborations for ceremonial use. These are middle-sized jars.

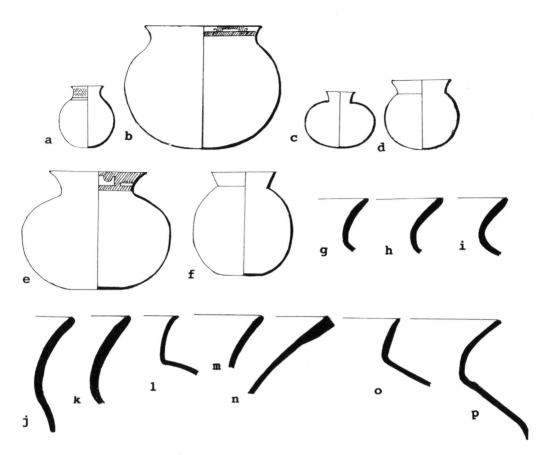

Figure 2.5. Form 2: jar with a high everted rim. *Reconstructed forms: a,* 3.J Level 5a; *b,* 3.G Level 5 (25 cm diam.); *c,* 3.H Level 4 (6 cm); *d,* 3.H Level 4; *e,* 3.G Level 2; *f,* 3.A Level 1. *Sherd profiles: g,* 3.G Level 5 (9 cm); *h,* 3.G Level 5 (20 cm); *i,* 3.G Level 5 (16 cm); *j,* 3.G Level 4 (28 cm); *k,* 3.G Level 4 (26 cm); *l,* 3.G Level 4 (6 cm), see *c* above; *m,* 3.D–F Level 2 (24 cm); *n,* 2.A Level 2 (30 cm); *o,* 3.J Level 1 (12 cm); *p,* 3.D Level 1 (13 cm). Average rim diameter 19 cm. These are generally the largest jars.

diameter is 10.2 cm, but the range is wide, from 3.5 and 4 to 32 cm, with a cluster in the 8–14 cm range. It is also the most varied in rim form. It was a medium-small jar in the early levels, but in Levels 2 and 1 (where it becomes a standard tecomate with a direct rim) it is much larger, rivaling the flared-neck jars. This form shows many distinctive variants (2.7b, d, e) that make it seem especially characteristic of Challuabamba. Vessels for serving food or drink are probably Forms 3 and 8. Forms 5 and 9 seem to have had ceremonial uses.

Form 5 is a bowl with a flat base and vertical walls (Figure 2.8). This is another distinctive Challuabamba product, probably a service vessel with some ceremonial uses, which are suggested by the two wares in which it was made, each with its special decorative style. We will discuss the styles later, but here it is sufficient to note that the Burnished Blackware bowls (Figure 2.8A: a–s) are more likely to have a break in the profile of the wall (e, h, m, o) and a sharp angle be-

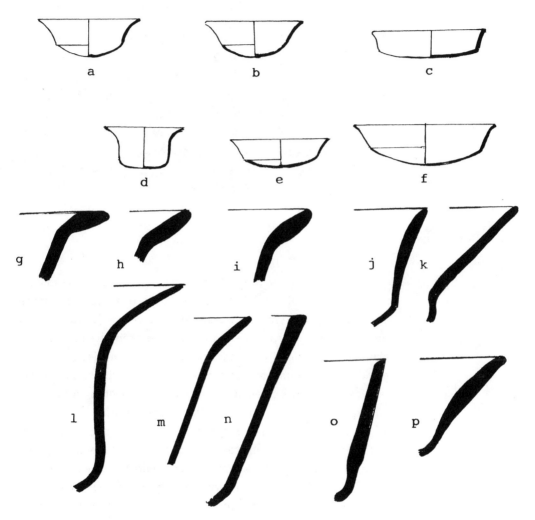

Figure 2.6. Form 3: open bowl, flared walls, rounded base. *Reconstructed forms: a,* 3.G Level 5 (17 cm diam.); *b,* 3.H Level 4b; *c,* 3.G Level 2; *d,* 3.E Level 2; *e,* 1 Level 1; *f,* 3.J Level 1. *Sherd profiles: g,* 3.H Level 5 (24 cm); *h,* 3.H Level 5; *i,* 3.H Level 4c (20 cm); *j,* 3.H Level 2 (24 cm); *k,* 3.I Level 2 (26 cm); *l,* 3.E Level 2 (13 cm); *m,* 3.A Level 1 (13.5 cm); *n,* 3.J Level 1 (34 cm); *o,* 3.I Level 1 (16 cm); *p,* 3.J Level 1 (28 cm). Average rim diameter is 21.5 cm. This is probably the common serving vessel for food or drink. Its form remains consistent throughout the sequence, with a slight tendency to become wider and shallower in later levels.

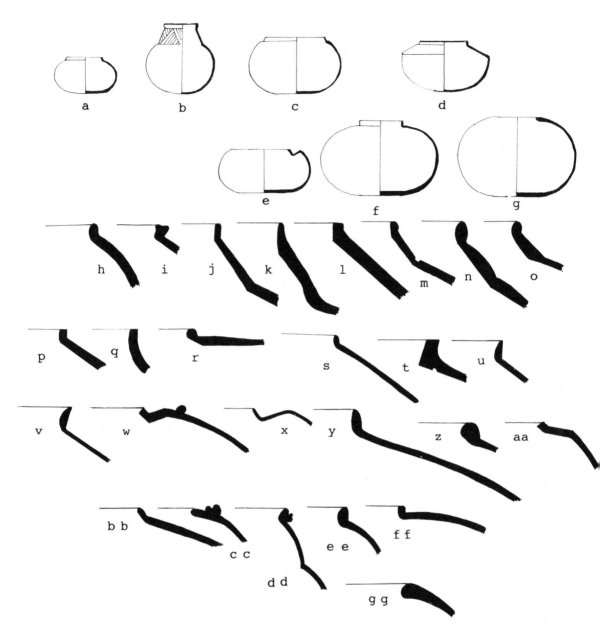

Figure 2.7. Form 4: jar with low vertical neck rim or neckless jars (tecomates). *Reconstructed forms: a,* 3.J Level 5a; *b,* 3.G Level 5; *c,* 3.G Level 4; *d,* 3.H Level 4b; *e,* 3.H Level 2; *f,* 3.G Level 2; *g,* 3.A Level 1. *Sherd profiles: h,* 3.H Level 5; *i,* 3.G Level 5a (12 cm); *j,* 3.J Level 5a (12 cm); *k,* 3.G Level 5; *l,* 3.G Level 5a (13 cm); *m,* 3.A Level 5 (32 cm); *n,* 3.A Level 5 (12 cm); *o,* 3.H Level 5; *p,* 3.H Level 4b; *q,* 3.H Level 4c; *r,* 3.H Level 4c (8 cm); *s,* 3.G Level 3 (17 cm); *t,* 3.I Level 2 (6 cm); *u,* 3.I Level 2 (10 cm); *v,* 3.I Level 2 (11 cm); *w,* 3.H Level 2 (10 cm); *x,* 3.G Level 2 (4 cm); *y,* 3.I Level 1 (3.5 cm); *z,* 3.I Level 1 (10 cm); *aa,* 3.I Level 1 (14 cm); *bb,* 3.I Level 1 (7 cm); *cc,* 3.I Level 1 (7 cm); *dd,* 3.I Level 1 (8 cm); *ee,* 3.J Level 1 (10 cm); *ff,* 2 Level 1 (8.8 cm); *gg,* 3.G Level 1 (20 cm). Average rim diameter is 10.2 cm, but the range is wide, from 3.5 to 32 cm, with a cluster in the 8–14 cm range.

tween the wall and base (i, n), while the Red-on-Cream bowls (Figure 2.8B) have a smooth wall and a curve where the wall meets the base (aa, bb, dd). The Red-Banded Incised (RBI) style is a Red-on-Cream version of this form.

Form 6 includes carinated bowls and basins (Figure 2.9). While carinated forms make up only 2% of the rim sample, they are a consistent presence throughout the levels. This is in part because carination was a decorative option for other general forms, such as bowls, small jars, and a wide, coarsely finished platter (2.9c, k, and l). While carination appeared as a rim elaboration in Valdivia III, it appears as an angle in the wall in Valdivia VI (2100–1950 BC) (Hill 1972–1974: Figures 36, 48), a likely source for Challuabamba's potters.

The form shown in 2.9c is one of the common forms throughout the sequence, from an early level in Cut 1 to all the levels from 4 to 1 in Cut 3. It is a low, wide serving vessel, round, with a thick flange at the shoulder decorated with punched holes on the outer edge of the flange.

Usually unslipped, these vessels look like potters' versions of the stone "ceremonial mortars" made and used at Cotocollao in all periods, which had probably already been translated into ceramic forms at Cotocollao (ceramic Forms 3, 5, 8, and 12 in Villalba 1988:461–464). While people at Challuabamba did work stone, there are no stone containers or mortars. At Cotocollao the earlier stone mortars (Period IA) appear mainly in residential areas, but later (Periods IB, IIA and B) they appear as offerings with human burials, many of them broken, perhaps ritually, despite being made of hard igneous stone (Villalba 1988:307). Although we cannot definitely connect our ceramic versions with burials or ritual locations, sherds of these platters are common in the middle levels of Cut 3, Sectors G–H, which had several burials, two intact and an uncertain number completely disrupted.

The distinctive form and its unusual coarseness of material and finish also suggest a ritual use. This implies that while utilitarian jars may be very well made and well finished, vessels with ritual uses may be either more finely finished or more coarsely finished. Several of the earliest examples were reduction-fired, and the form seems to originate without a definition of its ware, perhaps another indication of an origin in stone rather than ceramics.

The carinated forms at Challuabamba seem to be indicators of external contacts more than of local inventive powers. While such features usually spread rapidly (or not at all), carination was most widely used in mid–second millennium pottery (as we see, for example,

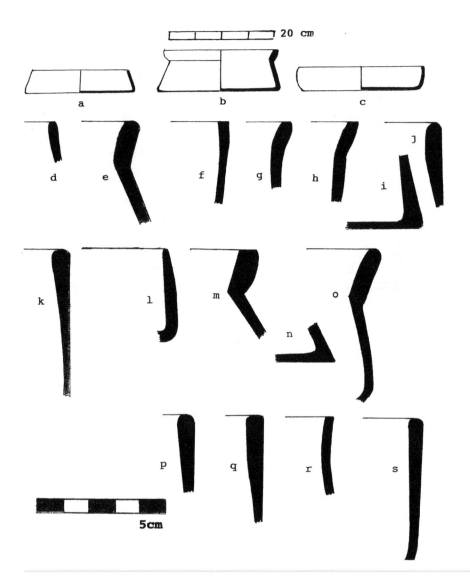

Above and facing page

Figures 2.8. Form 5: Bowl with flat base, vertical walls. *A. Burnished Black reconstructed forms: a,* 3.G Level 4; *b,* 3.G Level 4; *c,* 3.F Level 1. *Sherd profiles: d,* 3.J Level 7; *e,* 2.F Level 4 (diam. 24 cm); *f,* 3.H Level 4; *g,* 3.H Level 4c (20 cm); *h,* 3.H Level 4c (17 cm); *i,* 3.F Level 4 (16 cm); *j,* 3.H Level 4c (7 cm); *k,* 3.F Level 3 (31 cm); *l,* 3.J Level 3; *m,* 3.E Level 2 (22 cm); *n,* 3.G Level 2 (base); *o,* 2.A Level 2 (30 cm); *p,* 3.D–E Level 1; *q,* 3.E Level 1 (24 cm); *r,* 3.E Level 1 (12 cm); *s,* 3.G Level 1 (20 cm). Average rim diameter is 20.2 cm. *B. Red-on-Cream and Red-Banded Incised style. Red-Banded reconstructed forms: t,* 3.J Level 1; *u,* 3.G Level 5; *v,* 3.F Level 1. *Sherd profiles: w,* 3.G Level 5 (25 cm); *x,* 3.H Level 4 (upper is exterior; lower is interior); *y,* 3.F Level 3 (26 cm); *z,* 3.H Level 3 (31 cm); *aa,* 3.J Level 2 (36 cm); *bb,* 3.I Level 2 (18 cm); *cc,* 3.I Level 2 (20 cm); *dd,* 3.C Level 1 (24 cm); *ee,* X-surface. Average rim diameter is 25.7 cm.

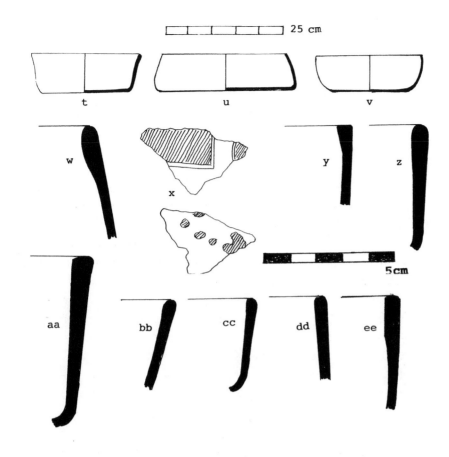

in Cotocollao and Machalilla), so its appearance at Challuabamba is not a very useful chronological marker.

Form 7 is a bowl with a round base and in-curving walls (Figure 2.10). A rare form (1.9% of the rim sample), it appears to be a service vessel for individual food or drink.

Form 8 is a plate with an expanded rim (Figure 2.11). Plates or relatively shallow bowls with rims reinforced on the interior and usually painted red are a late form. Hill (1972–1974: Figures 64, 65, Valdivia phase VII or VIII?) shows two examples from Valdivia, which can be dated after 1950 BC. They appear to be individual food service vessels.

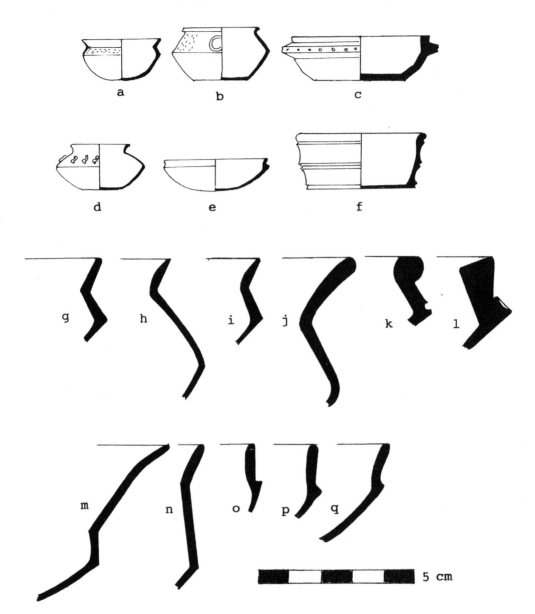

Figure 2.9. Form 6: carinated bowls and basins. *Reconstructed forms:* a, 3.G Level 5; b, 3.G Level 5; c, 3.H Level 4b; d, 3.H Level 4c; e, 3.G Level 2; f, X-1 surface. *Sherd profiles:* g, 3.F Level 4 (16 cm); h, 3.G Level 3 (17 cm); i, 3.F Level 2; j, 3.F Level 2 (22 cm); k, 3.G Level 2 (37 cm); l, 3.I Level 1 (26 cm); m, 3.D–E Level 1 (26 cm); n, 3.G Level 1 (32 cm); o, 3.E Level 1 (26 cm); p, 3.I Level 1 (35 cm); q, 3.E Level 1 (24 cm). Average rim diameter is 26.1 cm.

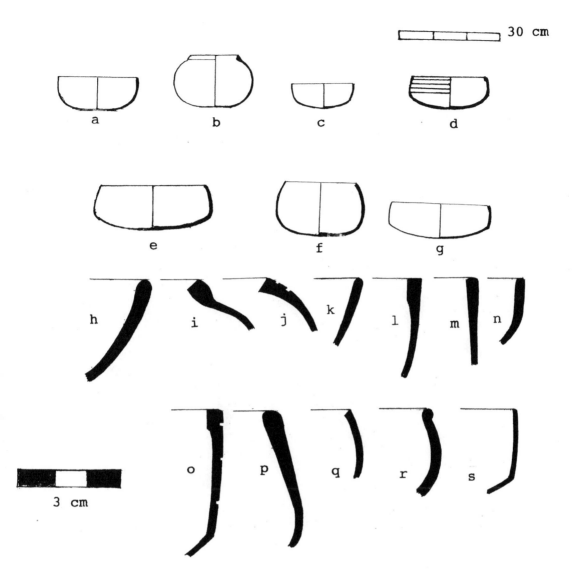

Figure 2.10. Form 7: bowl with round base, in-curving walls. *Reconstructed forms: a,* 3.G Level 5 (23 cm); *b,* 3.F Level 3 (14 cm); *c,* 3.G Level 2 (18 cm); *d,* 3.D–F Level 2 (22 cm); *e,* 3.J Level 1 (32 cm); *f,* 3.G Level 1 (20 cm); *g,* 3.G Level 1 (30 cm); *Sherd profiles: h,* 3.J Level 5a (31 cm); *i,* 3.G Level 3; *j,* 3.F Level 3 (26 cm); *k,* 3.G Level 2 (28 cm); *l,* 3.G Level 2 (18 cm); *m,* 3.G Level 2 (26 cm); *n,* 3.D–F Level 3 (28 cm); *o,* 3.J Level 1 (12 cm); *p,* 3.J Level 1 (12 cm); *q,* 3.G Level 1 (16 cm); *r,* 3.J Level 1 (12 cm); *s,* 3.E Level 1 (14 cm). Average rim diameter is 22.7 cm. This is a rare form, just 1.9% of the rim sample. It appears to be a service vessel for individual food or drink.

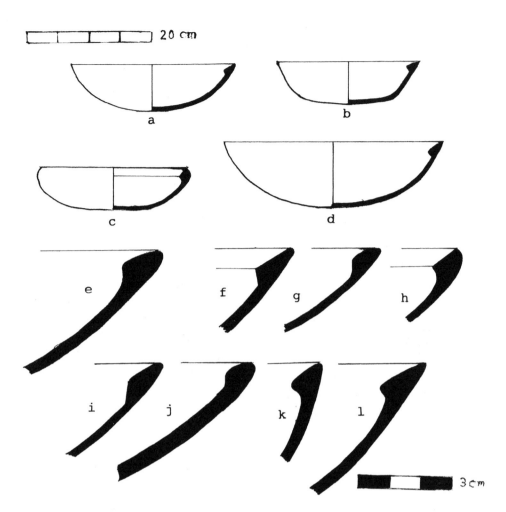

Figure 2.11. Form 8: plate with an expanded rim. *Reconstructed forms: a,* 3.H Level 3 (26 cm); *b,* 3.G Level 2 (22 cm); *c,* 3.I Level 1 (24 cm); *d,* 1 Level 1 (35 cm). *Sherd profiles: e,* 3.H Level 3 (26 cm); *f,* 3.E Level 1 (22 cm); *g,* 3.E Level 1 (24 cm); *h,* 3.I Level 1 (24 cm); *i,* 3.I Level 1 (26 cm); *j,* 3.J Level 1 (5 vessels of this form from this location); *k,* 3.G Level 1 (28 cm); *l,* 1 Level 1 (35 cm). (This is *d* in the reconstructions above.) Average rim diameter is 25.7 cm. Plates or shallow bowls with rims reinforced on the interior, usually slipped or painted red, are a late form. Hill (1972–1974: Figures 64, 65, Valdivia phase 7 or 8?) shows two examples from Valdivia which can be dated after 1950 BC. They appear to be individual food service vessels.

Form 9 is a single-spout bottle (Figure 2.12). Our earliest evidence of the single-spout bottle comes from Cut 3.H Level 5, a fragment of bottle neck in Red-and-Black ware (Figure 2.12e). The interior is rough black, the exterior a highly polished dark red slip. It is shorter than later necks (about 2.8 cm tall compared with about 6 cm in later examples) and narrows gradually, rather than being nearly vertical and widening at the rim as in later bottles. The early neck looks as if it grew gradually out of the body rather than being sharply differentiated, as in later examples. It probably had a globular body, which was the common form for jars in all periods (jars being likely prototypes for bottles). That seems to be supported by the next earliest examples, from 3.G.4a and Burial 6, which have a soft transition from the wall to the flattened base.

All the complete bottles that survive are long necked and globular, with bases that are flat or nearly flat. The composite or domed form appears as early as Level 4 in the bottles, and the most capacious body is in the latest example, which also bears an elaborate incised design with postfire red paint on the Burnished Black ware (decorative elements that were absent on earlier examples). The form appears to have been used for ceremonial service of liquids. All Challuabamba's bottles are in this category. There are no stirrup-spouts, and only the latest (Figure 2.12d), with its twin openings, appears to be a bridge-spout with perhaps a whistle and an effigy head on one of the perforations.

Figure 2.12 shows a sample of bottle necks from Cut 3, Levels 5 through 1, with one (2.12l) from Cut 2.A Level 1. The variation in form and ware is noteworthy, implying a long period of production of a form which was not absolutely standardized. All but two of our twenty examples come from Cut 3.

Challuabamba's bottles make an interesting comparison with the larger and more varied collection of bottle forms from Cotocollao, which includes numerous stirrup-spouts, single spouts set on a slight dome with a handle that has a protuberance with an air hole (formal class XVI: Botella Cotocollao), and single spouts with a handle with an air hole (whistle in some cases) (XVII: Botella Tipo Chorrera) (Villalba 1988:172–184). Stirrup-spouts at Cotocollao appear early and diminish over time, to be replaced by single-spout forms (Villalba 1988:173), but that sequence is not general for the region. The "Cotocollao type" is usually decorated with incisions and punching, while the "Chorrera type" at Cotocollao is always decorated with vertical red stripes between incisions. Challuabamba's bottles are all Burnished Black or Red-on-Cream or buff, or solid red with what may be

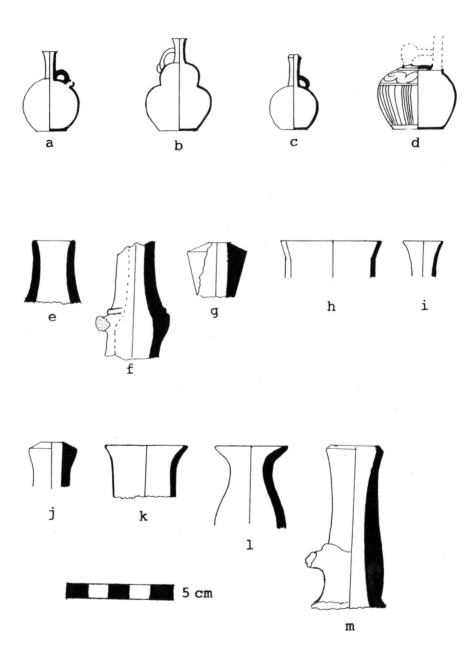

Figure 2.12. Form 9: Single-spout bottle. *Reconstructed forms: a*, 3.H Level 4; *b*, 3.H Level 4; *c*, 3.G Level 2; *d*, 3.L Level 1. *Sherd profiles: e*, 3.H Level 5 (2 cm); *f*, 3.G Level 4; *g*, 3.G Level 3; *h*, 3.G Level 2 (4.5 cm); *i*, 3.G Level 2 (1.8 cm); *j*, 3.J Level 2 (1.9 cm); *k*, 3.D–E Level 1 (3.7 cm); *l*, 2.A Level 1 (3.3 cm); *m*, 3.E Level 1 (2.5 cm). Average rim diameter is 2.8 cm.

intentional fire-clouding. The only incision is on the latest example (2.12d). The variations in the setting of the spout and design of the handle at Challuabamba include most of the Cotocollao variations, the great exception being stirrup-spouts. The often-reproduced incised stirrup-spout bottle from El Descanso in the Duran Collection (Collier and Murra 1943: Plate 10, no. 4) is unique and impossible to connect with anything known to be from Challuabamba.

The closest comparisons with Challuabamba's bottles are with the Chorrera style, as shown by Donald Lathrap et al. (1975), particularly Nos. 279, 280, 282, 284, 285, and 298 in the catalogue, all of which come from Manabí. Our bottles are less refined in design, lacking the incised decorations and the effigy elements and some of the elaborations of the wall (e.g., carination) as well as the wide reinforced rim. But the proportions, color, and burnish are generally comparable. Bottles, both single-spout and stirrup-spout, were in general use in the northern Andean areas of Peru and Ecuador in the middle and late Formative. The single-spout bottle, to which Challuabamba seems to have made an early contribution (Cut 3, Level 5, Figure 2.12e), was more widely distributed. Bottle forms in general were almost certainly containers for liquid in some ritualized service.

All but one (Form 8) of these nine forms were found in the lowest level. The standard set of forms was established early, with large and small jars, round-based and flat-based bowls with open or closed rims, and the bottle appearing in Level 5, leaving only plates to appear in Level 3. Among the jar forms, which are most numerous in all levels, the smaller jars (Form 1) with low everted rims far outnumber the larger jars (Form 2) with flaring rims. A third jar form (Form 4), with a very low vertical rim (we have lumped the few direct-rim tecomates made in the latest phase into this category), further expands the number of globular jars. While jars make up 73% of the total rim sample and 74% of the rims of the selected sample of forms, they appear to divide into three functional groups, the largest (Form 2), the second largest (Form 4) with low neck rims, and the smallest (Form 1), which is the most numerous. The flared-neck large jars (Form 2) appear to have gotten smaller over time, while Form 4 shows some increase in size and Form 1 remains about the same. The dominance of jars in Challuabamba pottery allies it with some of its early neighbors to the south, Catamayo and Paita (DeBoer 2003:305–308). While those three jar forms appear to have been employed as cooking and storage vessels, the bowls and plates were service forms and the bowls were probably also employed as drinking cups.

The numbers of vessels represented in this sample from a small area and the unusually varied forms given the standard types argue against the shorter interpretations of the sequence. While the vessel forms gave many opportunities for variety, the wares produced by differences in firing and surface treatment multiplied those opportunities, reserving certain forms for blackware, others for red or cream. The exploitation of those opportunities took time, so we are obliged to look for some at least tentative ways to divide this mass of material into phases or periods.

Summary and Comparisons of Pottery Morphology

Challuabamba pottery forms began with a few closely related forms. Globular containers (Forms 1, 2, and 4), varying mainly in size and rim elaborations, were presumably for cooking or storage. Forms 3, 5, 6, 7, 8, and 9 were presumably used for serving food or beverages. Form 3, usually in an oxidized ware, appears to have been the common service form, probably for both liquids and solids. All the others, at least in the possibly burial context in which we found some of them, appear to have been for special service. All these forms underwent development, and some unique variations are to be found, especially in the later phases.

In terms of form, some of the innovations led to simpler, more geometric forms, such as pure tecomates without rim elaboration, straight out-slanted necks for jars, and hemispherical bowls. At the same time potters added elaborations, such as multiple moldings on shoulders and rims, and enlarged capacity for bottles. But innovation in the later phases was not so much in vessel form as in ware and decoration.

Wendell Bennett's (1946:20–40) report on Huancarcuchu ceramics, from the locations closest to those reported here, shows two general forms: "constricted mouth bowls," which include all our smaller jar forms (1, 2, 4), and "open bowls," in which most of our Forms 3, 5, 7, and 8 would fall. The high percentage of jar forms (74%) noted in our collection is surpassed in Bennett's, in which 81.93% are in the "constricted mouth" category. The main differences are in the firing and decoration: Bennett found only 32 sherds of polished blackware, in contrast to 1,483 red painted and polished sherds. While the similarities suggest a general contemporaneity, the differences in our findings reflect the diversity within the site. More distant (20 km), but perhaps more similar in ceramic content, Pirincay shows all the bowl and plate rims in our sample except the commonest (Form 3) (Bruhns 1989: Figure 4).

Bibliography

Arnheim, Rudolf
1954 *Art and Visual Perception.* Berkeley: University of California Press, 1971.

Barton, Robert, and Russell Hill
2005 Red Enhances Human Performance in Contests. *Nature* 435, no. 7040 (May 19):293.

Bennett, Wendell C.
1946 *Excavations in the Cuenca Region, Ecuador.* Yale University Publications in Anthropology, No. 35. New Haven: Yale University Press.

Bruhns, Karen Olsen
1989 Intercambio entre la costa y la sierra en el Formativo Tardío: nuevas evidencias del Azuay. In *Relaciones interculturales en el área ecuatorial del Pacífico durante la época precolombina,* ed. J.-F. Bouchard and M. Guinea, 57–74. British Archaeological Reports, International Series 503. Oxford: BAR.

Burger, Richard L.
1992 *Chavín and the Origins of Andean Civilization.* New York: Thames and Hudson.

Caillavet, Chantal
1983 Ethno-histoire équatorienne: un testament indien inédit du XVI siècle. *Caravelle* (Toulouse) 41:5–23. Collier, Donald, and John Murra
1943 *Survey and Excavations in Southern Ecuador.* Anthropology Series 62. Chicago: Field Museum of Natural History.

DeBoer, Warren R.
2003 Ceramic Assemblage Variability in the Formative of Ecuador and Peru. In *Archaeology of Formative Ecuador,* ed. J. S. Raymond and R. L. Burger, pp. 289–336. Washington, D.C.: Dumbarton Oaks.

Guffroy, Jean
1994 *Cerro Ñañañique: un établissement monumental de la période formative, en limite de désert (Haut Piura, Pérou).* Paris: Orstom.

Helms, Mary W.
1987 Art Styles and Interaction Spheres in Central America and the Caribbean: Polished Black Wood in the Greater Antilles. In *Chiefdoms in the Americas,* ed. Robert D. Drennan and Carlos A. Uribe, 67–84. Lanham: University Press of America.

Hill, Betsy D.
1972– A New Chronology of the Valdivia Ceramic Complex from the Coastal
1974 Zone of Guayas Province, Ecuador. *Ñawpa Pacha* (Berkeley) 10–12:1–32.

Lanning, Edward P.
1963 *A Ceramic Sequence for the Piura and Chira Coast, North Peru.* University of California Publications in American Archaeology and Ethnology. Berkeley/Los Angeles: University of California Press.

Lathrap, Donald W., Donald Collier, and Helen Chandra
1975 *Ancient Ecuador: Culture, Clay and Creativity, 3000–300 BC.* Chicago: Field Museum of Natural History.

Oyuela-Caycedo, Augusto
1995 Rocks versus Clay: The Evolution of Pottery Technology in the Case

of San Jacinto I, Colombia. In *The Emergence of Pottery: Technology and Innovation in Ancient Societies,* ed. W. K. Barnett and J. W. Hoopes, 133–144. Washington, D.C.: Smithsonian.

Roosevelt, Anna C.

1995　Early Pottery in Amazonia: Twenty Years of Obscurity. In *The Emergence of Pottery: Technology and Innovation in Ancient Societies,* ed. W. K. Barnett and J. Hoopes, 115–131. Washington, D.C.: Smithsonian Institution.

Shepard, Anna O.

1965　*Ceramics for the Archaeologist.* Washington, D.C.: Carnegie Institution.

Shimada, Izumi, Carlos G. Elera, Victor Chang, Hector Neff, Michael Glascock, Ursel Wagner, and Rupert Gebhard

1994　Hornos y producción de cerámica durante el Período Formativo en Batán Grande, Costa Norte del Perú. In *Tecnología y organización de la producción de cerámica prehispánica en los Andes,* ed. I. Shimada, 67–119. Lima: Pontificia Universidad Católica del Perú.

Temme, Mathilde

1999　El Formativo en Putushío, Sierra Sur del Ecuador. In *Formativo sudamericano: una revaluación,* ed. P. Ledergerber-Crespo, 124–138. Quito: Abya-Yala.

Turner, Terence S.

1969　Tchikrin: A Central Brazilian Tribe and Its Symbolic Language of Body Adornment. *Natural History* 78(8):50–70.

Villalba O., Marcelo

1988　*Cotocollao: una aldea Formativa del valle de Quito.* Quito: Museos del Banco Central del Ecuador.

Wilbert, Johannes

1972　*Survivors of El Dorado: Four Indian Cultures of South America.* New York: Praeger.

Petrographic Analysis of Selected
Ceramics from Two Sites in Ecuador

DAVID V. HILL

Nine potsherds from the excavations at Challuabamba and two reliably reported to be from a Chorrera site in the province of Los Ríos were analyzed by the author using a Nikon Optiphot-2 petrographic microscope. The sizes of the natural inclusions and tempering agents were described in terms of the Wentworth Scale, a standard method for characterizing particle sizes in sedimentology. These sizes were derived from measuring a series of grains using a graduated reticle built into one of the microscope optics. The percentages of inclusions in the ceramics and clay samples were estimated using comparative charts (Terry and Chilingar 1955; Matthew et al. 1991).

Analysis was conducted by first going through the total ceramic collection and generating a brief description of each of the sherds. A second phase was then conducted, consisting of the creation of classification groups based on the similarity of the paste and temper of those sherds to one another. This process also allowed for the examination of the variability within each grouping. Additional comments about the composition of individual sherds were made at this time.

ECU-1: Brown Paste, Red Exterior Slip

The paste of this sherd is light grayish yellow. A distinctive characteristic of the paste is the presence of about 10% submicron-sized rectangular features. The majority of these features represent voids: whatever was present is now gone. A few contain an amorphous grayish white material whose composition is unknown.

Also present in the sherd are about 15% inclusions that consist predominantly of isolated grains of andesine plagioclase and quartz in roughly equal proportions. These isolated grains range from very fine to medium in size. A few particles of untwinned potassium are also present in trace amounts. The feldspars appear fresh and unweathered. Green-brown hornblende and biotite are present in trace amounts. The biotite is present as slightly weathered to completely weathered black inclusions.

Rock fragments are also present in the paste of this sherd. The most common type is a dacite characterized by a very fine-grained to glassy groundmass. Contained porphyritically within the groundmass is andesine plagioclase, which often exhibits incomplete crystallization in the centers of the crystals, which contain glassy groundmass. Sparse, very fine ferro-manganese cubes are present in the dacite fragments, usually staining the rock fragments a brownish-orange. Also present but less common than the dacite are fragments of weathered rhyolitic tuff having a cryptocrystalline-to-glassy groundmass. The rhyolite has a weathered to a grayish white color. A single fragment of highly weathered fine-grained basalt is also present. The basalt is trachyitic in texture and contains abundant magnetite that has weathered to the point of staining the andesine plagioclase a brownish-orange color. All the rock fragments range in size from fine to medium. A single coarse void was observed, surrounded by a carbonaceous halo. The void had formed as the result of the combustion of some type of plant material accidentally present in the clay.

ECU-2: Tan Paste, Red Slip

The paste of this sherd is quite similar to that of ECU-1 and is likely to have been derived from the same clay source. There are several differences between the two sherds that provide some insight into the variability in the source material. The paste is a darker brown than in ECU-1. The very fine rectangular features observed in ECU-1 are found in this sherd only in trace amounts. The mineral grains and rock fragments in this specimen are similar in composition and amount but are generally larger, ranging up to medium in size. The major isolated mineral grains consist predominantly of plagioclase, with a slightly smaller amount of quartz and sparse untwinned potassium feldspar. One of the dacite grains contains a single euhedral hornblende crystal. Also present are six fine to medium black, rounded silty inclusions that contain grains too small to identify through optical means. These round black inclusions could represent either soil pisolites or fecal pellets. A single rounded void with a carbonaceous halo was observed, the result of combustion of plant material in the clay.

ECU-3: Tan Body, Red Slip

This sherd was mounted in cross section in order to examine the surface treatment of the vessel. An iron-rich slip on the vessel surface produced a hematitic reddish brown stain that permeates less than 1 mm into the vessel wall. Below the slip the paste is a light yellowish brown to a depth between 2 and 3 mm. The interior of the sherd is an opaque black.

The paste contains about 30% rounded sand grains dominated by untwinned potassium feldspar along with quartz and sparse plagioclase. The sands are moderately well sorted and range in size from fine to medium. The feldspars appear fresh. Also present is a single medium-sized grain of weathered grayish-brown rhyolitic tuff with a cryptocrystalline groundmass. The tuff grain has altered in places to clay minerals. A single medium-sized fragment of fine-grained quartzite is also present.

If we define ECU-1 and -2 as the basic local clay body, ECU-3 is probably not from the immediate locality.

ECU-4: Dark Brown Paste

The paste of this sherd is a golden brown color. It contains about 15% fine subrounded sands, consisting of about even amounts of untwinned potassium feldspar and quartz. A sparse amount of plagioclase is also present. The feldspars are slightly to heavily altered to clay minerals. Trace amounts of green-brown hornblende and brown biotite were also observed. Depending on the degree of weathering, the biotite has altered to hematite and clay minerals, resulting in the appearance of reddish stains or small black inclusions.

About 10% of the sands consist of rounded grains of rhyolitic tuff and dacite. In general the tuff has a brownish gray groundmass that is altered to clay minerals. A few dacite fragments contain plagioclase porphyritically. The plagioclase in the dacite was incompletely crystallized, leaving the center open. A very coarse fragment of quartz monzonite is present, with mineral particles of variable size. Hematitic staining was observed between the mineral grains of this rock fragment.

This specimen probably originated close to the locality, although the dacite and monzonite are different.

ECU-5: Polished Dark Brown Surface, Yellowish Paste

This sherd was examined in cross section to contrast the composition of the surface with that of the body. The surface has a dark brown iron-rich slip that contrasts with the lighter-colored yellow-ish brown paste. The slip appears to diffuse into the lighter paste.

The paste contains about 15% naturally occurring sand and fragments of rhyolitic tuff. The sand particles are well sorted and fine grained. The majority of the isolated mineral grains are untwinned potassium feldspar, with grains of plagioclase only slightly less common. Quartz makes up about 10% of the sands. A few fine to medium-sized fragments of rhyolitic tuff are present, highly weathered and with a grayish brown groundmass. One tuff grain contains weathered plagioclase laths. Four round, medium-sized opaque black inclusions are present, either soil pisolites or fecal pellets.

ECU-6: Light Brownish-Yellow Paste, Burnished Tan-to-Brown Interior Surface

The paste contains about 10% very fine rectangular voids, a few of them containing an amorphous white substance. The majority of the inclusions (about 15%) are untwinned potassium feldspar. Most of the feldspars are highly weathered, occasionally obscuring their optical characteristics. Weathered grains of plagioclase are less common. Trace amounts of rounded grains of quartz are present, as well as limited quantities of brown biotite, often weathered to hematite, clay minerals, and green-brown hornblende.

Fragments of intrusive and extrusive rock are also found. About 60% of the isolated rock fragments appear to be highly weathered rhyolitic tuff with a microcrystalline to crystalline groundmass. They are light gray, very fine grained, and highly weathered. Brown biotite altered to hematite and clay minerals is present in a few rock fragments. Porphyritic sanidine is present in two of the rhyolite fragments. Fragments of intrusive rock are uncommon in the paste of this sherd, but there are fragments of monzonite and others containing untwinned feldspar and stained with hematite.

ECU-7: Yellow-Brown Paste, Burnished Brown Surface

This sherd was examined in cross section to show the relationship of the surface to the interior. Along one edge the exterior surface is a slightly darker layer, but the surface does not contrast with the underlying body. It is likely that the vessel was self-slipped.

The paste of this specimen is quite similar to that of ECU-6 in terms of color and the presence of untwinned potassium feldspar, plagioclase, and sparse quartz. Rhyolitic tuff is also present (one fragment with a reddish hematitic stain) as well as a single medium-sized fragment of gneiss.

ECU-8: Reddish-Brown Paste, Eroded Surface

The paste of this specimen is similar to that of ECU-6 and ECU-7. The clay body contains about 20% isolated mineral grains and rock fragments. These represent materials that were in the source clay rather than added material. The continuous distribution of particle sizes from silt-sized to fine and the high degree of weathering in the feldspars present in the rock fragments indicate that the materials are natural inclusions in the clay. The majority of the grains are rounded, indicating that the source of the clay was likely an alluvial deposit.

The majority of the inclusions (about 15%) are untwinned potassium feldspar. Most of the feldspars are highly weathered, making their identification difficult. A single medium-sized fragment of monzonite could be the source of the untwinned feldspar in the paste. Less common are weathered grains of plagioclase. There are also trace amounts of rounded quartz grains and brown biotite, often weathered to hematite, clay minerals, and green-brown hornblende.

More common in the paste are fragments of intrusive and extrusive rock, about 80% of them highly weathered rhyolitic tuff with a microcrystalline to cryptocrystalline groundmass. These rock fragments are light gray and have a very fine-grained texture. Brown biotite altered to hematite and clay minerals is found in a few rock fragments. Porphyritic sanidine is present in two of the rhyolite fragments. One tuff fragment displays compaction of glassy vesicles. Intrusive rock is uncommon in the paste of the sherd. Besides the fragments of monzonite mentioned previously, there are also a few fragments containing untwinned feldspar stained with hematite. A single fragment of very fine-grained basalt is present. It has a trachytic texture and contains very abundant magnetite, which shows some iron staining from weathering.

This specimen, which is especially rich in tuff, may not originate in the immediate locality but somewhere closer to the volcanoes.

ECU-9: Red-Banded Incised Sherd, Dark Brown Paste

A single sherd of Red Banded Incised was submitted for petrographic analysis. The analysis was oriented toward comparison with a previous study.

The paste of the sherd is dark brown. The paste of the sherd contains isolated mineral grains and fragments of several types of rock. The isolated mineral grains range in size from a coarse silt to medium sand (0.031–0.5 mm). Isolated mineral grains compose about 10% of the ceramic paste, which is composed of roughly equal amounts of quartz and untwinned alkali feldspar, with quartz slightly predominating. Plagioclase accounts for an additional 5% of the isolated mineral grains. Brown biotite constitutes about 1% of the isolated mineral grains. Trace amounts of muscovite and augite are also present as isolated grains.

The rock fragments fall into the same size range as the isolated mineral grains: 0.031–0.5 mm. Rock fragments account for an additional 3% of the ceramic paste. The most common rock type present in the ceramic paste was derived from a weathered volcanic tuff. The groundmass of the tuff ranges from reddish gray to gray and aphanitic or eutaxitic in texture. The tuff contains weathered biotite and occasionally untwinned alkali feldspar or plagioclase. The untwinned alkali feldspar ranges from fresh to highly weathered. The isolated fragments of brown biotite are occasionally weathered to hematite and clay minerals, resulting in reddish or opaque black inclusions.

Trace amounts of other types of rock and sparse inclusions of glassy pumice are also present in the paste of this sherd. Two fragments of basalt were observed in the ceramic paste. One fragment has a groundmass composed of laths of plagioclase in a glassy matrix. Plagioclase was also contained porphyritically. The other basalt grain was holocrystalline and trachyitic.

Two fragments of plutonic rock were observed in the ceramic paste as well. One fragment consists of a fragment of quartzite. A fragment of biotite gneiss was also present in the ceramic paste.

The similarity of the size of the isolated mineral grains and rock fragments and the presence of similar sizes and compositions of minerals in the rock fragments that also occur as isolated mineral grains indicate that the two types of inclusions share a common source. The inclusions are likely natural materials that are present in the clay used to produce the ceramic vessel. Without collection and analysis of clay sources that would have been available locally, the source of the vessel will remain unknown.

Previous analysis of RBI reported both volcanic and metamorphic rock fragments in the same ceramic paste, as in the current specimen. However, in addition to the vitreous volcanic ash that appears similar to the glassy pumice of the current specimen, the comparative specimen lacks the eutaxitic tuff observed in the present sample. Previous analysis also suggested that the rock and mineral inclusions represent an added tempering agent rather than natural inclusions in the original ceramic clay.

The following two specimens were examined as a control. They are reported to have been collected in the Babahoyo River Valley in the western lowlands of Ecuador and have been identified as Chorrera style.

CHO-1 (Chorrera Region): Brown Paste, Red Slip

The dark brown paste of this sherd contains about 20% well-sorted, subrounded fine sands. Untwinned potassium feldspar and plagioclase are present in nearly equal amounts (less than 5%), and quartz is slightly more common. The feldspar grains display alteration, often obscuring the optical characteristics of the minerals. There are trace amounts of green-brown hornblende and biotite, which appears as either reddish-brown stains or black opaque inclusions. These sediments originate in an extrusive source.

About 15% of the sands are rounded fragments of highly weathered rhyolitic tuff with a cryptocrystalline-to-glassy groundmass. The tuff fragments are usually weathered to a grayish brown. A single grain of weathered basalt was observed, with a reddish glassy groundmass and containing sparse laths of andesine plagioclase.

CHO-2 (Chorrera Region): Burnished Brown on Yellow-Brown Paste

This sherd was mounted in cross section to observe the presence of a possible slip. The paste shows zones with light yellowish brown within 3 mm of the edge and a dark brown within the interior of the vessel wall. The possible slip was not observed using a light microscope.

The paste contains sediments derived from a heavily eroded black-spotted, hard dark rock, an intrusive geologic source. The sediments of hornblende and andesite porphyry make up about 25% of the body. The rock fragments range between medium and coarse in size, and the individual mineral grains range from fine to medium. The andesite is characterized by a microcrystalline groundmass consisting of plagioclase. Andesine plagioclase is contained porphyritically within the andesite fragments, as is brown hornblende. Sparse magnetite cubes are present in the groundmass of the andesite as well.

Trace amounts of light gray rock fragments appear to represent highly weathered fragments of tuff, some stained slightly reddish from iron minerals in the tuff grains.

Discussion

A single group of four sherds possessing a common paste was identified through petrographic analysis. Samples ECU-1, 2, 6, and 7 make up this compositional group. The outstanding characteristic of these sherds is a variable amount of rectangular void or voids filled with a white amorphous substance in a light yellow-brown paste. The inclusions present in the four sherds include an abundance of untwinned potassium feldspar and less commonly quartz and plagioclase. Also present were fragments of highly weathered dacite and rhyolitic tuff.

Sample ECU-5 may also belong to the above group. This sherd has a light yellowish-brown paste that contains predominantly untwinned potassium feldspar, quartz, and plagioclase as well as weathered fragments of dacite and rhyolitic tuff. This sherd also contains the rounded soil pisolites observed in the paste of ECU-2. However, the rectangular voids present in the pastes of the previously described four sherds were not observed in this specimen.

Samples ECU-3, 4, and 8 are unique paste groups in this collection. It is likely that they represent vessels derived from clay source different from that of the other five in the ECU group. The two samples from the Chorrera region were produced from clays from entirely different sources than those in the ECU specimens. One sherd was made of clay containing sands that also contained fragments of rhyolitic tuff. The other contains sediments derived from hornblende andesite porphyry. Thus it is most likely they were made in two different places.

Bibliography

Folk, R. L.
1974   *Petrology of Sedimentary Rocks.* Austin: Hemphill Publishing.
Mason, R. B.
1995   Criteria for the Petrographic Characterization of Stonepaste Ceramics. *Archaeometry* 7(2):307–321.
Matthew, A. J., A. J. Woods, and C. Oliver
1991   Spots before the Eyes: New Comparison Charts for Visual Percentage Estimation in Archaeological Material. In *Recent Developments in Ceramic Petrology,* ed. Andrew Middleton and Ian Freestone, 211–264. British Museum Occasional Paper No. 81. London: British Museum Research Laboratory.
Terry, R. D., and V. G. Chilingar
1955   Summary of "Concerning Some Additional Aids in Studying Sedimentary Formations" by M. S. Shvetsov. *Journal of Sedimentary Petrology* 25:229–234.

Pottery Decoration

4

The most important decorative effects were achieved by the firing, which dictated surface color and hardness and affected burnish and fire-clouding. While modeling, carving and incision, brushing, painting, and differential burnishing were all important, they still took second place for potters whose principal interest was in the firing. All early pottery was fired just once (since it was not glazed, unlike most modern pottery, which has a bisque firing and a glaze firing), but some pots were subjected to a second exposure to a smoky fire to deposit carbon. Red-and-Black ware is defined by this practice, but some other vessels were given intentional fire-clouds as part of their decoration. Since the type of firing to be used for any particular vessel was chosen in advance, we can consider the firing part of the decoration as well as a technical requirement.

It seems likely that the colors and designs had particular associations with spiritual powers and cosmological realms. Although we speak of these as "decorative effects," whether they were pleasing to the eye was probably incidental. All the ceramic products to some extent, and the finest examples certainly, expressed ideas and values that were understood by those who saw or handled them. Although we sometimes think of pots as merely instrumental (meaningless except as tools for cooking or serving), early pottery, along with all the ceramic arts, was a carrier of ideology. It is usually in the decoration that ideas and values seem most intentionally and explicitly presented. Having no access to the ancient unwritten languages, we must seek ideological content in the decorative arts. If we are to know anything of what was in the minds of ancient artists and artisans, we must learn to read the language of their designs.

Two-Dimensional Abstract Designs

The following set of designs was the basis for most Challuabamba decorative art:

1. zigzag incisions or nested chevrons (Figure 4.1 a–d), sometimes in very cursive pattern burnish (Figure 4.1e);

2. triangles, hatchmarked, in series (Figures 4.1f and g);

3. X alone or in a series of Xs or a net (Figure 4.2a–c) or with dots in the net, the tie-dye design (Figure 4.2d);

4. squares or rectangles, usually part of a larger design such as the scroll-and-bar (Figure 4.3a, c, and d);

5. steps: may be extended into up-and-down steps, sometimes forming acute angles (Figure 4.4a);

6. spirals: a circle expanding from a center (Figure 4.4b);

7. double curves: S or Z, originating in a straight line with opposed curves at the ends (Figure 4.4c).

Although this set of designs clearly derives from Valdivia's long tradition, it makes quite a different impression. While Valdivia pottery is dark and tactile, Challuabamba's is mostly light (both in weight and color) and smooth, with defined areas of design. Nos. 3 and 7 ordinarily appear on reduced wares, while the others are usually found on oxidized wares. Although Valdivia artisans preceded Challuabamba's potters in the use of these designs, they can hardly be considered the property of Valdivia, since they are all part of a universal graphic design vocabulary, with the general symbolic tendencies dictated by tradition. The universality of these designs may be a result of their simplicity as manual gestures or possibly derived from the use of psychoactive substances to produce hallucinations (Stahl 1985, 1986). (Since I have made an extended exposition of this subject elsewhere [Grieder 1982], I will not repeat it here.)

The immediate ancestry of the zigzag is in Valdivia Incised (Meggers et al. 1965: Plate 67; Marcos 1988:258) of Phase 2a. Challuabamba's use of the design is far more disciplined, set between incised borders, with the incisions regular and of the same depth, in contrast to Valdivia's slashing manner. This design remained in use through at least Phase 7 at Real Alto. It is found at La Emerenciana in Phases 7 and 8 (Staller 1994:362, Figure 40a), with borders similar to those at Challuabamba. It forms constricting belts around the necks of jars, enhancing the contrast of the bulge of the wall and the narrowing of the neck.

The second design, hatched triangles, like the first, derives from Valdivia Fine-Line Incised jars and bowls of Valdivia Phases 1 and 2 (Meggers et al. 1965: Plates 62, 63; Hill 1972–1974: Plate IV; Marcos 1988:237). The common Challuabamba version is interlocking triangles on the in-slanted neck of the early "trompudo" jar form

(Figure 4.1f–g); Cut 3 Levels 4, 5). The accepted date for this design in Valdivia is before 2800 BC, though simplified versions appear at La Emerenciana (Staller 1994:362, Figure 40b), contemporary with Challuabamba. It was retained in Machalilla Ayangue Incised after 1500 BC. It may originate in basket weaving and may have remained popular because it emphasizes the built form of the vessel wall.

The incised or pattern-burnished X (Figure 4.2a–c), and its developments into series and nets, looks like a controlled development from Valdivia zigzag. Although Betsy Hill (1972–1974: Plate IV:9) shows a wide net on a jar neck of Phase 1, it was not common in Valdivia. For Challuabamba it was commonly pattern-burnished on

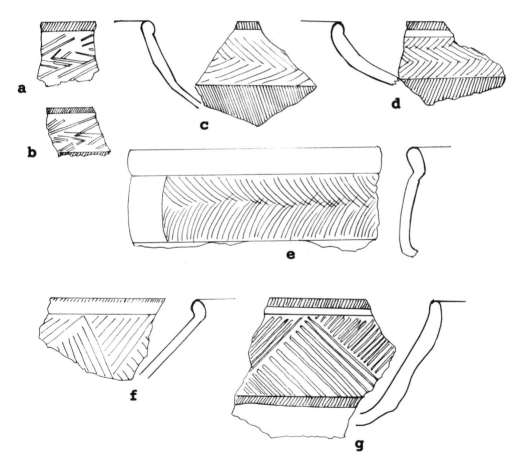

Figure 4.1. Designs incised and pattern burnished: *a* and *b,* zigzag or nested chevrons, Cut 3.G. Level 5; *c* and *d,* Red-on-Cream, Cut 3.G Level 4; *e,* pattern burnish on Burnished Black, 3.G Level 4; *f,* incised nested triangles, Red-on-Cream, 3.G Level 4; *g,* incised nested triangles, 3.G Level 5.

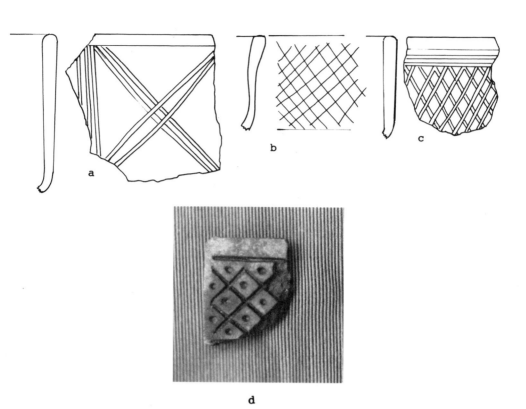

Figure 4.2. *a, b,* and *c,* Pattern-burnished X and net designs on reduced ware; all Cut 3 Level 4; *d,* tie-dye design, Cut 1.1.

the matte vertical exterior wall panels of black flat-based bowls. That location suggests associations with ceremonial drinking and probably with the night and hence may represent the network of stars. Although clearly in the regional tradition, this design was especially characteristic of Burnished Black at Challuabamba, and its expression in pattern-burnish enhances its local character. It was also a basic part of the Machalilla Ayangue Incised design vocabulary.

The square or rectangle is best represented in Valdivia in Broad-Line Incised and Excised bowls (where it appears as frames for lines, faces, equal-arm crosses, etc.) (Meggers et al. 1965: Plates 32f–i, 42a, 58f, 59b), characteristic of Phase 3. At Challuabamba it appears as a plain square or rectangle, most commonly as the center of the scroll-and-bar motif in Red-on-Cream jar rims (Figure 4.3). It is also the center of the complex design on the fragmentary cylinder seal No. 7 (Figure 7.8), where it is the center of the design, flanked by "wings" rather than a frame. This use of squares and rectangles is the opposite of that found in Valdivia: at Challuabamba they are the main

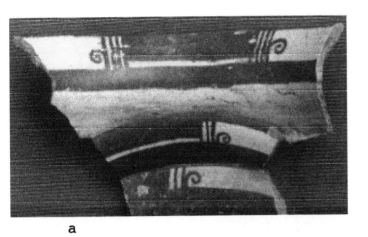

a

b

c

d

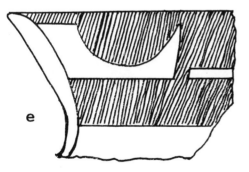

e

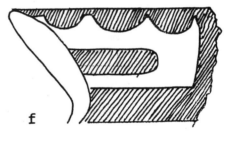

f

Figure 4.3. Rectangle or square, usually part of a larger design, as in *a*, scroll-
and-bars, Cut 3.H Level 4c; and *b*, Pucara Stela No. 1 (Lima: Museo Nacional
de Antropología y Arqueología); *c* and *d*, scroll-and-bar, both Cut 3.G Level 2;
e and *f*, late developments of scroll-and-bar, 3.G Level 2.

subject, not a frame for another design. That is interesting, because a square or rectangle was widely conceived as a symbol of the earth's surface (opposed to the circle of the sky) or sometimes as the "square" formed by the annual path of the sun across the sky. Although we have too little variety in the examples to assign a definite identity to the square, we can be sure that it had an identity for the people at Challuabamba. They also extended squares into the square-and-dot of the tie-dye motif (Figure 4.2d). That design, at least to the Aztec, represented the starry sky, again as a netlike pattern.

Design 5, rectangular steps, appears on a cylinder seal (No. 5) (Figure 7.6), in painted Red-Banded Incised vertical wall bowls and jars (Figure 4.4a), and incised on a Black bowl in Cut 1.1. In an Andean context it seems likely that it stands for the earth (or a mountain representing the earth) or the throne of sacred powers associated with the earth. This design is absent in Valdivia but is part of some incised designs at Machalilla (Meggers et al. 1965: Plate 133r).

The volute or spiral (Figure 4.4b) expanding from a center point and forming an even band was used to represent the snout of the jaguar on flat stamps and is part of the scroll-and-bar motif in Red-on-Cream jar rims (Figure 4.3a). The energy implied by its tightly coiled shape (the opposite of a perfect circle or square, which are seen as at rest) must refer to some active principle, a creator spirit perhaps, which might be seen in feline form. Even as a purely formal design, as on Cylinder Seal No. 14, it no doubt recalled some energetic spirit or principle (Figure 7.15).

The double spiral (Figure 4.4c), an S-shape created with one straight line with opposing hooks at the ends or a bar with curled ends or a double spiral, appears in appliqué fillets or incised on a variety of vessels throughout the sequence. The S-design is known first on Chinese pottery of the fourth millennium BC, where it may have had symbolism connected with female fertility (Chang 1977:110), but it survives in modern Peru under the Quechua name *pawsa*, a female fertility symbol used on women's shawls in imitation of the shawl of the Earth Mother, her *pawsa lliklla* (Isbell 1978:143; Grieder 1982:118–128).

Phases of Pottery Decoration

Challuabamba's pottery shows continuous change and development in its decoration, as in its forms and wares, with certain motifs remaining popular for long periods while others make only a brief appearance. The development of the decoration can be conveniently

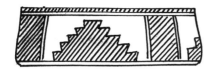

a

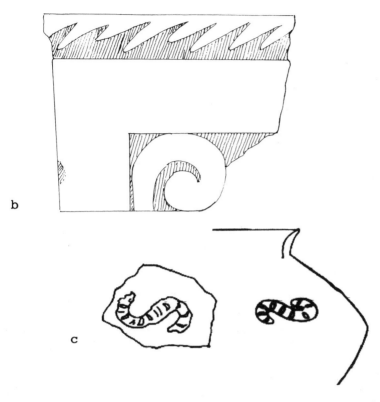

b

c

Figure 4.4. *a,* Stepped pyramid, Red-Banded Incised ware, Cut 3.G Level 5; *b,* volute, Cylinder Seal No. 11, Cut 3 Level 1; *c,* S-design, appliqué fillet, Cut 3.H Level 4.

summarized in four phases, based on the general stratigraphy but largely on Cut 3, in which Levels 5 and below are represented in Phase I, Level 4 in Phase II, Levels 3 and 2 in Phase III, and Level 1 and the surface in Phase IV. While the duration and the dating of the phases remain in doubt, the stratigraphy of Cut 3 provides an objective order and content for them. Since the decoration is somewhat independent of the vessel form, and to some lesser degree of the ware, the phases of development in decoration, while based on the stratigraphy, have a rate of change largely independent of the forms and wares.

Most of the pottery was decorated in some way; even jars, the quintessential utilitarian form, were commonly decorated with cream or white slip inside the rim with a red painted design. There is little pottery at Challuabamba that would not be considered "fine ware" (thin-walled and lightweight for the Red-on-Cream; sometimes heavier, but well-made, for the Burnished Black), almost all of it smoothed or burnished at least in part, and bearing some painted, incised, appliqué, or pattern-burnished decoration. Observers seem to agree that the designs added a layer of significance to the vessels that bore them, but only in rare cases can we guess with any confidence what they meant to the original audience. Nonetheless, simply putting them in sequential order is a step toward understanding.

The overall quality of the ceramic production suggests that it was considered important, the "high tech" of its period. It seems to have lost that status in later periods when the quality of the ceramic products declined, their prestige perhaps lost to the newer metal arts and crafts.

Phase I

In the earliest phase Red-on-Cream jars (Forms 1, 2, and 4) were the commonest forms and the fundamental decorative design was simple stripes, most commonly around the rim on the most visible surface (interior or exterior). Additional elaboration of the exterior usually consisted of incisions, either zigzag or hatched triangles (Figure 4.1a–g). There are a few decorations that run throughout the sequence, changing only slightly over the centuries. Two of those appeared in the earliest phase, in Red-on-Cream, and it would be useful to look at those before we examine the designs that make their appearance in later phases.

The most common painted elaboration of the rim stripes in the first half of the sequence is shown in Figure 4.3a. That scroll-and-bars design is found on the interior of the rim of jars, which is almost always decorated with burnished cream slip and one or more red stripes. The design starts with red stripes at the rim and at the base of the everted neck. Pendant from the upper stripe is a red rectangle, much wider than deep, with one to four red bars and a standing red curl at each end. The design was so popular and so consistent that it must have had a well-understood meaning, presumably connected in some way with the use of the large globular jars, which were perhaps cooking vessels for food or for brewing beer. The symmetry of the design and its definite top and bottom suggest that it may possibly represent a frontal face, though probably not a human one. The pair of scrolls at the sides can be compared with the curled snake tails that form an eye of one of the figures on a stela at Kuntur Wasi (Burger 1992: Figure 102, left) and the eye of a tenoned head at Chavín de Huantar (Burger 1992: Figure 154). They might also be compared with the curls (eyes?) at the sides of the top of the plaza stela (or Stela 1) from Pucara (Figure 4.3b) in the Titicaca basin (Chavez 1975: Plate 5). In the later phases the scroll-and-bars design was sometimes simplified, as in the examples from 3.G Level 2 (Figure 4.3e, f), which suggest that the motif was losing its meaning.

Another oxidized design that began in the early phase is much more complex and sophisticated and less common because the usual vessel forms are rarer, especially in Red-on-Cream. It is named Red-Banded Incised (RBI) for the exterior design. Figure 4.5 shows examples from three levels from early to late in Cut 3 and one from a surface find. At Challuabamba this design was applied to flat-based bowls (a form much more common in Burnished Blackware than in the oxidized wares) and was defined for both the exterior and the interior. One of the more complete early examples (Figure 4.5a) shows the exterior with incised lines outlining a rim stripe with vertical bands pendant from it and a scattering of circles in the cream field between the bands. Red paint fills the areas within the incised lines, which were cut before the red paint was applied. Later exteriors show bands with hooked, curved, or angular ends on the red bands (Figure 4.5c, d). At Challuabamba the interior also had a defined design. While the exterior is formal and controlled, with the paint areas ruled by the prior incisions, the interior is free in a way that we associate with the word "modernistic," painted with splashes of red on the cream slip. It appears that the artist had a brush that could contain a load of wet paint that could be scattered over the surface with a flip of the wrist, though it could have been done with flicks of the fingers. The slightly curving lines of red spatters indicate the gesture. We have called this the "splashed design." Uhle (1922: Figures 15, 56) and Gomis (1999:155, "poroto") mention similar bowl interiors from Challuabamba splashed with red paint.

Bruhns and her team have encountered both the interior splashed design (Bruhns et al. 1990:228) and the incised red-banded exterior (ibid., p. 230) at Pirincay, the interior design "in the earliest levels" and the exterior in the "later phases" (ibid., p. 228), but not together. Bruhns et al. (1994) have made a study of the type defined by its external design, Red-Banded Incised (RBI) (or Incisa en Franjas Rojas: IFR), finding it at several sites (Macas, Sucua, Sangay) in the Upano River–Sangay volcano region, united by volcanic inclusions in the

Figure 4.5. Red-Banded Incised (RBI) with Splashed interior (exterior on left, interior on right): *a*, Cut 3.G Level 5; *b*, 3.G Level 4, with reconstruction; *c*, 3.H Level 4; *d*, surface find, X1-2.

paste, as well as at Pirincay, Challuabamba, Cerro Narrío, and the Jubones Valley. Their conclusion is that the authentic RBI must be defined by paste rather than by decoration and, dated by Pirincay's radiocarbon dates, belongs to the period 400 BC–AD 100 (Bruhns et al. 1994:58).

This defines an interesting art historical sequence: the splashed interior/RBI exterior appears in Level 5 of Cut 3 at Challuabamba in a very confident, expert rendition (Figure 4.5a). The interior alone was used at Pirincay in its earliest period in crudely made bowls, and many years later the exterior design spread very widely and was adopted for local production somewhere in the Upano Valley (Bruhns et al. 1994:61), becoming one of the standard Late Formative types along the eastern fringe of the highlands. While people of the various regions used whatever materials were available to make their pottery, they were eager to adopt a new design or a good old design that retained its appeal, reviving it on new vessel forms (e.g., a large jar, Bruhns et al. 1990:230, Figure 10). With the present evidence, which is clearly incomplete, it appears that the original conception is found in Challuabamba's Level 5, where interior and exterior are inseparable.

We can trace this design into later phases at Challuabamba. Figure 4.5b shows its use in Level 4 of Cut 3.G, and it remained in use in later phases, sometimes showing slight revisions in style, as in Figure 4.5c and d. Figure 4.5c is a revision of the earlier vessel form, with an updated decoration showing the curves and hooks, perhaps related to the nascent Chavín style. The highly burnished exterior has Red-on-Cream within incised boundaries, and the interior has a red splash pattern on highly burnished cream slip. Figure 4.5d is a surface find, with the exterior also showing the hooked shape that anticipates Chavín design and a traditional splashed interior. The lines on the exterior were incised after the red paint was applied, which shows the painter defining the style with the brush, not merely filling in the lines, a change from the earlier practice.

A set of sherds from the late Level 2 in Cut 3.H (Figure 4.6, top row) shows the latest version of this RBI/Splashed style, with stepped pyramid designs in cream on a red ground both interior and exterior. This suggests that the ideology expressed by the design was losing its clarity, and the design may have gone out of use in the last years of the local sequence.

To modern eyes this design suggests a "Cubist" exterior and an "Abstract Expressionist" interior, a contrast of the formal and the informal that was on the minds of its creators. The persistence of the

Figure 4.6. Red-Banded Incised/Splashed sherds, Cut 3.H Level 2. These late versions of RBI/Splashed style add step-pyramids both inside and out, mixed with incised exteriors and splashed interiors.

design and its relative resistance to change show that it had some important symbolism in the local culture. Purely formal designs of this type are among the easiest to translate into words. In this case the interior is subject to chance and largely free of intellectual control, while the exterior is premeditated and subject to precise control. We might state this dichotomy in terms of a formal public behavior versus a spontaneous private life. One wonders how they would have expressed in words this idea that they have expressed so clearly in their art: perhaps as a contrast between the freedom of the dream or vision and the bounding form of a conventional life in the group. The idea was important to them, or they would not have expressed it over and over in very similar forms during several centuries.

Having surveyed these two examples of designs that persisted throughout several phases, we can return to decorations mainly confined to the first phase. While Blackwares were usually simply burnished and Red-and-Black decorated by simple areas of those colors, there were several common methods of ornamenting oxidized wares by incision, filleting, and punching (Figure 4.7). Notched fillets beginning in Phase I remained common throughout the sequence, usually in vertical lines but fairly often as nubbins or as S-shaped appliqués on jar bodies (Forms 2, 3, 4). (See Figures 2.3 #21, 2.9d, 4.4c.)

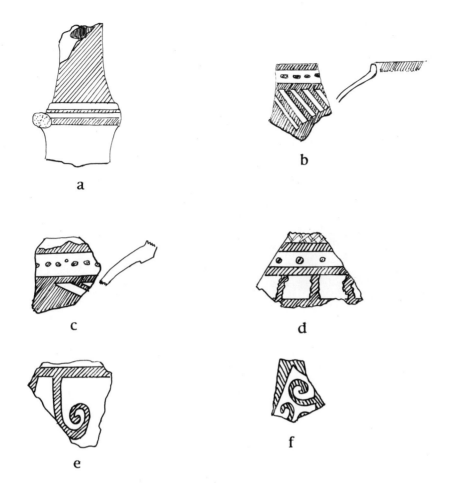

Figure 4.7. Red-on-Cream painterly style, all from Cut 3.G Level 4, Phases I and II: *a,* dark red on cream, bottle neck; *b,* red on burnished buff, rim of very small jar; *c,* red on cream, cream interior, very small jar; *d,* red on orange, cream interior, fine incisions at top; *e,* red-brown on gray, shoulder of jar; *f,* red on burnished buff, body sherd, scraped interior.

Burnishing in the first phase tended to cover the whole vessel or large surfaces and was often less thorough than in later phases. Pattern burnish is rare in the first phase and became popular in the second. While Blackwares were usually burnished, Red-on-Cream vessels were usually just smoothed overall and burnished only on the interior of the rim.

During Phase I and II the painters of Red-on-Cream small jars and basins (Forms 3 and 4) developed a free painterly style beyond rim stripes, with Xs and dots, red areas on jar shoulders augmented with lines of dots, diagonal stripes, and especially curling shapes. This painterly style belongs to this early period, beginning in Phase

Figure 4.8. Selected rims from Cut 3.H Level 4. Note the unique representational (?) rim painted black on buff.

I in Level 5 (Figure 4.7) and continuing into II (Figure 4.8; all examples from Cut 3, Level 4). It was largely executed in red paint with a fairly large brush, but an unusual example (Figure 4.8, center, from 3.H Level 4) is a rim and shoulder of a jar with two black shapes—a paw and tail?—unique in its color and its possible representation. The Red-on-Cream painterly style differs from the Late Formative Red-Banded Incised (Bruhns et al. 1994) and Machalilla Red-Banded (Meggers et al. 1965:133–135, Plates 149–153) in lacking incision and in its more varied designs, controlled lines, and generally smaller brush. The style does not appear in later levels at Challuabamba.

Phase II

The second phase shows a general refinement of vessel forms and a great increase in decoration. The incised triangles on in-slanting neck jars (Form 1c) went out of style with the vessel form, but the designs began to appear in pattern-burnish on matte areas of Burnished Blackware.

Phase II saw the expansion and development of pattern burnished designs on the exterior walls of Burnished Black bowls (Form 6). Contrasting areas of burnished and matte surface permitted the addition of pattern-burnished lines on the matte areas. The artists realized that the natural way to draw on the smooth, soft carbonized surface was with a smooth point—perhaps a stick—with a quick, cursive stroke (Figure 4.1e). In general, the best designs are the most cursive, done very quickly and freely following the surfaces of the vessels. None of the designs are representational and the commonest by far are diagonal lines or Xs, often expanded into nets. One of the earliest (Figure 4.1e) has free curving lines from the upper and lower borders, making a pattern suited to the gently curving wall. Uhle (1922: Plates XIX, XXI) shows several other examples of X patterns, nets, and other burnish/matte designs from Challuabamba.

The second phase, when Level 4 material in Cut 3 was deposited, was a period of experimentation, evident in the variety of decorative techniques. Modeling, burnishing, incision, and colored slips and paints were all used separately but also in combination, as we see in the sherds in Figure 4.9. All of these were parts of vessels that

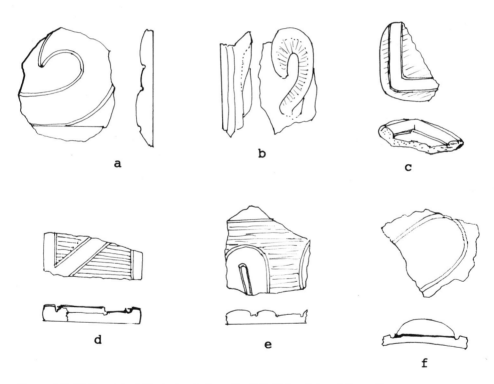

Figure 4.9. All Burnished Black sherds from Cut 3.G–H Level 4: *a,* feline tail (?) in relief with incision, relief burnished, matte background; *b,* ear of an effigy head?; *c,* relief with incision, burnished; *d,* wide strap handle with raised Z between borders (bottle handle?); *e,* burnished modeled forms, background incised; *f,* raised form, burnished, outline incised.

are hard to visualize, because they were clearly very labor-intensive, employing modeling, incising, grooving, and burnishing. Even Figure 4.9b, which we have been calling a feline tail, may be one end of an S-shaped bar, as shown by Uhle (1922: Figure 58). Figure 4.9d is part of the handle of a bottle, wider than usual, ornamented with a Z design; other fragments identify the form, but the vessel remains unrestorable.

Phase III

Burnished X and net patterns on matte areas continued to be made, sometimes growing more controlled and densely patterned. A variety of fine bowls (Form 5a or b) continued into Phase III, and contrasting areas of burnished and matte with pattern burnish lines are still found. The bowls in 4.10a and b have burnished and matte areas separated by very precise incisions.

The third phase is largely based on Level 2 in Cut 3 and on contemporary material from the other cuts. Among the new traits is the use of unslipped Matte Orange ware fired under variable conditions to produce orange-to-gray tones (Figure 7.1, top left). The light color of the Matte Orange ware seems to be part of a general development toward oxidation and light-colored pottery at Challuabamba. During this phase gray wares in the Burnished Black/Gray category began to be more common, rivaling the dominance of the pure blackwares.

In this phase we see the first use of postfire red paint, which was to become a common feature of later Formative pottery. It came in with a new or revived preference for textural or sculptural effects, different from the earlier preference for graphic or painterly surfaces done with pattern burnish or fired paint. An early example (Figure 4.11), from Level 2, is the small sherd probably from the wall of a jar or bottle with notched fillets and postfire red pigment applied to scraped areas between the fillets.

Postfire paint was part of the slowly coalescing wider style we call Chavín that was forming in a large area of northern Peru by this period. Red was by far the most common postfire color. Although it has not been analyzed, it may be cinnabar (mercuric sulfide), which was favored for funerary rites at Chavín-related sites in Peru (e.g., Cupisnique, Kuntur Wasi; Burger 1992:127, 205). The Peruvian source of cinnabar is at Huancavelica in the central highlands. If the red at Challuabamba is cinnabar, it is an indication that the site was participating in the long-distance trade network that grew up and declined along with the Chavín style. There is also the possibility that a closer Ecuadorian source remains unknown.

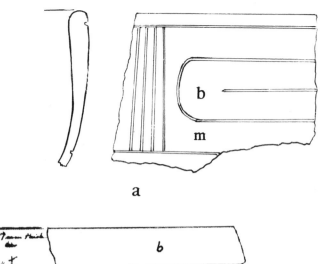

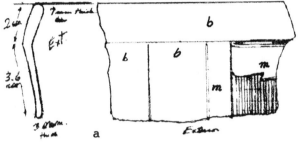

Figure 4.10. Burnished Black bowls, Form 5 (b = burnished; m = matte): *a*, Cut 3.D–F Level 4 (diam. 28 cm); *b*, Cut 3.A Level 2 (diam. 30 cm).

One of the most interesting potsherds decorated with postfire red is Figure 4.12a. It is a good example of late innovations in vessel form as well as in decoration. Another rim sherd (Figure 4.12b) is a Burnished Black bowl (Form 6) of traditional form and color, but with an innovative excised area containing white postfire paint. That color is rare at Challuabamba in postfire color but was found at Shillacoto and Kotosh in pre-Chavín styles (Kano 1979:13).

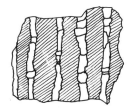

Figure 4.11. Postfire red, with notched fillets: sherd from Cut 3.I Level 2. Early use of postfire paint.

Phase IV

Other new stylistic features were appearing by about 1400 BC: some of the finest vessels have larger capacities, with thicker and more articulated walls. Textural effects such as fillets and incision (which were part of Phase I style) are returning, and effigy attachments are becoming more common. Fragments of various large jars in Level 1 show a Phase IV approach to large effigy forms (Figure 4.13). We cannot be sure what the subject is, both because the design is simplified and because the largest parts of the vessels are missing, but the shoulders of these vessels bulge and bear red linear designs that suggest wings. Sherds in the same level (Cut 3.E Level 1) include several bird head effigies, perhaps owls, which might have been attached to the smaller of the jars.

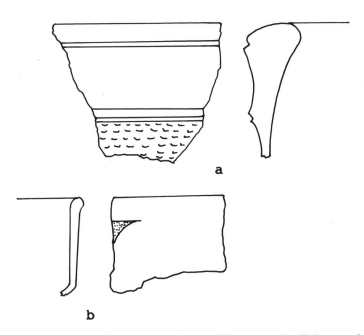

a

b

Figure 4.12. *a,* Burnished Gray, Phase IV elaboration of wall, fingernail punch with postfire red, X-2 surface find; *b,* Burnished Black bowl (22 cm rim diam.), Cut 3.J Level 1. Excised area has white postfire paint.

Figure 4.13. Jars of Forms 1 and 2, Red-on-Cream, Cut 3.D Level 1.

Two vessels are notable examples of the local style in this phase. The earlier is an oxidized tecomate that was a burial offering in Cut 2.B Level 1 and was largely restorable in the field (Figure 4.14). It measures 13 cm high and 8.8 cm rim diameter, with a wall thickness between 2 and 3 mm and a body circumference of 59 cm. It is a well-fired cream paste. The slightly raised rim is red and burnished; the remainder of the exterior is unslipped, very smooth but matte with a subtle pattern of burnish lines extending downward from the rim. A very small solid figure 8 mm high and 14 mm long makes a slight bulge just below the rim.

A large irregular patch of orange was applied to one side of the base, and a slight spatter of orange can be found over parts of the exterior. Within the orange patch is a small elongated area of black, probably applied by fire-clouding. Its combination of extremely light weight, scale, light color with accidental-appearing color fields, and subtle texture makes it an exceptional work of ceramic art.

This was not a unique item, but it is the only one that is complete enough that we can appreciate its quality. Level 1 in Cut 3 produced several rim sherds of what must have been similar vessels (Figure 4.15a, b). Both of the vessels shown have lightly burnished cream

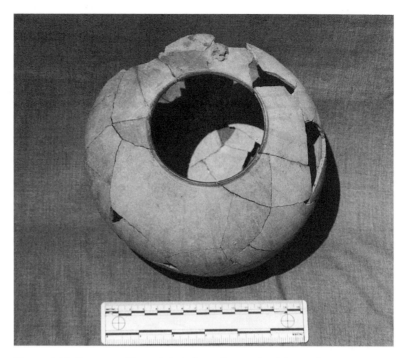

Figure 4.14. Tecomate (Form 4g), Red-on-Cream, Cut 2.B Level 1.

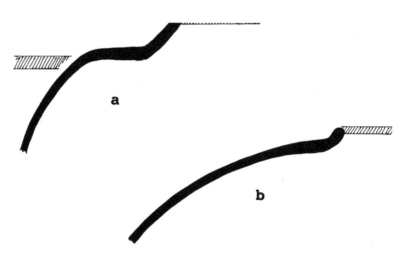

Figure 4.15. Rim sherds from Forms 4g, Cut 3 Level 1, Red-on-Cream (*a*, 14 cm rim diam.; *b*, 7 cm rim diam.).

slip on the exterior, with red rim stripes. These are typical rim forms for Challuabamba tecomates; the "comma-shaped" reinforced rim common in the earlier Peruvian and Mesoamerican tecomates is absent here.

The later of the two exceptional examples (Figures 4.16a, b, c) was found crushed, but missing only the upper parts, at the edge of an area of presumed feast debris of bone and antler fragments very near the surface in Cut 3.L Level 1. It is a bottle which appears to have had an effigy-head at the top center with a bridge to the off-center spout. The body seems to have had about twice the capacity of the earlier bottle forms, but the vessel walls are very thin and well made. The

a

Figure 4.16. *a,* Burnished Black bridge-spout bottle, Cut 3.L Level 1 (incised designs held postfire red pigment); *b,* side; *c,* top view. Fragment is 15 cm high, top design 16 cm diam.

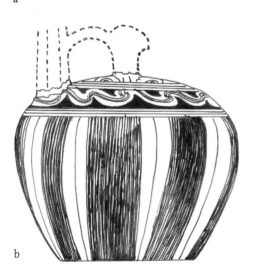

b

c

remaining fragment is 15 cm high; the base is 11 cm diameter, at the shoulder 18 cm. It is made of a soft sandy yellow-brown clay, with walls 2–3 mm thick, with a solid black (but eroded) surface which was given a good burnish. The decoration was precisely incised through the black surface. The walls were set off from the top by four incised lines. Straight vertical incised lines went from that border to the base in a set pattern alternating two plain areas divided by one line followed by a set of eleven, fifteen, or twenty-two lines.

On the top of the vessel, inside the boundaries of four incised lines, is a frieze of swirling S-shapes, with the center circle divided into four fields, each containing a half-circle with five petals. Red postfire pigment was rubbed into the design, making the effect a bright red design on burnished black. This vessel was a spectacular item, but it was lying so near the surface that about half the sherds were lost.

Stylistically the latest published material from Challuabamba known to me is a set of nine potsherds excavated by Gomis (Hocquenghem et al. 1993:457, Figure 3). All of them appear to be developments of techniques and designs found in our collection but considerably closer to Late Formative Peruvian styles and motifs and perhaps at least a few centuries later than our material. If still local products, they show the continued occupation of the site into the first millennium BC.

Bibliography

Bruhns, Karen Olsen, James H. Burton, and George R. Miller
1990 Excavations at Pirincay in the Paute Valley of Southern Ecuador, 1985–1988. *Antiquity* 64:221–233.
Bruhns, Karen Olsen, James H. Burton, and Arthur Rostoker
1994 La cerámica incisa en franjas rojas: evidencia de intercambio entre la sierra y el oriente en el Formativo Tardío del Ecuador. In *Tecnología y organización de la producción de cerámica prehispánica en los Andes*, ed. Izumi Shimada, 53–66. Lima: Pontificia Universidad Católica del Perú, Fondo Editorial.
Burger, Richard L.
1992 *Chavín and the Origins of Andean Civilization*. New York: Thames and Hudson.
Chang, Kwang-chi
1977 *The Archaeology of Ancient China*. 3rd ed. New Haven: Yale University Press.
Chavez, Sergio Jorge
1975 The Arapa and Thunderbolt Stelae: A Case of Stylistic Identity with Implications for Pucara Influences in the Area of Tiahuanaco. *Ñawpa Pacha* (Berkeley) 13:3–26.

Gomis, Dominique

1999 La cerámica Formativa Tardía de la sierra austral del Ecuador. In *Formativo sudamericano: una revaluación,* ed. P. Ledergerber-Crespo, 139–159. Quito: Abya-Yala.

Grieder, Terence

1982 *Origins of Pre-Columbian Art.* Austin: University of Texas Press.

Hill, Betsy D.

1972– A New Chronology of the Valdivia Ceramic Complex from the Coastal
1974 Zone of Guayas Province, Ecuador. *Ñawpa Pacha* (Berkeley) 10–12:1–32.

Hocquenghem, Anne-Marie, Jaime Idrovo, Peter Kaulicke, and Dominique Gomis

1993 Bases de intercambio entre las sociedades norperuanas y surecuatorianas: una zona de transición entre 1500 A.C. y 600 D.C. *Bulletin de l'Institut Français d'Études Andines* 22(2):443–466.

Isbell, Billie Jean

1978 *To Defend Ourselves: Ecology and Ritual in an Andean Village.* Latin American Monographs 47. Austin: Institute of Latin American Studies, University of Texas.

Jijón y Caamaño, Jacinto

1951 *Antropología prehispánica del Ecuador.* Quito: La Prensa Católica.

Kano, Chiaki

1979 *The Origins of the Chavín Culture.* Studies in Pre-Columbian Art. Washington, D.C.: Dumbarton Oaks.

Marcos, Jorge G.

1988 *Real Alto: la historia de un centro ceremonial Valdivia.* Quito: Corporación Editora Nacional.

Meggers, Betty J., Clifford Evans, and Emilio Estrada

1965 *Early Formative Period of Coastal Ecuador: The Valdivia and Machalilla Phases.* Washington, D.C.: Smithsonian Institution.

Stahl, Peter W.

1985 The Hallucinogenic Basis of Early Valdivia Phase Ceramic Bowl Iconography. *Journal of Psychoactive Drugs* 17:105–123.

1986 Hallucinatory Imagery and the Origin of Early South American Figurine Art. *World Archaeology* 18(1):134–150.

Staller, John Edward

1994 Late Valdivia Occupation in Southern Coastal El Oro Province, Ecuador: Excavations at the Early Formative Period (3500–1500 BC) Site of La Emerenciana. Doctoral dissertation, Southern Methodist University.

Uhle, Max

1922 *Influencias mayas en el Alto Ecuador.* Boletín de la Academia Nacional de Historia 4, Nos. 10–12. Quito: Tipografía y Encuadernación Salesianas.

5

Pottery Comparisons

While knowledge of the technical history of Ecuador and Peru in ancient times is still far from complete, it is already clear that knowledge and skills were being shared between communities over long distances. Pottery vessels and other ceramic products provide some of the best evidence of connections, or lack of connections, among these early communities. As Shepard argued (1965:347), "As a means of establishing contemporaneity, pottery has advantages over other kinds of artifacts because of the variety of its features and the richness of its development." Pottery techniques, forms, and especially decorative styles spread rapidly, or not at all, which contributes to the definition of periods (Shepard 1965:344–345). Recent years have produced a number of well-reported ceramic collections which make interesting comparisons with Challuabamba. In this we may be guided by Henning Bischof's suggestion that we should consider that "works of art throughout the world constitute the most secure chronological indicator, after inscribed dates—which they sometimes replace" (Bischof 1998:62; my translation). The common use of stylistic comparisons, along with radiocarbon dates, has resulted in the gradual emergence of a generally accepted and broadly consistent picture of Andean cultural development.

The story of the spread of ceramics into the highlands of Ecuador and Peru is multifaceted. One route was from the Amazon basin up the Ucayali River to the central Peruvian site of Kotosh, another down the Peruvian coast from Valdivian sites in southern Ecuador. At the same time a separate route carried ceramics into the high country of the Ecuadorian Andes to places which may have had some preceramic population but which were essentially newly established as pottery-making communities. That story can be told by looking at a few pots from four sites: the Valdivia site of Real Alto on the southwest coast, Cotocollao at Quito in the northern highlands, Challuabamba in the southern highlands, and the Peruvian site of Cerro Ñañañique in the upper valley of the Piura River about 100 km from the coast.

While Valdivia ceramics had a long history (beginning about 4400 BC; Zeidler 2003:519), it became part of this story about 2100 BC, in its Phase 6. Figure 5.1 (a, b, c) shows just three pots to represent the Valdivian contribution to Challuabamba's pottery. The neck of a large globular jar (5.1a) has a common incised design of slash marks in rows forming a zigzag. Variations on that design were common over a long period but particularly in Phase 6 (Hill 1972–1974: Figure 51). That style of globular jar with a neck bearing incised designs, frequently the zigzag, appears in the earliest levels at Challuabamba.

Another important early contribution from Valdivia to Challuabamba was the red and black color scheme, commonly applied to low restricted bowls, which were a new fashion in Valdivia Phases 5 and 6. Jorge Marcos (1988) shows a burnished black exterior to which a burnished red rim and shoulder were added (No. 303), a small jar (No. 327) with a smudged black body with an incised design filled with resinous red paint, and three jars (Nos. 375, 376, and 377) with a red body and a blackened shoulder and rim. These burnished red-and-black designs were likely models for the Red-and-Black ware which appears in the earliest levels at Challuabamba (see Marcos 1988:128–129, 166–168, and 178–180).

While the styles represented by Figure 5.1a and b appear in the earliest levels at Challuabamba and suggest contacts during the period 2100–1900 BC (or Phase 6 of Valdivia style), Figure 5.1c, a wide shallow serving bowl that I have called a "plate" at Challuabamba, appears in Valdivia Phases 7 and 8 (Hill 1972–1974: Plate VII), between 1950 and 1450 BC. At Challuabamba the plate form appears in Cut 3 Levels 3, 2, and 1, dated after 1510 BC by the radiocarbon tests, which places it in a late phase at that site. The influence of Valdivia pottery was clear throughout the Challuabamba sequence, basic in its first phase but still continuing in its latest.

Cotocollao, located about 300 km north of Challuabamba, shows some especially interesting connections and disconnections.

The main disconnection is the early appearance of the stirrup-spout bottle (Figure 5.1f), which seems never to have been made at Challuabamba. The later and apparently preferred bottle was the single-spout (5.1j), which is still quite different from the Challuabamba form. The variety and abundance of bottles (889 examples; Villalba 1988:459) suggest that Cotocollao was the source of bottle forms during this period, perhaps even of Challuabamba's earliest small single-spout form.

Beginning in Cotocollao's earliest period there are 111 stone bowls (Figure 5.1d), "beautifully worked and decorated, made in various

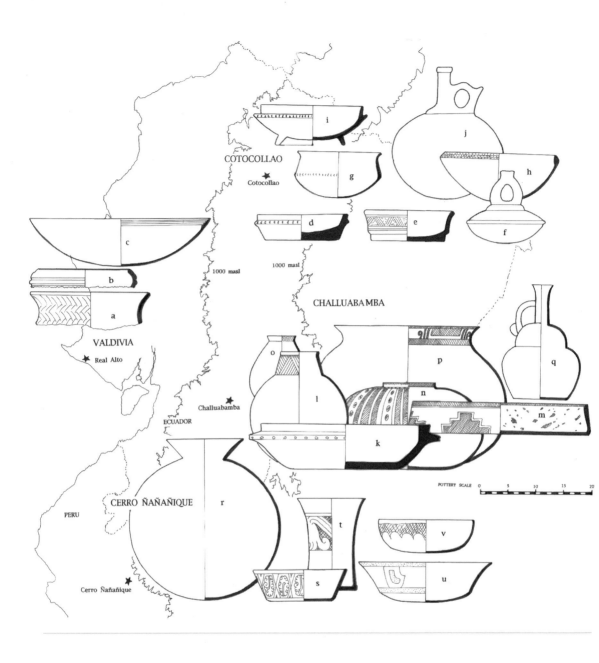

kinds of stone" (Villalba 1988:261, 307–308; Plates 40–50), all but seven of them broken, probably sacrificially. Although stone vessels did not disappear with the introduction of ceramics, they represent an earlier technical stage, and some of them may actually be pre-ceramic products. At Cotocollao their forms inspired pottery forms (Figure 5.1e; Form 4; Villalba 1988: Plate 43) that copied their flat bases, articulated walls, and incised decoration. In the Valdivia tradition pottery bases were rounded, and the Cotocollao vessels may

Facing page

Figure 5.1. Pottery from four Formative sites: Valdivia style at Real Alto, Cotocollao, Challuabamba, and Cerro Ñañañique: characteristic vessels of the period 2000–800 BC Valdivia: *a,* globular jar with a high everted neck with zigzag incision (Real Alto: Marcos 1988:I:258 no. 350), found as early as Phase 2 (c. 3000 BC; see also Phase 6, c. 2000 BC) (Marcos 1988:II:162 no. 351); *b,* small neckless closed bowl, burnished black with excised horizontal bands (Marcos 1988:II:100 no. 272), first found in Phase 5 (c. 2200 BC); *c,* shallow open bowl or plate (Hill 1972–1974: Plate VII no. 64, 65; Staller 2000:132), found in Phases 7 and 8 (c. 1800 BC). The order of appearance of these forms in Valdivia is reproduced in the Challuabamba sequence.

Cotocollao, at Quito, occupied c. 1500–500 BC (Villalba 1988:244; the following page/plate citations are to this volume): *d,* reconstruction of stone ceremonial mortar (Villalba 1988: Plate 41b); *e,* pottery ceremonial bowl, Form 4 (p. 462); *f,* early stirrup spout, Form 15 (p. 464); *g,* Form 14, small carinated basin, everted rim (p. 464); *h,* bowl with restricted rim, carinated with incision or punched ornament on rim, Form 1 (p. 461); *i,* carinated bowl with ring foot, late (c. 700 BC), Form 8 (p. 463); *j,* "Cotocollao Type" bottle, which appears early and gradually increases in popularity, Form 16 (p. 465).

Challuabamba: *k,* carinated bowl or ceremonial basin, Form 6c; *l,* globular jar with "trompudo" in-slanted neck with incised nested triangle design, Form 4b; *m,* Red-Banded Incised/Splashed interior, Form 5; *n,* globular jar with low vertical rim, Form 4f; *o,* globular jar with low neck, everted rim, Form 1c; *p,* large globular jar with high flared neck, scroll-and-bar on interior neck, Form 2b; *q,* single-spout bottle with dome, handle with whistle, Form 9.

Cerro Ñañañique, in northern Peru c. 1100–800 BC, shows large globular jars (*r*) comparable to Challuabamba's late Form 2 and bowl forms (*s, u, v*) comparable to Forms 5t, 3, and 7. The tall goblet form (*t*) is absent at Challuabamba and is a later development.

have been the first in the region with flat bases, following their stone models. The stone bowls were also copied at Challuabamba in pottery (Figure 5.1k) and may have been the inspiration for the use of flat bases on ceremonial vessels at that site (Figure 5.1m).

The Cotocollao basin and bowl forms (Figures 5.1g, h) appeared early and had a long life at the site (Villalba 1988:119ff., 150ff.) and may have contributed to some of the carinated forms at Challuabamba (Form 6). The flanged bowl with a ring foot (Figure 5.1i) is a late version of the type. Villalba (1988:157–161) shows two earlier deep bowls with ring feet, a form that was rare or imported (three sherds) at Challuabamba. The ring foot was not part of the Valdivia style, and the appearance at Cotocollao would seem to be the first in the region.

So far we have been describing Challuabamba as the recipient of features developed elsewhere, but its potters were creative in their use of the adoptions. Their earliest pottery copies of Cotocollao stone basins were painted in the Valdivia Red-and-Black style, and only later were they given a stonelike appearance by a rough, unslipped surface (Figure 5.1k).

Challuabamba's early phase shows adoptions such as the incised necks on jars, but the form of the neck is often not found elsewhere during that period, as in the "trompudo" in-slanted neck (Figure 5.1l). The tall jar (5.1o) is a local form, in the adopted Red-and-Black ware. The jar (5.1n) with a low vertical neck rim, painted red, with a decoration of incisions, nicked nubbins, and red stripes shows an original local style emerging. The low neck rim remained common at Challuabamba until it was superseded by the adoption of the neck-less rim (tecomate form).

The other three Challuabamba examples in the figure (Figures 5.1m, p, q) show early and mid-sequence types. The two painted vessels are part of the earliest local developments, in Level 5. The scroll-and-bars design in red on cream slip (5.1p) was the common decoration of the interior of large necked jars throughout the earlier phases, gradually decaying into abstract shapes in the last phase. It seems to be a purely local design (though found rarely at nearby Pirincay; Hammond and Bruhns 1987: Figure 5). The other painted style (5.1m, Red-Banded Incised with Splashed interior) is found early on flat-base vertical-wall bowls (Form 5), a form which later became standard in Burnished Black, while the painting style continued on related forms in Red-on-Cream. The Burnished Black bowls are relatively rare and very finely made, and it appears that the Red-on-Cream version is the ceremonial type in the more common oxidized wares. That would imply that the painted design, Red-Banded Incised on the exterior and Splashed on the interior, is also of special ceremonial significance. Red-Banded Incised decoration requires a separate discussion (see "The Red-Banded Incised Style" in Chapter 12).

The domed bottle (Figure 5.1q) seems to be an early example of a form associated with Chorrera and, being part of the Burial 6 offering, which has several imported items, casts doubt on it as a local product. The Burial 6 offering can hardly be later than 1300 BC, however, which would be early for a Chorrera product. Since several other domed forms are known at Challuabamba and other ceramic forms (e.g., cylinder seals) anticipate Chorrera forms, it may be considered local until proven otherwise.

Figure 5.1 (k–q) barely scratches the surface of Challuabamba creativity. Solid figurines, effigy vessels and effigy attachments on jars, stamps and cylinder seals, and modeled, painted, and incised designs on vessels remind us of the range of expression in clay found there.

The last phase in this condensed summary of the regional style is represented by Cerro Ñañañique, located at Chulucanas on the upper Piura River in northern Peru. The site is dated 1100–700 BC by Guffroy (1994), who has defined two pottery styles (A and B) in local production. Style A is the expression of the majority, believed by Guffroy to represent an ancient population spread across the region from Bagua to Tumbes, from the Amazon forests to the Pacific coast. Its forms are necked jars (Figure 5.1r) and bowls (u, v), fired in an oxidizing atmosphere to red or brown. Style B (s, t) is fired to black or dark brown and appears in service wares associated with a small group of people "close to the systems of power" and the functions of a ceremonial center (Guffroy 1994:422; my translation). The complex iconography found in Style B has been attributed to sources as diverse as Valdivia and Kotosh. The typical forms are bowls, round based or flat with straight walls, fired to a uniform dark brown or black, in a reducing atmosphere (ibid., 375). Guffroy (ibid., 375) comments that "the most complex motifs, of classic technique, are nearly systematically associated with very dark colored, highly burnished vessels."

The paired styles at Cerro Ñañañique follow the pattern found at Challuabamba, an oxidized light-colored majority ware, which includes storage and culinary wares, and a minority smudged or reduced black or brown ware of service vessels with highly finished decorations. Guffroy (1994:421) finds similar paired ceramic styles at a number of sites contemporary with Cerro Ñañañique: Machalilla (red-banded/Ayangue incised), Bagua (polychrome/incised), Pacopampa (incised and painted postfire/incised or engraved). "More generally," writes Guffroy, "the coexistence of a painted style and an incised style is evident, beginning in the 15th century BC, in the whole region (Cerro Narrío, Catamayo C, Pechiche, Huacaloma), without necessarily implying two groups of producers or a multicultural population." Challuabamba is clearly part of this category at an earlier stage.

Ñañanique's vessel forms are generally similar to Challuabamba's later phases: globular flared-neck jars, carinated wide-mouthed basins, numerous bowls with round or flat bases, various single-spout bottles, flat-based or globular, plus rare stirrup-spouts. The two styles (A and B) divide not only in color but in forms: flat-based bowls with straight out-slanting walls are a major form in reduced wares, while round-based slightly restricted bowls or bowls with flared walls (an early form at Challuabamba) are oxidized. The decorations of those two bowl types are also different: the oxidized type is painted (frequently gray and white) on natural slip, while the reduced type is incised on the black or dark brown surface. All of these characteristics recall Challuabamba, though the two ensembles are easy to tell apart. The tall form (5.1t), which Guffroy calls a goblet, has no antecedent form and seems to be Ñañanique's elegant answer to the vessel for ritual service of liquids, anticipating the much later *kero* form.

While in many respects (morphology, techniques) Challuabamba and Cerro Ñañanique appear closely related, in the incised designs on reduced wares the differences indicate a chronological distinction: Challuabamba's geometric incised or pattern-burnished lines provide frames for Ñañanique's flowing curvilinear "monster" designs (Figure 5.2a–d), "the principal image in the iconography of the Upper Piura during the Formative Period" (Guffroy 1994:315). The monster seems to be both fishlike and mammal or a winged feline, perhaps best called a "dragon," the designation chosen by Luis Lumbreras for similar designs at Chavín de Huantar. Challuabamba's Xs (Figure 4.2a) may be the model for the frames around designs of the monster that developed in Figure 5.2d at Ñañanique.

The two great Late Formative ceramic styles, Chavín in Peru and Chorrera in Ecuador, have both been thought to have played some part in the development of Challuabamba's pottery. Both those styles made their first appearance about 1300 BC and reached their greatest development after 800 BC. The most famous single pot supposedly found on the Challuabamba site (Figure 5.3), more precisely from the part of the site called El Descanso, was first published by Collier and Murra (1943: Plate 10, Figure 4), who called it a "Coastal Chavín type." The frieze of abstract profile monster heads incised on the body is in a style closest to a well-known vase from Morropón in the highlands east of Cerro Ñañanique. The El Descanso stirrup-spout was certainly imported into the Tomebamba Valley, probably from some Chavín-related site in northern Peru, several centuries after the end of our ceramic sequence. Although we can largely elimi-

Figure 5.2. Incised decorations at Cerro Ñañañique, "the principal image in the iconography of the Upper Piura during the Formative Period" (Guffroy 1994:315; my translation): *a–d:* "monster" designs: *a*, male, *b*, female, *c*, "monsters" in series, *d*, "monsters" in frames.

nate Chavín as an influential connection with Challuabamba, there still remains the major question of the significance of Chorrera in the ceramic production of our site.

The middle and later part of the sequence was the high point in Challuabamba's ceramic art. It was also a period when connections westward with the nascent Chorrera culture seem to have increased. Domed forms became more common on bottles and jars and carinated walls on bowls and basins, with modeled relief, effigy vessels and effigy attachments, cylinder seals, and stamps. These features

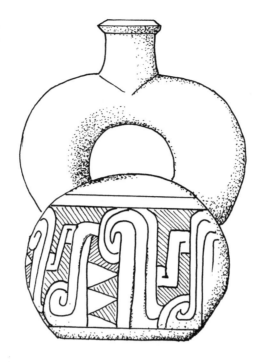

Figure 5.3. Black incised stirrup-spout bottle supposedly found at Puente de El Descanso, part of Challuabamba site, in the Duran Collection, Cuenca. Redrawn from Collier and Murra (1943: Plate 10, no. 4).

account for the "Chorrera de la Sierra" title given (most recently by Idrovo Urigüen 1999:121) to Challuabamba's work, since many of those features are also found in coastal Chorrera ceramics. James Zeidler (2003:494–508) provides an assessment of Chorrera's dates, concluding that the Chorrera style (incorporating Tabuchila and Engoroy) appeared earliest in Manabí and western Pichincha about 1300–1200 BC and ended about 350–300 BC. The definition of "The Tabuchila Complex (Chorrera)" by James Zeidler and M. J. Sutliff (in Zeidler and Pearsall 1994:114–115) provides a good excavated sample of Chorrera pottery from the Jama River valley in northern Manabí (Figure 5.4a–f). The jar forms (5.4a, b) are globular or subglobular with low everted rims similar to Form 1 at Challuabamba (Figure 2.4a, d, and e). The wide-mouthed basin (5.4c) is a common form "diagnostic of the Chorrera culture throughout the western Ecuadorian lowlands" (Zeidler and Pearsall 1994:114–115). Described as a "squat, wide-mouthed 'cuspidor' olla," it is closest to our Form 6 (Figure 2.9) but appears lower and wider.

The bowls (5.4d, e, f) are all common Chorrera forms. 5.4f is the earliest, associated with C[14] sample AA-4140, dated 2845±95 RCYBP, cal. 95.4% to 1300–810 BC, or 1055 BC±245 (Zeidler 2003:506, 516), which the authors consider Tabuchila 1. The Figure 5.4d and e forms are assigned to Tabuchila 2. Those shown had round bases, but a common variant of 5.4e had a wide pedestal base. While Challuabamba pots have flat or round bases, the Chorrera style and its lowland contemporaries often have ring bases (Figure 5.4g, from Beckwith [1996: Figure 6.9, no. 4]), which developed in later phases into pedestals or tripod (or more) legs. The undulating rim of 5.4i carries on a Valdivia tradition, but one absent at Challuabamba. The napkin-ring earspool (5.4h), however, is represented at Challuabamba (Figure 9.11).

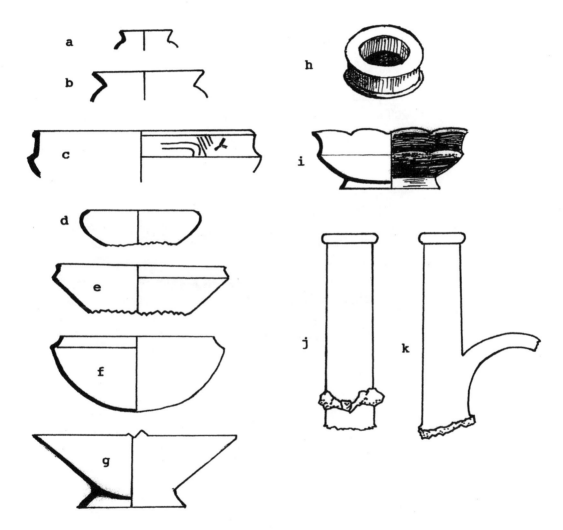

Figure 5.4. A selection of diagnostic Chorrera ceramic forms from the western lowlands of Ecuador, redrawn from various sources. Items *a–f* from Zeidler and Sutliff, Figure 7.2 (recoded), in Zeidler and Pearsall (1994:114–115). Bowl *g* is from Beckwith (1996: Figure 6.9, no. 4), to show the common ring foot in Chorrera pottery. Items *h–k* are redrawn from Estrada (1958:76, 88, 86).

Among the earliest-appearing vessel forms in the Chorrera group are single-spout bottles, with handles incorporating whistles, from Ayangue on the southern Manabí coast, shown by Emilio Estrada (1958:86–88). That form is certainly older at Challuabamba, where it appears in Cut 3, Levels 5 and 4 (Figure 2.12e); Level 5 has a C[14] date of 2039 BC±295. The early Chorrera bottle spouts (Figure 5.4j, k) are fairly wide and untapered with reinforced rims. A spout in that style was found in our Cut 3, Sector D, Level 1 (Figure 5.5, top row, third column from left). It is the tallest and most roughly finished spout in our sample and the only one with this type of reinforced rim. To its left in Figure 5.5 is a Challuabamba spout, found in Level 1 of the adjoining Sector E of Cut 3. It is typical of the style of Challuabamba's later bottles, although the other eight spouts show the range of variation in form and finish. If an early "Chorrera (Tabuchila)" phase at San Isidro can be dated by C[14] to 1300–810 BC (Zeidler 2003:506, 516), then the early Chorrera-style spout at Challuabamba provides a plausible period for the end of our ceramic sequence at Challuabamba at about 1055 BC±245 years. The elegant tall spouts

Figure 5.5. Ten spouts from single-spout bottles from Cut 3 Level 1 at Challuabamba. The tallest (*center right*) is early Chorrera style, an import. All the others are Challuabamba style, with the possible exception of the one in the lower left. Most or all should date about 1300–1100 BC.

on later Chorrera bottles are closer in finish to Challuabamba's late spouts, although they often retain a reinforced rim (Lathrap et al. 1975: catalog Nos. 396, 406), which was always rare at Challuabamba (as in the lower left example in Figure 5.5).

Another feature of Chorrera ceramics that provides objective evidence of a temporal difference compared with Challuabamba is the use of molds in the production of hollow figurines. Pedro Porras G. and Luis Piana Bruno (1976:75; my translation) remark: "It appears that the majority of the [Chorrera] figurines are modeled by hand, but there exist examples with characteristics suggesting the use of molds"; and Tom Cummins (2003:431, note 13) writes: "In many cases single piece molds were used to make the front of the figure, and the back was modeled by hand. . . ." The prototype for the ceramic mold is the stamp or seal, which leaves its imprint just as does a mold, and Challuabamba made an important early contribution to that stage. Chorrera potters and figurine sculptors achieved the next stage, the one-piece mold for parts of figures intended to represent a likeness of a sacred being (Cummins 2003:438). In the later centuries of the first millennium BC that technique spread widely in the Pre-Columbian world.

The role of Challuabamba relative to Late Formative ceramics in the Ecuadorian western lowlands was clearly as a stimulant. Only rarely did the highland potters produce effigy forms that might be mistaken for Chorrera products, or vessels with the formal perfection of Chorrera's, but they do provide an answer to the mystery of where Chorrera potters found inspiration.

Bibliography

Beckwith, Laurie Anne
1996 Late Formative Period Ceramics from Southwestern Ecuador. Doctoral dissertation, University of Calgary, Department of Archaeology.
Bischof, Henning
1998 El Período Inicial, el horizonte temprano, el estilo Chavín y la realidad del proceso formativo en los Andes Centrales. *Primer Encuentro Internacional de Peruanistas, Lima, Set. de 1996:* 57–76.
Collier, Donald, and John Murra
1943 *Survey and Excavations in Southern Ecuador.* Anthropology Series 62. Chicago: Field Museum of Natural History.
Cummins, Tom
2003 Nature as Culture's Representation: A Change of Focus in Late Formative Iconography. In *Archaeology of Formative Ecuador,* ed. by J. S. Raymond and R. L. Burger (J. Quilter, general editor), 423–464. Washington, D.C.: Dumbarton Oaks.

DeBoer, Warren R.

2003   Ceramic Assemblage Variability in the Formative of Ecuador and Peru. In *Archaeology of Formative Ecuador*, ed. J. S. Raymond and R. L. Burger, 289–336. Washington, D.C.: Dumbarton Oaks.

Estrada, Emilio

1958   *Las culturas Pre-Clásicas, Formativas o Arcaicas del Ecuador*. Guayaquil: Museo Victor Emilio Estrada.

Guffroy, Jean

1994   *Cerro Nañañique: un établissement monumental de la période formative, en limite de désert (Haut Piura, Pérou)*. Paris: Orstom.

Hammond, Norman, and Karen Olsen Bruhns

1987   The Paute Valley Project in Ecuador, 1984. *Antiquity* 61:50–56.

Hill, Betsy D.

1972–   A New Chronology of the Valdivia Ceramic Complex from the Coastal
1974   Zone of Guayas Province, Ecuador. *Ñawpa Pacha* (Berkeley) 10–12:1–32.

Idrovo Urigüen, Jaime

1999   El Formativo en la sierra ecuatoriana. In *Formativo sudamericano: una revaluación*, ed. P. Ledergerber-Crespo, 114–123. Quito: Abya-Yala.

Lathrap, Donald W., Donald Collier, and Helen Chandra

1975   *Ancient Ecuador: Culture, Clay and Creativity, 3000–300 B.C.* Chicago: Field Museum of Natural History.

Marcos, Jorge G.

1988   *Real Alto: la historia de un centro ceremonial Valdivia*. Biblioteca Ecuatoriana de Arqueología, 4 and 5. Quito: Corporación Editora Nacional.

Porras G., Pedro I., and Luis Piana Bruno

1976   *Ecuador Prehistórico*. 2nd ed. Quito: Instituto Geográfico Militar.

Shepard, Anna O.

1965   *Ceramics for the Archaeologist*. Washington, D.C.: Carnegie Institution.

Staller, John Edward

2000   The Jelí Phase Complex at La Emerenciana: A Late Valdivia Site in Southern El Oro Province, Ecuador. *Andean Past* 6:117–174.

Villalba O., Marcelo

1988   *Cotocollao: una aldea Formativa del valle de Quito*. Quito: Museos del Banco Central del Ecuador.

Zeidler, James A.

2003   Formative Period Chronology for the Coast and Western Lowlands of Ecuador. In *Archaeology of Formative Ecuador*, ed. J. Scott Raymond and Richard L. Burger, 487–527. Washington, D.C.: Dumbarton Oaks.

Zeidler, James A., and Deborah Pearsall

1994   *Regional Archaeology in Northern Manabí, Ecuador*. Vol. 1. Pittsburgh: University of Pittsburgh, Dept. of Anthropology; and Quito: Libri Mundi.

Effigy Vessels and Figurines

6

When we lay out the figurines, effigy vessels, and effigy attachments to vessels according to their stratigraphic locations, it becomes apparent that certain features of form and style cluster at different stratigraphic levels. Level being in general a function of time, it follows that the clusters represent conventions accepted during certain periods. Since form and style can be defined and their conventions represent social agreements ("A work of art is a statement about the nature of reality": Arnheim: 1964:21), we can reconstruct some of the conventions of the periods when those clusters of works were made.

The general term "effigy" refers to a representation of a human figure or other natural form (which at Challuabamba was often a bird but might be a fish, frog, jaguar, etc.). The examples under discussion here are three-dimensional ceramic forms: freestanding small clay sculptures, pots modeled into the forms of living creatures, or modeled effigies attached to standard pot forms. The general order of development was solid clay figurines, then solid effigy elements (usually heads) attached to pots, then pots modeled into an effigy form, and finally hollow effigy heads attached to pots and, probably about the same time, hollow figurines and finally faces modeled on the exterior walls of bowls.

Solid Figurines

There are only five independent, free-standing human figures in the ceramic collection from Challuabamba. Three come from Level 5 of Cut 3, which places them among the earliest items in our sequence (Figure 6.1a–c). Although they vary in size from small to very small, they share several traits. All are solid clay, well fired, with no postfire additions, roughly modeled. The heads are all simple masses without indications of hair or ears, with large noses without nostrils, slashed mouths, and punched or slashed eyes. The neck of Figure 6.1a is so long that it probably had no arms; and while 6.1b had arms, 6.1c had no arms but did have divided legs. There are no indications of gender on 6.1a and b, but 6.1c is clearly female. These are stratigraphically the earliest effigy forms, and their general consistency implies an early local type. Figurines already had a long history in the Valdivia culture by the time Challuabamba was occupied, so we must assume a derivation from Valdivia. Few published examples of Valdivia figurines are very directly comparable, but an early publication (Evans et al. 1959:115) shows several figurines of the "coarse variety" ("variedad tosca"), which share the bald head and slashed or punched features that compare with our examples. At Real Alto, in a Valdivia IV deposit, Marcos (1988:96–99; my translation) found four figurines "en las que se marcan por primera vez la nariz" (in which for the first

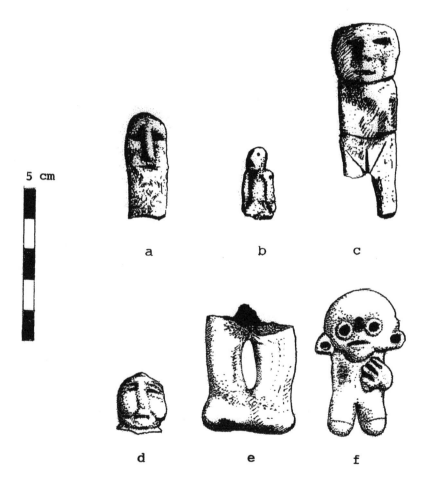

5 cm

a

b

c

d

e

f

Figure 6.1. Solid figurines: *a*, Cut 3.J Level 5 (3.5 cm high); *b*, Cut 3.G Level 5b (2.4 cm); *c*, Cut 3.K Level 5 (6.5 cm); *d*, Cut 2 Level 2 (2.1 cm); *e*, Cut 3.E Level 3 (4.0 cm); *f*, Cut 3.C Level 2 (4.9 cm): this has a break on the back where it was attached to a surface.

time the nose is indicated). That feature as well as blocklike bodies and less emphasis on the hair show some similarity to Challuabamba's earliest figurines. But in general it appears that the Challuabamba figurine makers began with an independent vision of a female figure with a face but no secondary sexual characteristics or cultural attributes or actions.

The figurine 6.1f, found in Level 2, introduces many new features: although solid and a complete figure (with the right arm broken off), it was not freestanding, and the treatment of eyes, ears, hands, and feet is new. A broken area down the middle of the flat back shows where it was attached, presumably to a pot. The round eyes, punched into an appliquéd button, depart from the older slashed eye; the same technique is used to indicate earplugs, a new feature, as are the modeled hands and the feet indicated by the line separating them from the legs. In Level 2 of Cut 3 it is apparent that we have entered a new period. The fragments 6.1d and e show other steps in the development of figurines: 6.1d retains the slashed eyes and mouth and small scale, while 6.1e is on a much larger scale but still solid. Hollow figurines, if ever made at Challuabamba, were very rare and found mostly in surface levels (Figure 6.7, Nos. 9, 30–37). Effigy vessels were slightly more common, but most common were attached effigy heads on standard vessel forms.

Early Effigy Vessels

The early steps in the development of this art form at Challuabamba were, first, purely functional pottery forms and very rough solid figurines, followed by a few pots modeled as effigies. The two best examples of effigy pots were both placed among the offerings with burials, one in Burial 6 in Cut 3 Level 4 (Figure 6.2), the other in Offering 2 with the burials in Cut 2 (Figure 6.5).

The most complete and most interesting vessel (Figure 6.2) is a Burnished Black vase apparently showing a fish undergoing metamorphosis into a jaguar, with the vertical tail fin of a fish but pairs of pawlike fins at the base on both sides. It has a pattern of engraved circles on the body and a face with protruding button eyes and a wide mouth with curling lines at the corners, which probably stand for fangs or perhaps whiskers. This adds up to a fish with jaguar spots and fangs, perhaps a concept somewhat like the underwater panther of the Algonkians.

This vessel is of special interest because it brings together a set of features that in many other Pre-Columbian groups have ceremonial or religious importance: placement in a burial offering, burnished

Figure 6.2. Jaguar-catfish effigy vase, Burnished Black with postfire engraving, from Cut 3.H Level 4, Burial 6 offering. (Photo by J. Farmer)

black color, the effigy figure, and feline traits (especially the spots and the fanged mouth). While fish are not a common subject in Challuabamba art, this being the only one so far identified, the proximity of the river makes it seem natural there. Feline features, as we shall see in the discussion of carved wares, are fairly common and varied in the local style. The ware and high level of craft indicate that this was produced locally. The most unusual feature in the technique is the engraving of the spots and mouth, done after firing, which indicates that they were afterthoughts. They are also the crudest work on the vessel. Without those features the feline quality is much reduced, remaining perhaps only in the four pawlike fins. It could be that the vessel was delivered to the patron as a fish effigy but was returned for further work to give it the feline traits, or they might have been added by a later owner. Perhaps this gives us some information about the interaction between artists and their patrons, since an offering in a burial may be a commissioned piece. The quality of the original work makes it virtually certain that the artist was a specialist who fulfilled orders from elite patrons, but the engraving is amateurish.

Offering 2 with the set of four burials in Cut 2 contains another very fine, thin-walled jar, still only partly restored, of unslipped brown micaceous clay (Figure 9.10c). Its lobed form suggests a fruit or vegetal form, but the punched circle and grooved lines that remain on one side might be the eye and snout of an animal. These two exceptional pieces suggest that effigy vessels may have been more common than the excavated material suggests and, along with the carved wares, represented the highest level of art production of the site and its period.

Solid Effigy Attachments

At about the same time when these two effigy pots were made, many small, solid effigy heads (birdlike or humanlike) were also being made. A tiny (1.5 cm high) solid head broken from a jar and perhaps made into a pendant, to judge by a hole drilled in the top of the head, is typical (Figure 6.3d). Note the pressed-in eyes, similar to the eyes of the small relief face in Figure 6.3e. That face, perhaps representing an owl on the basis of its beaklike mouth and large round eyes, is formed by a fillet of clay that marks the top of the head, ending with a clay button. The features—pressed-in eyes and a pressed button mouth—are of the same orange-buff clay as the vessel. Set just

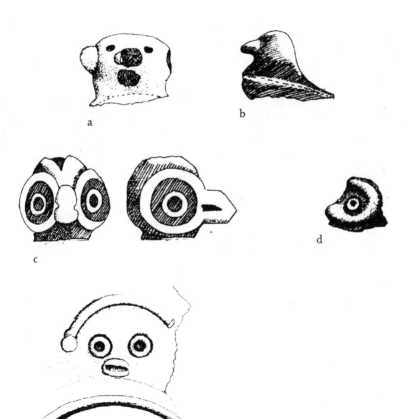

Figure 6.3. Solid effigy heads, attachments to small jars: *a*, Cut 2 Level 2; *b*, 3.F Level 4; *c*, 4.B (30 cm level); *d*, 4.I (30–40 cm level); *e*, Cut 1 Level 1.

below the vessel rim, as if looking over it, this is a flat version of what had already become the standard modeled attached head on small jars.

Solid effigy heads were most common in Cut 3 Level 4, an indication that they represent an early period, in contrast to the much more numerous hollow heads, which are most common in Levels 1 and 2 of Cut 3. Two solid bird heads show an earlier and a slightly later style in solid effigy attachments: Figure 6.3b (from Cut 3.F Level 4) and Figure 6.3c (from Cut 4.B at 30 cm). The most humanlike version of the solid effigy attachment, Figure 6.3a has punched eyes in common with the rare human figurines, but the smooth hollow under the base of this head was the interior of the pot it was attached to, which proves that this head was an effigy attachment, not a freestanding figurine. Small figures formed of fillets attached just below the rim of large or small jars were fairly common in the late levels, as found in the large tecomate from Offering 2 in Cut 2 (Figure 4.14).

One of the most realistic of these small solid attached heads, from Cut 2 Level 2, represents a bat. Like all the other attached heads, it faces inward into the vessel. The common vessel for attached heads was a restricted jar with a low vertical rim (Figure 6.4), but the bat ornaments the flared rim of a Red-on-Cream bowl, facing inward as effigies on jar rims always do.

Figure 6.4. Solid effigy head of a bat attached to the rim of a Red-on-Cream bowl from Cut 2 Level 2.

Hollow Effigy Heads

The offerings with Burial 1 in Cut 2 show the transition from solid to hollow attachments, which resulted in the reduction of the attachment in most cases to just the head or the head with solid arms. The jar with the hollow head attachment (Figure 6.5) is just 6.2 cm high; the attached head is a separate hollow from the vessel interior, with the eyes punched through. Originally it had both arms holding something to the mouth, the common motif among the hollow attachments. Frequently the arms, and rarely the lower body and legs, were modeled in solid clay and attached to the wall of the jar.

This type of effigy attachment was very common in the later levels (Levels 1 and 2 of Cut 3 and the equivalent levels in the other excavations), differing from the earlier examples only in the hollow of the head being joined to the hollow of the jar, showing that the head was not merely attached but conceived as part of the vessel form. Maria Naula (1997) discusses seventy-nine examples of this type from Challuabamba, comparing them with examples in collections and publications (thirty-eight in the Museo Municipal in Cuenca; thirty-three in the Museo de las Culturas Aborígenes in Cuenca; six from Cerro Narrío published by Collier and Murra [1943]; two from Huancarcuchu and Azogues published by Bennett [1946]). Several

Figure 6.5. Jar with effigy head from Cut 2, offering with Burial 1. The jar is 6.2 cm high. The hollow of the head is separate from the interior of the jar.

more examples have been found since Naula completed her study, making a total of ninety-four small heads attached to pots at Challuabamba (including solid and hollow, human and bird or animal). Although this large sample can be divided into subject types—for example, the Roundhead, Birdhead, Mouth, Special, and Anthropomorphic types which Naula defined—the variation within the types is wide (Figures 6.6, 6.7). The essence of the applied effigy elements is individuality within broad categories: helmetlike roundheads with a visor fillet, beaked faces of birds, froglike large-mouthed heads, and varied humanlike heads with punched eyes.

The essential feature of these vessels with attached heads seems to be that the face stares over the rim. The examples which are intact enough to give us an idea of the complete composition consist of a small globular jar of a size to hold cupped in one hand, with an opening wide enough that the other hand can easily take something out of the jar. The natural way to hold the vessel is with the effigy head facing you. Many of the effigy figures have one or both hands (or paws) to their mouth, as if they were eating something. It is easy to imagine that the effigy head was meant to witness, and share in, the taking of some ritual substance. With the evidence available we cannot be sure what that substance was, but it is likely that coca was used at Challuabamba (see the bone pick in the offering of Burial 6 in Cut 3 Level 4 in Figure 9.5f, which probably served to draw lime from a shell container to mix with coca leaves for chewing). Whatever the substance may have been that was taken from these jars under the eyes of the effigies, it was a ritual in which many people participated, not something reserved for the elite. The appearance of little effigy heads on (or broken from) small jars at many other sites in the region attests to the widespread popularity of this practice.

Figures 6.6 and 6.7 show some typical examples. The difficulty of interpreting their significance is evident. Some appear to be birds, foxes, and frogs, but the sculptors probably intended to represent a mysterious being who was part of the nonhuman natural world and yet could communicate with a human intelligence. Figure 6.7 gives a schematic sample of the figurines and effigy heads: numbers 1–3 represent the early solid figurines; 4–8, later solid attached figures or heads; 9, an early head (discussed below); and all the remainder, hollow attached heads.

Among the most naturalistic are a couple of head fragments from 3.C Level 2 (Nos. 31 and 32 in Figure 6.7). Despite the loss of the upper half of the faces, they provide us with some useful information. Both seem to have a hand to the mouth, like the gesture of the non-

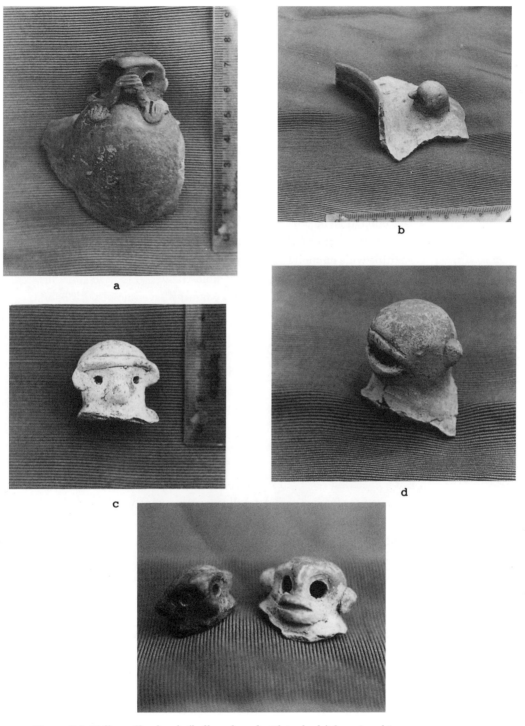

Figure 6.6. Hollow effigy heads (hollow shared with jar body) from Level 1: *a*, 3.D; *b*, 3.A; *c*, 3.A; *d*, 3.D; *e*, 3.C; *f*, 3.D.

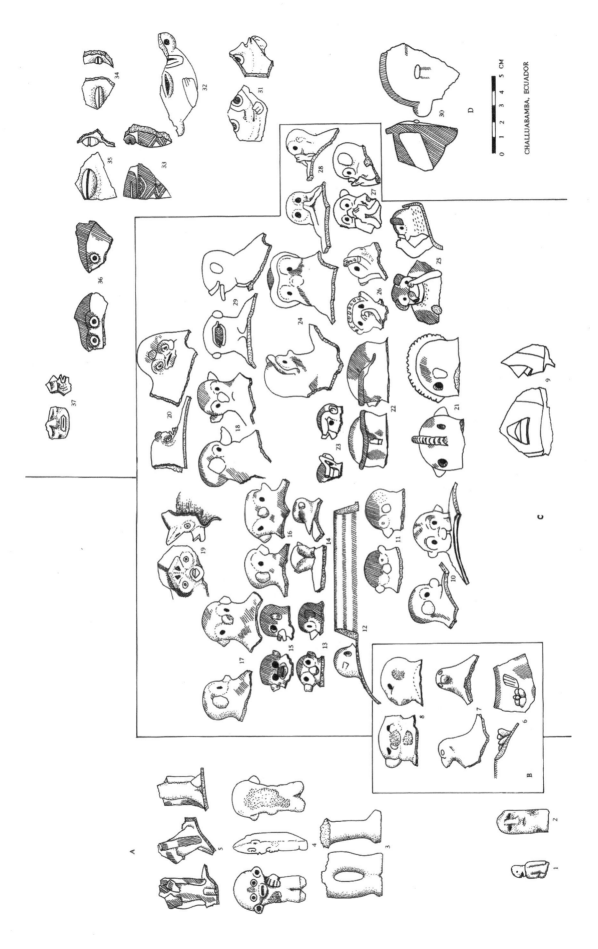

CHALLUABAMBA, ECUADOR

Figure 6.7. The figure is divided into four groups (A, B, C, D). Group A: solid figurines on the left (*1–5*: note that *4* and *5* were attached to some support). Group B (*6–8*): solid attachments to vases. Group C (*9–29*): front and side views of all but *12*, all being hollow attached heads. Group D (*30–37*): miscellaneous heads or fragments of heads (most seem to be imports). Stratigraphic source for items in Figure 6.7: *1*: 3/G Level 5b; *2*: 3.J Level 5; *3*: 3.E Level 3; *4*: 3.C Level 2; *5*: 3.C Level 1; *6*: 3.E Level 1; *7*: 3.F Level 4; *8*: 2.A Level 4; *9*: 3.B Level 4; *10*: 3.C Level 1; *11*: 3.C Level 2; *12*: 3.A Level 1; *13*: 3.C Level 2; *14*: 3.C Level 1; *15*: 3.C Level 2; *16*: 3.C Level 1; *17*: 3.C Level 1; *18*: 3.C Level 1; *19*: 3.C Level 2; *20*: 3.E Level 1; *21*: 3.A Level 1; *22*: 3.A Level 1; *23*: 3.E Level 1; *24*: 3.E Level 1; *25*: 3.A Level 1; *26*: 3.B Level 1; *27*: 3.D Level 1; *28*: 3.E Level 1; *29*: 3.D Level 1; *30*: 3.A Level 1; *31*: 3.C Level 2; *32*: 3.C Level 2; *33*: 3.A Level 2; *34*: 3.E Level 1; *35*: 3.E Level 1; *36*: 3.E Level 1; *37*: 3.H Level 1.

human creatures attached to other vessels. Most important are the earspools on No. 32, which also appear on the attached full figurine (No. 4 in Figure 6.7).

The identification of these elements is supported by an actual earspool found with Burial 3 in Cut 2 (Figure 9.11). Ear ornaments, which by Inca times were worn by all adult Inca males, in earlier times were a sign of special status. For example, the ear pendants on the Lanzón at Chavín de Huantar are an early example, and the Late Preceramic or early Initial Period wooden plugs found at Asia (Engel 1963) and at La Galgada (Grieder et al. 1988:75) were unique pieces at their sites. The ceramic spool from Cut 2, Offering 2, is also unique among the artifacts recovered at Challuabamba and is presumably an indication of special status. Even among the Moche (who produced some of the most spectacular examples of ear ornaments known anywhere), ear ornaments are shown only on individuals of high rank or supernatural status. Presumably, then, the person in the burial associated with Offering 2 was of special distinction, and the people represented in ceramic heads wearing ear ornaments were meant to be understood as having special status.

Hollow Figurines and Face Bowls

Face bowls and hollow figurines never became common at Challuabamba; there may be no more than twenty traces of them in fragments of eyes, noses, and ears. The earliest and one of the largest (No. 9 in Figure 6.7 and Figure 6.8) (at 4.2 cm high, 4.4 cm wide) is from Level 4 of Cut 3. It is the lower half of a face with a sharp (now eroded) nose, thin lips, and a square chin, with a band of black (presumably hair) at the edges. The clay was modeled precisely into shape, oxidized to buff and smudged to black, then the hair was burnished to a shiny surface while the flesh was left matte. We found no other pieces of this, so it was evidently broken when it reached Level 4, which may contain debris from destroyed burials. The ceramic technique could be local, and this could be a portrait of a human individual. It may be part of a category that includes the stone carvings, which belong to a later period. The face seems to be looking upward, as if it might have been supported by a base such as a jar or possibly by a full seated figure. It is hard to imagine the appearance of this unique piece when complete.

Figure 6.8. Hollow head fragment from Cut 3.B Level 4: Burnished Black, matte face (4.2 cm high, 4.4 cm wide).

A Burnished Black fragment is another unique item in our inventory: a hollow human body, unfortunately lacking the head as well as the base (Figure 6.9). The design of the body is tubular, with a straight vertical indentation up the center of the body, with its arms emerging from the form at the elbows and nearly meeting at the center. This simple form angles inward at the shoulders and hips; at the hips we can see how abstract the design really is, as it forms a smooth angular surface. This is quite different from the more organic forms found in the stone sculpture and in most of the small attached effigies and effigy heads on pots. Its reduction firing and its high burnish may suggest an unusually formal design.

All the other fragments that appear to have been parts of hollow figurines were found in the latest levels. The two best examples, from Cut 3.A Level 1 (Figure 6.7, No. 30) and Cut 4 Level 1, are hard to assign to a source, but they are both likely imports. The former, made of gray clay 3 to 5 mm thick, is 5.4 cm high but shows only an eye, an ear, and the top of the head. The skin color is a cream slip, with reddish-brown paint around the top of the head, leaving a diagonal band of cream across the back of the head, and reddish lines from the incised eye and a horizontal line on the forehead. It has most in common with Machalilla figurines, particularly the painted examples from La Ponga shown by Ronald David Lippi (1983:170, 173), which share the general form and scale as well as some of the painted features. Still, the source cannot be specified: the incised oval for the eye, the flat face, and the lump for the ear are unlike any of the local styles known to me. Its thin walls, smooth forms with a cream slip, and carefully applied red slip paint show an established style that might be contemporary with later Challuabamba.

The half of a face from Cut 4, about 6 cm high in Red-on-Cream, shows a coffee-bean eye, a red nose, and wide lips, with red stripes on the cheek and chin. While quite different in style from the former example, it shares the face paint pattern. An anonymous reader has suggested that the distinctive face type might be assignable to the Panzaleo of the Quito area, which would make it an import of a much later period.

All the remaining hollow fragments are very small. Only one shows a nearly complete face on a thin surface broken all around its edges, measuring 2 cm wide by 1.5 cm high (Figure 6.7, No. 37). Three others (Figure 6.7, Nos. 33–35) show eyes with a bulge or button with a slash to make a "coffee-bean eye," a common feature in Machalilla figurines (cf. Meggers et al. 1965: Plate 158a–d; Lippi 1983:167, Figure 41). An interesting variant (Cut 3.A Level 2, Figure 6.7, No. 33) has a coffee-bean eye with a painted eye just below it, on a fine burnished Red-on-Cream surface. The clay is 6 mm thick but varies, which suggests that it may be a sculptural piece, not attached to a container.

The rarity of hollow figurines separates Challuabamba from the coastal Machalilla style, to which it is in other respects somewhat related. The general development on the coast was from small solid figurines in Valdivia to larger hollow figurines in Machalilla and Chorrera and their successors. This would tend to place Challuabamba somewhere between Valdivia and Machalilla in the technical sequence, but the highlands never showed as much interest in ceramic sculpture as the coastal lowlands, where it became a major art form.

Bowls with faces modeled on the exterior just below the rim seem to be the latest of these types, evident in our excavations in fragments in Levels 1 and 2 of Cuts 1, 2, and 3. The identifiable sherds are parts of faces, none having sufficient rim to allow description of the bowl. We recorded one ear (Cut 3.2) and six noses (1.2, 2.1 and 2.2, 3.2 [two] and 3.1), all a little under life size (about 5 cm long) but naturalistic in style, and two coffee-bean eyes, both in Burnished Blackware (both at 3.E Level 1 and about 2 cm wide). This type has been recorded at Pirincay (Hammond and Bruhns 1987: Figure 4; Bruhns 1989:60, Figure 8), differing only in the presence of rims (everted), an eye and mouth, an apparent carination below the face, and a slightly heavier wall. That suggests local production of the type at both sites, with slightly different vessel characteristics very late in the sequence.

Figure 6.9. Small hollow figurine body fragment, Cut 3.J Level 2: Burnished Black ware (5.0 cm high).

Bibliography

Arnheim, Rudolf
1964 *Art and Visual Perception.* Berkeley and Los Angeles: University of California Press.

Bennett, Wendell C.

1946 *Excavations in the Cuenca Region, Ecuador.* Yale University Publications in Anthropology, No. 35. New Haven: Yale University Press.

Bruhns, Karen Olsen

1989 Intercambio entre la costa y la sierra en el Formativo Tardío: nuevas evidencias del Azuay. In *Relaciones interculturales en el área ecuatorial del Pacífico durante la época precolombina,* ed. J.-F. Bouchard and M. Guinea, 57–74. British Archaeological Reports, International Series 503. Oxford: BAR.

Collier, Donald, and John Murra

1943 *Survey and Excavations in Southern Ecuador.* Anthropology Series 62. Chicago: Field Museum of Natural History.

Engel, Frederic

1963 *A Preceramic Settlement on the Central Coast of Peru: Asia, Unit I.* Transactions of the American Philosophical Society n.s. 53(3). Philadelphia: American Philosophical Society.

Evans, Clifford, Betty Meggers, and Emilio Estrada

1959 *Cultura Valdivia.* Guayaquil: Museo Arqueológico "Víctor Emilio Estrada."

Grieder, Terence, Alberto Bueno Mendoza, C. Earle Smith, Jr., and Robert M. Malina

1988 *La Galgada, Peru: A Preceramic Culture in Transition.* Austin: University of Texas Press.

Hammond, Norman, and Karen Olsen Bruhns

1987 The Paute Valley Project in Ecuador, 1984. *Antiquity* 61:50–56.

Lippi, Ronald David

1983 La Ponga and the Machalilla Phase of Coastal Ecuador. Doctoral dissertation, University of Wisconsin–Madison.

Marcos, Jorge G.

1988 *Real Alto: la historia de un centro ceremonial Valdivia.* Quito: Corporación Editora Nacional.

Meggers, Betty J., Clifford Evans, and Emilio Estrada

1965 *Early Formative Period of Coastal Ecuador: The Valdivia and Machalilla Phases.* Washington, D.C.: Smithsonian Institution.

Naula, Maria Isabel

1997 A Stylistic and Iconographic Analysis of Seventy-nine Ceramic Heads from Challuabamba, Ecuador. M.A. thesis in the History of Art, Virginia Commonwealth University, Richmond.

Stamps and Seals

7

Among the most interesting items of ceramic art at Challuabamba are the pieces bearing deeply carved designs. They are found in a variety of forms: flat stamps, large hollow circular forms which have been called "bracelets" (Uhle 1922:222) or roller stamps, which I will call cylinder seals, and other forms (Figure 7.1).

There can be no doubt that they are local products, for their variations fall within the range of local ceramic production. Flat stamps and roller stamps (or cylinder seals) have been found at several sites in northern Peru and southern Ecuador. They "are very common items in Chorrera refuse" (Lathrap et al. 1975:51), and a large cylinder seal was found in Machalilla deposits at La Ponga (ibid.: cat. 233), but stamps and seals are rare in Andean Formative sites in general (Guffroy 1994:246). The largest collections outside the Ecuadorian coastal region come from Challuabamba (first shown by Uhle) (1922:221–223, Plate XXXV) and from Cerro Ñañañique. Guffroy (1994:248, Figure 15h) illustrates twelve flat ceramic stamps from Cerro Ñañañique and finds them similar to those from Chorrera collections illustrated by Lathrap et al. (1975: Nos. 521, 524, 533). As we might expect, unique individual examples have been found at several other sites (e.g., Pirincay: Hammond and Bruhns 1987:55; see Tellenbach 1998: Plate 35 for a selection from various sites). Although every one of the fourteen cylinder seals and thirty-seven flat stamps in our collection at Challuabamba is fragmentary, they are still the finest examples in terms of precision and design quality, as Uhle also asserted for the twelve cylinder seals in his collection.

It is noteworthy that the carved items bear designs that have very little overlap with those found on containers. That suggests that the makers of those artifacts were members of two distinct social groups. The term "carved," which I have applied to the stamps and seals, refers to the technique, rare on containers, of cutting deep lines, dots, and shapes into smooth, leather-hard surfaces. This technique is easily distinguished from incision, modeling, and so forth, in which the

Figure 7.1. Twelve of the fourteen cylinder seals are shown in the upper left corner of photo. *Top row:* No. 14, No. 7, No. 1, and No. 8; *second row:* No. 2, a flat stamp, No. 5, No. 9, No. 10; *third row:* No. 3, No. 11, a flat stamp, No. 4, No. 12. Cm scale at bottom. Photo by B. Jones. Cylinders Nos. 6 and 13 are shown in Figures 7.7 and 7.14. The three rows on the right and two rows on the bottom are flat or curved stamps.

clay is softer and can be treated more freely, and changes made by adding more clay. Uhle referred to the technique as engraving, but in current use that term refers to incision on a surface already fired, while these were cut into the clay before firing when partly dry.

Since the large hollow cylinders are the earliest (six of the fourteen examples coming from Level 4 of Cut 3), we will first look at all the cylinders and then go on to the flat stamps, which are mostly later, from Levels 1 and 2. Finally, we will look into the range of variation and the external relationships of the carved designs and into the question of their significance.

Cylinder Seals

All but two of the cylinder seals are shown in Figure 7.1 (the second from left in row 2 and the third in row 3 are flat stamps). Missing in this picture are cylinders numbered 6 and 12, shown in Figures 7.7 and 7.13. All are relatively large curving pottery fragments with carved designs on the external surface, all but one (No. 14) reduction-fired to a black or gray surface. All of them have at least one finished rim (at the top in Figure 7.1 except the first on the upper left) and Nos. 2 and 13 have finished rims at both top and bottom. The designs on cylinder seals do not necessarily have a top and bottom if, for example, they were used to print a pattern on textiles, but many of these designs do seem to have a top (Nos. 5 and 9 in the second row, for example). That might indicate a pictorial or inscription-like significance to the designs rather than a purely decorative one.

The fourteen cylinder seals fall into two groups: an earlier group of six coming from Level 4 and a later group of eight from Levels 1 and 2. The early group is Nos. 1–6 (Figures 7.2–7.7), the later Nos. 7–14 (Figures 7.8–7.15). (A 1-cm scale is shown below each figure.) In general, if we can judge by these fragments, it appears that the earlier group is slightly finer than the later group. The examples found by Uhle (1922: Figures 102–105) can be compared with both groups. For example, in Uhle's Figure 105 (1922:222), identified by him as a jaw with small triangular teeth (upper left) and a volute tongue; the "teeth" are similar to those in the lower right corner of No. 1 (Figure 7.2). Our No. 13 (Figure 7.14) shares crescent-and-dot and picket elements with Uhle's Figure 102.

Considering the abundance of artifacts identified as "cylinder seals" in Late Formative and later Ecuadorian collections, it seems reasonable to accept that designation; but it would be reassuring to have one complete example, preferably with some paint traces on it. Examination of the surfaces, however, shows not only the absence of paint but some uneven surfaces (e.g., Nos. 4, 6, 9) which would not print evenly. The deep carving of their relatively thin walls might not resist the pressure that repeated printing would impose. The question was first posed by Uhle (1922:222; my translation):

> We also found in Challuabamba, in the fill above the ancient altar, twelve fragments of large rolls or hollow rings, at first glance appearing to be cylinder seals for their general form, being engraved on their exterior more or less deeply, and for their repetition of designs found on other fragments of stamps. But they are different from the stamps in their much larger size (diameters from 6.5 to 10.3 cm, widths from 5 to 8.8

Figure 7.2. Cylinder Seal No. 1, Cut 3.G Level 4.

Figure 7.3. Cylinder Seal No. 2, Cut 3.H Level 4.

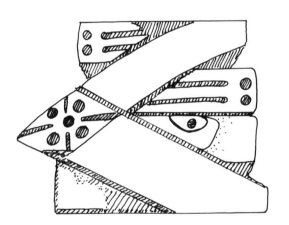

Figure 7.4. Cylinder Seal No. 3, Cut 3.G Level 4.

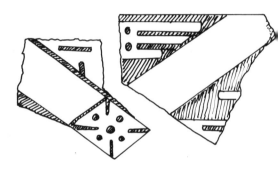

Figure 7.5. Cylinder Seal No. 4, Cut 3.G Level 4 (12 cm diam.).

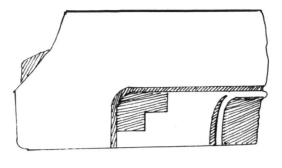

Figure 7.6. Cylinder Seal No. 5, Cut 3.H Level 4.

Figure 7.7. Cylinder Seal No. 6, Cut 3.G Level 4.

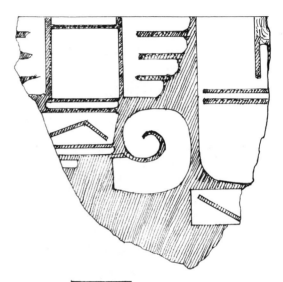

Figure 7.8. Cylinder Seal No. 7, Cut 3.G Level 2 (10 cm diam.).

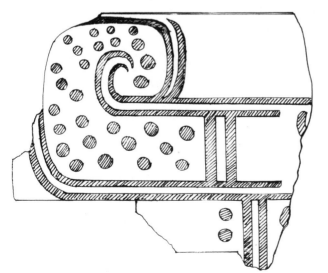

Figure 7.9. Cylinder Seal No. 8, Cut 3.G Level 1.

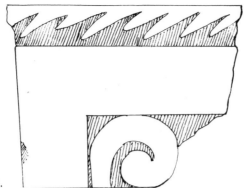

Figure 7.10. Cylinder Seal No. 9, Cut 3 Level 1.

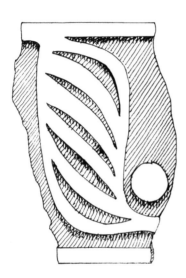

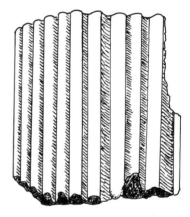

Figure 7.12. Cylinder Seal No. 11, Cut 3 Level 1.

Figure 7.11. Cylinder Seal No. 10, Cut 3.G Level 1.

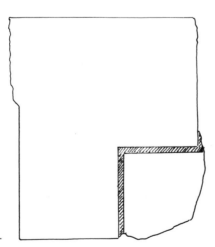

Figure 7.13. Cylinder Seal No. 12, Cut 3 Level 1.

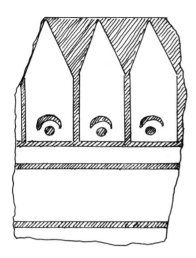

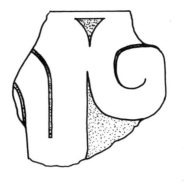

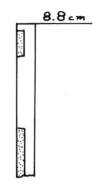

Figure 7.15. Cylinder Seal No. 14,
Cut 3.G Level 1 (8.8 cm diam.).

Figure 7.14. Cylinder Seal No. 13,
Cut 2 Level 1.

cm), and their slight thickness (4 to 7 cm), so that they appear more like rings than like cylinder seals. Considering their length and interior width (5.7 to 9.2 cm) they could be worn as bracelets. For their variation in color (there are also various black examples) [actually all of these are reduced blackware], for their much finer execution and surface finish, and for the engraved designs in a special style found only on these objects, they exceed in quality all the other artifacts of the same period.

The exterior diameters of several of our examples can be estimated from their curve. Nos. 4 and 7 suggest diameters between 8 and 12 cm. Some, such as No. 3, were surely smaller, too small to serve as bracelets. Although the function of the cylinders is uncertain, I provisionally classify them with the forms that seem most clearly their descendants, the cylinder seals. That name has long been attached to the seals of later cultural groups, notably Chorrera and Jama Coaque (Meggers 1966: Plate 35), in which the cylinders on average are a little longer (6–8 cm) than our examples (3–6 cm) but are much smaller in diameter. Although none of our examples are complete, it seems certain that they were hollow rings that might have been used to roll paint or dye on a surface such as cloth or the human body. I first identified No. 14 as a carved cup, thinking of a Chavín-style soapstone cup (Rowe 1962: Figure 30) and stone and pottery cups from the Pacopampa region (Burger 1992:107, Figures

95, 97), but the lack of any remains of the floor of the cup casts doubt on that identification. Until a more complete example is found, their intended use is in doubt. The one aspect of their use which seems certain is their sacrifice in burials; they were apparently broken in pieces which were divided among several burials, since No. 3 is the only one of which we have found more than one sherd, though still much less than half the original.

All but one (No. 14) of our examples belong to the reduction-fired group, and that one is of the rare unslipped Matte Orange ware. None of these examples belong to the technical tradition of oxidized Red-on-Cream pottery, which composed about 90 percent of the local pottery production. If we consider that reduction-fired pottery was just about 10 percent of local production, and most of that was of unusually good quality, the carved wares were among the most elaborate of the best ceramics. They were clearly the work of specialists who had exceptional knowledge and skills. Their products were presumably designed for the use of specialists in intellectual, spiritual, or governmental activities.

Although each seal is unique, they share a general style. The most common design elements are the volute and the punched dot (five examples each), and fingers/feathers appear on four. The designs are so sophisticated that we may imagine that they must convey some profound religion or philosophy (see Nos. 3 and 7) or emerge from a tradition of architectural ornament using designs such as No. 5 or No. 8.

A rich vocabulary of designs is evident in the early set. In the six earliest examples, all from Level 4, we can identify the volute, sets of "fingers" or "feathers," punches, wide plain bands which were sometimes crossed, a quincunx, sets of steps, and parallel lines. (The names are arbitrary: "fingers" or "feathers" may have merely a formal resemblance to the things named.) Examples of the later group (Nos. 7 to 14) are simpler: parallel strips in No. 11, a right angle in No. 12. The earliest of the later group (No. 7 from Level 2) retains the greater variety of the early group in what seems one of the most complex designs. Many design elements, such as the volute, punched circles, a border of slashes, wide straight bands, or a right angle, or bands bent back on themselves, are retained from the early set; but the simpler designs hint at a decline in intellectual and design power in the later group.

Only a few additional design elements appear in the later examples: the central rectangle and blocks with incised lines (No. 7), the crescent-and-dot and picket (No. 13), the wide plain bands flanking a depressed right angle (No. 12) and a series of raised parallel strips (No. 11), twisting lines on an S shape and raised circle (No. 10), and a single element, the volute, simplified and broadened into bands that double back on themselves (No. 14).

The Craft of Carving

We can learn a little about the artists' tools and craft by close examination of the designs, as in the magnified view of No. 2, from Cut 3.H Level 4 (Figure 7.16). It appears that the clay was leather-hard when the work was done, not yet fired (which means it was not "engraved"), so it could be cut smoothly with a sharp blade. The design was made with very straight cuts with smooth walls. Some of the debris in the cuts may be dirt left by imperfect washing, but some of it is bits of soft clay left in the channel where the cuts for the two walls meet. The ends of each cut are sharply pointed; where wide, flat-floored channels end, as between the fingers, there was not a tool adapted to making a neat end. That makes it surprising that the artist got such clean floors on the wide channels, such as the border below the spiral. For the curved lines the two cuts for the walls angled to make a V and the channels have sharply pointed ends. The basic tool must have been a very sharp, very small blade, probably of obsidian.

Four kinds of cuts are basic: a long slash with the blade held vertically for the sides of wide straight channels and for one side of the curves, an angled cut to make the V-shaped channel of the curves, a series of short chopping horizontal cuts to remove background areas or angled to make soft transitions between background and relief areas, and finally circular pits made with a sharp point which had a narrow blade behind the point.

Figure 7.16. Cylinder Seal No. 2, Cut 3.H Level 4. Cm scale at top.

Magnification reveals the smoothness of the fine clay ring and the sharpness of its edges, the excellence of the tools, and the steady, confident strokes that make the design. But the slight wavering of some lines, the minor differences in matching parts such as the "fingers," and the roughness of the pits and the ends of the spaces between the "fingers" all reassure us that it was the handwork of a human artist, not the product of a mold or other industrial practice once removed from the creative eye and hand.

Design Elements on the Flat Stamps

The thirty-seven fragments of flat ceramic stamps and related small carvings have a number of the same design elements as the cylinders, and the additional elements are included in Figure 7.17. These smaller items share several technical features: most of them have a carved surface ("the front") that could be used as a stamp, and some have a nubbin on the opposite surface ("the back") that could serve as a handle. Most are flat on both front and back, many have one or more finished edges, and only a very few have any traces of slip or paint. Another important feature is that all are black or gray to nearly white ware produced by reduction or partial reduction, a feature shared with all but one of the cylinder seals.

If we take the designs on the flat stamps as the basis for analysis, we can define a couple of themes that may serve to define groups of stamps. A "theme" is a subject or topic of discourse. Although Challuabamba art, as Christopher Donnan (1976:117) said of Moche art, "gives the impression of having an almost infinite variety of subject matter, analysis of a large sample of it indicates that it is limited to

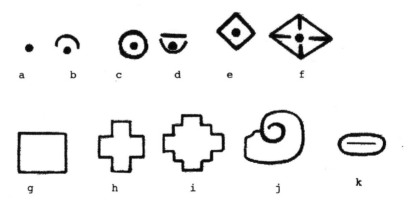

Figure 7.17. Design elements on the flat stamps: *a,* dot; *b,* crescent and dot; *c,* circle and dot (eye); *d,* eye; *e,* diamond and dot; *f,* cosmic center; *g,* rectangle; *h,* cross; *i,* cross and square; *j,* volute (feline snout); *k,* mouth of feline mask.

the representation of a very small number of basic themes." By studying a number of examples assignable to one of the basic themes, "it would be possible to identify a specific set of symbolic elements that are characteristic of it," as Donnan noted. In our case, with a much smaller sample than that supplied by the Moche and a relative absence of naturalistic representation, we find that we are in fact isolating certain repeated design elements and defining a theme by the cluster of elements that cohere in the design. To assign symbolism to these design elements is speculative, but we need only return to the Pucara Stela No. 1 (Figure 4.3b) to find design elements similar to those used much earlier at Challuabamba with what appears to be related symbolism. That whole monument represents the curly-horned beast that symbolizes the cosmos (Chavez 1975), and volutes appear again as the snakelike bodies of feline-headed creatures accompanying diamonds, stepped squares, and nine-square checkerboards, all having cosmic implications (Grieder 1982:147–148).

Two main themes, the cosmic and the feline, resonate so persistently through Pre-Columbian art that it is no surprise to find them represented in Challuabamba's designs. They are found in earlier styles on textiles and ceramics, where the feline mask seems to make an early appearance on the handles of a pottery basin (Figure 7.18a), on Valdivia bowls (Figure 7.18b), and on a preceramic bag (Figure 7.18c). So ubiquitous and so intertwined are the feline and the cosmos in Andean art that it would be more accurate to describe them as aspects of one grand theme. Nevertheless, each aspect has its own symbolic designs.

The Feline Theme

The earliest of the examples (Figure 7.18a), from Puerto Hormiga, Colombia, emphasizes the eyes with circles, proportions the face twice as wide as high, and places bulges suggesting animal ears at the top, with slashes suggesting fur all around the rim. The proportions, the punched eyes encircled with grooves, and the punch-groove-punch of the mouth also relate the Puerto Hormiga example to Valdivia-style frontal faces and ultimately to those produced at Challuabamba.

Figure 7.17c, d, j, and k show the basic elements of feline designs at Challuabamba. With few exceptions, they tend to divide into at least two groups, with 7.17c and k forming the eyes and mouth of a frontal feline mask, and 7.17c or d as eyes in a profile head with 7.17j as the profile snout. The frontal mask and the profile head both probably represent a jaguar or puma monster. The frontal face is the most com-

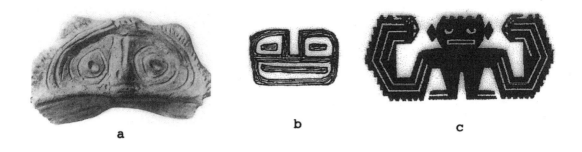

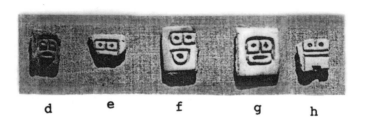

Figure 7.18. Antecedents of Challuabamba's feline designs: *a,* Puerto Hormiga, c. 3000 BC (after Reichel-Dolmatoff 1965); *b,* Valdivia Phases 3–4 (after Hill 1972–1974: Figure 30); *c,* textile design, La Galgada, c. 2300 BC (Grieder et al. 1988:179). Challuabamba feline mask designs: *d,* Cut 2 Level 2; *e,* Cut 3 Level 2; *f,* Cut 3.B Level 1; *g,* 3.E Level 1; *h,* Cut 2 Level 1; *i,* Cut 3.F Level 1; *j,* Cut 2 Level 1.

mon representational design, with seven examples (Figure 7.18d–j) stylized in a manner very common in Valdivia ceramics of Phase 4 (cf. Lathrap et al. 1975: cat. 24, 25; Meggers et al. 1965: Plate 58f, h, i, etc.).

Added weight is given to the identification of a feline theme by the frontal smiling toothy mouth on another fragment (Figure 7.18k). The nearly flat clay slab has no handle and its right edge is finished, but it is impossible to say how it was used. Yet it surely represents a feline mouth, conventionalized in an early Chavín way.

The profile feline may have a simple squared muzzle (Figure 7.19a), but so often has a volute (Figure 7.19b, c, e) as the snout that it may always have carried that association.

Although the designs on stamps and seals are largely separate from those on pottery vessels, both the feline and the cosmic themes appear on both. Two designs from the exterior walls of Burnished Black bowls (Figure 7.20) may be appropriate here since they seem to show feline tails, which are not shown on any of our stamps. We lack sherds to complete either design. The two basic themes, the cosmos and the feline, transcend the limits of stamps, or any particular expressive form, but they are fundamental ideas in the ancient conception of reality.

If the feline and the human may be merged in designs of faces, that may also be true of hand and paw designs. Two examples bracket the history of Challuabamba ceramics: Cylinder seal No. 2 from Level 4 of Cut 3.H (Figure 7.3), the other from Level 1 of Cut 2 (Figure 7.21). The early cylinder shows three fingers with punched nails and a volute for the heel of the hand or paw. If the volute has a general association with the feline theme, that would strengthen the feline character of this design. The later example (Figure 7.21) is one of the finest of the small flat stamps, with four fingers and a thumb, all

a   b   c   d   e

Figure 7.19. Profile feline head stamps: *a*, Cut 3.A Level 1; *b*, 3 Level 1; *c*, 3.C Level 1; *d* and *e* (Uhle 1922: Figure 98a, b).

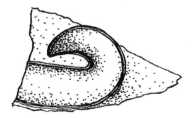 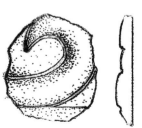

Figure 7.20. Feline tails in relief on Burnished Black bowls: *a*, from Cut 3.H Level 4 (2.8 cm high); *b*, from 3.G Level 4 (3.5 cm high).

Figure 7.21. Black incised flat stamp (2.5 cm high, 2.8 cm wide, 6 mm thick), Cut 2 Level 1. Broken at base; shows back of left hand (or paw?), nails, thumb, bracelet, or fur at wrist.

with crescent-shaped nails, and an elegant leaflike or perhaps fur bracelet at the wrist.

None of these design elements is a naturalistic representation, and we can see that particularly in the case of the volute. Cylinder No. 8 (Figure 7.9), with its large volute marked with an array of punched dots, can be explained as a feline symbol bearing spots, which would be a jaguar. In that metonymical sense many of these design elements are representational, but the volute seems to be purely symbolic in its relation to felines. Perhaps its energetic curl suggested the powerful movement of the animal. Challuabamba was one of the early users of that design, which was widespread and long-lived.

The Cosmic Theme

Another theme can be defined around Figure 7.17e, f, g, h, and i. In later times the square, cross, and stepped cross were widely accepted symbols for the earth's surface. The square was also used to refer to the sky, defining the path of the sun as it moved across the sky during a year or the imagined layers of cosmic levels (underworld, earth's surface, and levels of the heavens). We might suppose they share that kind of cosmic symbolism at Challuabamba. Variations of the quincunx (a square with a center dot and four dots in the corners) occur on Cylinder No. 3 (Figures 7.1, third row, and 7.4) and on flat stamps (Figure 7.22c and d). (See Gomis 1999: Plate 3a, b, for other uses of the quincunx.) On Cylinder No. 3 the quincunx lies at the crossing of two wide plain diagonal bands, which might signify the galaxy or Milky Way. In the triangular spaces between the bands are small triangular shapes containing a dot, which I take to be a bird's eye and beak, because associated with them is a set of horizontal stripes which could be a wing. Since birds travel between the cosmic levels (flying, walking on the earth, and diving under the water), they are appropriate in a cosmic design. The small flat wing (Figure 7.22e), perhaps not a stamp but broken from some small effigy form, provides an alternative design for a wing. We can associate this whole group with a cosmic theme: a vision of the multilevel universe.

The element in Figure 7.22f is a special case. That element forms a net of diagonal squares or diamonds on a flat stamp from Cut 1 Level 2, and Gomis (1999: Plate 3e, g) shows other variations. That net-with-dots design is very widely known in Asian and Pre-Columbian art and is derived from a tie-dye textile pattern usually printed with indigo and standing for a starry sky. Mesoamerican uses of the motif associated it with sky symbols. The design is linked to high rank, probably because the tie-dye method on such a small scale is very difficult to make. The dot was the top of a small bit of white cloth bound tightly, with the bound area protected from the indigo dye. Each dot and the narrow strips between bound areas were dyed blue. The design is so hard to produce by tie-dye that it was often counterfeited by painting or stamping, which may account for the presence of this little stamp. The deep areas of the dots and lines give the effect of

Figure 7.22. Crosses, star, wing, and tie-dye designs: *a*, Cut 3.F Level 1 (cosmic symbol); *b* and *c*, after Uhle (1922: Figure 106) (cosmic symbols); *d*, Cut 3.H Level 1 (star); *e*, Cut 2 Level 1 (wing); *f*, Cut 1 Level 2 (tie dye); *g*, Cut 3.G Level 1 (volute, spiral: probably celestial symbol).

Figure 7.23. Small curved relief stamp (3 cm long, 7 mm wide), Cut 3.E Level 2. Top shows pattern carved on stamp, black areas are incised; bottom shows black lines as printed.

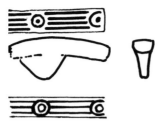

the dyed areas of cloth. The several examples of the design at Challuabamba are among the earliest known.

Most of the flat stamps were found in Levels 1 and 2 of Cuts 2 and 3, and at least some may have been associated with disturbed burials in those areas. There are several very small stamps classified among the flat stamps, which have a curved surface and may have been used for stamping on the human body (Figure 7.23). The designs are abstract but perhaps had a conventional meaning to their makers. None can be assigned to a theme.

Bibliography

Burger, Richard L.
1992   *Chavín and the Origins of Andean Civilization*. New York: Thames and Hudson.
Chavez, Sergio Jorge
1975   The Arapa and Thunderbolt Stelae: A Case of Stylistic Identity with Implications for Pucara Influences in the Area of Tiahuanaco. *Ñawpa Pacha* (Berkeley) 13:3–26.
Donnan, Christopher B.
1976   *Moche Art and Iconography*. Los Angeles: UCLA Latin American Center.
Gomis, Dominique
1999   La cerámica Formativa Tardía de la sierra austral del Ecuador. In *Formativo sudamericano: una revaluación*, ed. P. Ledergerber, 139–159. Quito: Abya-Yala.
Grieder, Terence
1982   *Origins of Pre-Columbian Art*. Austin: University of Texas Press.
Grieder, Terence, A. Bueno Mendoza, C. E. Smith, Jr., and R. M. Malina
1988   *La Galgada, Peru*. Austin: University of Texas Press.
Guffroy, Jean
1994   *Cerro Nañañique: un établissement monumental de la période formative, en limite de désert (Haut Piura, Pérou)*. Paris: Orstom.
Hammond, Norman, and Karen Olsen Bruhns
1987   The Paute Valley Project in Ecuador, 1984. *Antiquity* 61:50–56.
Hill, Betsy D.
1972–   A New Chronology of the Valdivia Ceramic Complex from the Coastal
1974   Zone of Guayas Province, Ecuador. *Ñawpa Pacha* (Berkeley) 10–12:1–32.

Kano, Chiaki

1979   *The Origins of the Chavín Culture.* Studies in Pre-Columbian Art. Washington, D.C.: Dumbarton Oaks.

Lathrap, Donald W., Donald Collier, and Helen Chandra

1975   *Ancient Ecuador: Culture, Clay and Creativity, 3000–300 B.C.* Chicago: Field Museum of Natural History.

Meggers, Betty J.

1966   *Ecuador.* New York: Praeger.

Meggers, Betty J., Clifford Evans, and Emilio Estrada

1965   *Early Formative Period of Coastal Ecuador: The Valdivia and Machalilla Phases.* Washington, D.C.: Smithsonian Institution.

Reichel-Dolmatoff, Gerardo

1965   *Colombia.* New York: Praeger.

Rowe, John Howland

1962   *Chavín Art.* New York: Museum of Primitive Art.

Tellenbach, Michael

1998   Acerca de las investigaciones de Max Uhle sobre las culturas tempranas de Surecuador. *Indiana* 15:269–353.

Uhle, Max

1922   *Influencias mayas en el Alto Ecuador.* Boletín de la Academia Nacional de Historia 4, Nos. 10–12. Quito: Tipografía y Encuadernación Salesianas.

8

Stone and Shell

There is no question that the working of stone preceded the making of ceramics, but in our excavations the ancient art of stone toolmaking is very rare: two ground stone axes, one possible fragment of a small ground stone saw, a pendant with an unfinished drill hole, a few broken stones which might have been used but show no signs of wear, and no blades or pressure-flaked forms. Stone was used most often unworked, in its natural form, selected for size or color and placed in a foundation or burial. While lithic blades, bowls, and metates are found at Cotocollao (Villalba 1988:260–315), none of those forms appear in our collections from Challuabamba.

On the other hand, nearby Pirincay shows an array of lithic material (Bruhns et al. 1990:231–232), including the gathering of "abundant coloured stones from nearby highland zones," which seems to be part of a pattern shared by Challuabamba. Fourteen colored quartz (flint, chert, etc.) rough pebbles (not waterworn) were found in the earlier levels of Cut 1 (Figure 8.1). There are no indications of use or of pressure-flaked edges, although the sharp points might have served as burins. The assembled group, all close to the same size (longest dimensions about 5 cm), suggests that their color may have been the reason for the collection: four are white or light gray, three are yellow, four are deep red, two are brown, and one is black. In Cut 2 Level 1 an additional piece of red chert was found beside the head of an undisturbed burial, which may indicate that burial ritual or symbolism may have played a part in its use. Stothert (2003:373–377) describes the widespread use of small stones in shamanic or burial rituals as soul receptacles in Preceramic Las Vegas culture and among more recent Ecuadorian societies. The variety of colors at Challuabamba might be another example of a regional interest in color, also manifested in pottery.

Turquoise and several other varieties of green stone were probably all imported at Challuabamba. Twenty-four turquoise beads were found in Cut 3, scattered through Levels 4 to 1. Typical examples

Figure 8.1. Fourteen colored quartz pebbles from Cut 1 Levels 2–5. None show shaping or wear.

are rectangular (just two are round), between 5 x 6 mm and 11 x 14 mm and 2 mm thick. Bruhns also found turquoise in a necklace with *Spondylus* shell beads, assigning its source to Ecuador's southern coast, also the source of the worked shells at Pirincay (Bruhns et al. 1990:231–232).

Obsidian is represented by five small chips of black obsidian from Cut 3 Levels 2, 3, and 4. Such scarcity is surprising since the highlands of Ecuador were a major source of obsidian, but at Pirincay obsidian is also "rare," an import from the highlands around Quito (Bruhns et al. 1990:231). Distribution of obsidian from sources near Quito was uneven in Formative times, reaching La Emerenciana, on the coast near Machala, but hardly appearing in the southern highlands.

Two specimens of the standard Andean T-shaped axe were found in surface levels at Challuabamba, a broken fragment in Cut 3.A Level 1, and a complete axe outside our excavations at what we believe is the southern edge of the site (Figure 8.2). The greenish granite of these axes could have been obtained from stones in the river; but they may be imports, since the type is widely known.

Figure 8.2. Stone axe of greenish granite found in surface levels outside our excavations, similar to a broken fragment from Cut 3.A Level 1.

A flat subcircular disk, of greenish-gray slate, was found in Cut 4 Level 1, above 25 cm. It measures 8.2 × 7.5 cm and 4 mm thick. Its surface is unpolished, with an unfinished drill hole in the center. Presumably a pendant, it was left unfinished, an indication it was a local product, dating late in our sequence.

There are many similarities in the stone artifacts found at Pirincay and Challuabamba, but they differ in one important respect. Rock-crystal beads were manufactured at Pirincay throughout the sequence, with "some 45" workshops located, presumably for trade with Chorrera centers in the western lowlands (Bruhns et al. 1990:232). This resource, based on a rock-crystal deposit about 15 km from Pirincay (Bruhns 2003:153, citing Burton n.d.), provided an economic foundation for Pirincay. No specimens of rock crystal were encountered in our Challuabamba excavations.

Stone Sculptures

A small collection of stone sculptures comes from a relatively small area in Cut 3 Levels 1 and 2 and Cut 4 Level 2, about 40 cm deep. It seems to represent a short period associated with or perhaps just before the building of the large stone revetments. All but two (No. 1 and No. 6) of the seven are broken, apparently intentionally; the destruction and disposal occurred during the period of the building of the large stone platform foundations. They were all made of the yellow-to-gray tuff common in the local environment, a soft compacted volcanic ash suitable only for small sculptures. They are numbered in the order of their discovery.

Two reliefs, Sculptures Nos. 1 and 2, appear to be abstract curvilinear designs. Sculpture No. 1 is of white compacted volcanic ash with rough linear incisions into the flat surface of the thin block (Figure 8.3). Since the design follows the irregular pattern of the stone and the only break is the chip out of the surface on the right side, the design appears to be complete. This could be an abstract design, but it can also be seen as two spiral eyes and a drooping nose. That reading is given more credibility by the other representations of heads and faces. This sculpture was found at a slightly higher level than any of the others (above 30 cm depth), and its flatness and linearity are different from the more massive style of the other carvings. It is also unbroken, perhaps postdating the period in which all the more lifelike human heads were broken. It is hard to define the base, but the only flat surfaces are the back and the left side as it is shown; if it was set vertically resting on its left side, the reading of the design as

a face would be largely lost. In that position we might think of it as a snail, whose shell was common in the excavations.

Sculpture No. 2 is roughly cut into a half-circle of gray tuff; the lower half is lost (Figure 8.4). It appears to be a spiral, but further interpretation does not seem possible.

Sculpture No. 3, found in Cut 3.F Level 2, is carved in relief but has a flat back, presumably to be mounted on a flat surface (Figure 8.5). The subject is uncertain. Note that the photograph has an additional block in the center, and the drawing an additional block at the bottom (no. 5). The right side (edge of block 2) is broken; presumably the folded curved area at lower left (of blocks 1, 4, and 5) continued onto that area. Another dozen small fragments cannot be placed. This sculpture is near the size of those that represent human heads, although no facial features can be identified; nor is the symmetry we expect in a head evident. Whatever the subject, it appears to have been broken by an intentional blow to the center of the relief, a trait that it shares with the other sculptures that seem to show human heads.

Figure 8.4. Stone Sculpture No. 2, from Cut 3.G Level 2 (9 cm thick, 22 cm wide, 12 cm high).

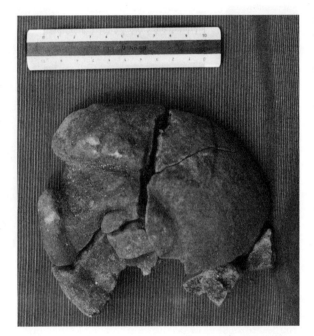

Figure 8.5. Stone Sculpture No. 3, from Cut 3.F Level 2 (4.5 cm thick, 12 cm wide, 9 cm high).

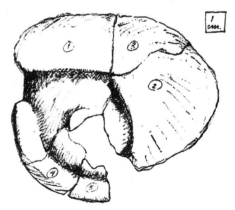
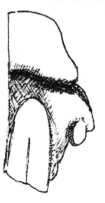

Of the sculptures representing human heads (No. 4, 5, and 7), No. 4 is the most complete, since the fragments can be reassembled to form a nearly complete head (Figure 8.6). The neck takes up about half the height, with a broken base, and it is conceivable that it might have served as a tenon for placement in a wall, particularly as the head is tilted back. The breaks suggest that it was intentionally smashed by a blow between the eyes. The heads are carved in different styles, this being the simplest, with large masses, projecting circles for eyes, and only the eyes, nose, and chin showing, with a hint of lips.

Sculpture No. 5 was found in Cut 4.I (Figure 8.7). The stone is a fine-grained soft volcanic tuff. It lay on its side at about 40 cm depth, about 2 m distant from the stone used as a pedestal in the photograph. The original setting of all these sculptures is unknown and hard to imagine since stone walls and pedestals are absent, with the possible exception of the one shown here. The sculpture is only 10 cm tall, with a rough, broken base which suggests that it was set in a socket, perhaps on a post. The sculpture shows a carefully designed abstraction of the head, emphasizing the forms that represent the eye and the ear. Battered as it is, it was clearly made for display and retains sufficient sculptural interest to make us regret the loss of half the form.

The shaped "pedestal" shows a similar careful production. The photograph does not pretend to show an original setting, but the stone pedestal was unusual and seems to have been worked to make

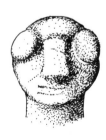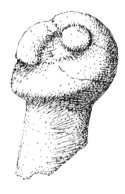

Figure 8.6. Stone Sculpture No. 4, from Cut 3.J Level 2 (22 cm high; width of face 18 cm).

Figure 8.7. Stone Sculpture No. 5, from Cut 4.I at about 40 cm depth (10 cm high).

smooth surfaces on several sides, with a flat area on top, as shown. It lay in the same level as the sculpture, in Cut 4.F.

The subject of Sculpture No. 6 is uncertain, but it is probably an animal, perhaps a snake (Figure 8.8). Although the stone has been shaped, the features are very simple: deep pits for eyes, slight modeling around the muzzle, and a rough incised line for the mouth. This sculpture shows no signs of intentional damage and may be complete. It appears to have been set on its own flat base.

Sculpture No. 7 is of a speckled, grainy yellowish tuff (Figure 8.9). Like all the human heads (Nos. 4, 5, and probably 3), this one is less than half life-size. The only remaining details seem to show a cloth cap or turban. The damage appears to have been intentional destruction of the face. The headdress suggests that the face might have been more naturalistic in style than those of the other heads, which are made up of conventionalized forms, different from the apparently naturalistic aim of No. 7.

Uhle (1922:224–225, Figures 108–112) shows four small stone sculptures from Challuabamba and one, a relief, from nearby Sigsig. Uhle's Figure 108 is clearly a human head, although only one eye and the top of the head remain. It is in better condition and more natural in form than our examples. His Figure 109, identified as a torso with the arms crossed, seems to show a human with the lower part of the face upturned. Figure 110 has a human profile supported on what Uhle identifies as animal legs, perhaps an armadillo. Figure 111 is an incised relief comparable to our No. 1. His Figure 112, from Sigsig, is a similar relief, slightly more complex in design.

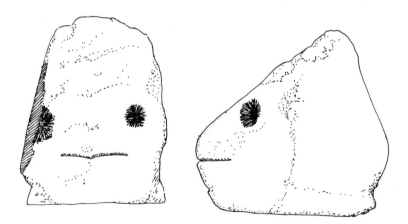

Figure 8.8. Stone Sculpture No. 6, from Cut 4.I (6 cm high, 9 cm thick, 7 cm wide).

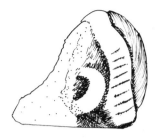

Figure 8.9. Stone Sculpture No. 7, from Cut 4.J 40–50 cm depth (10 cm high, 12 cm front to back).

Putting Uhle's collection together with ours makes a dozen small sculptures, most of them broken, made of a soft local stone in styles that do not seem to associate with any other regional style. Their dating is uncertain since we have no radiocarbon samples that date Levels 1 and 2 exclusively, but the two latest dates (on mixed Levels 1–3) give confidence for a dating of about 1300 BC. Probably 1300–1100 BC would cover the whole group.

Perhaps the most interesting feature of these modest carvings is the lack of an apparent rationale for their display. Carved stones, at least until the era of modernism, were expected to represent or memorialize some religious, political, or mythic principle, movement, or personality. All these stones, including those shown by Uhle, had been cast off, losing whatever setting they originally had. The breakage of Nos. 3, 4, 5, and 7, which appears intentional, suggests that whatever they represented was controversial. No. 5, more than the others, suggests that the sculptor, at least, aimed at a display of abstract form for its own sake, along with whatever representational motive may have inspired it.

This small sample is insufficient to serve as the definition of a sculptural tradition, but it is interesting to see how different it is from other early stone sculptures from the general region.

Close to Challuabamba, but later in time, is a small stone sculpture found at Cerro Narrío (Figure 8.10, from Uhle 1922:224, Figure 107). In its geometric forms it shows a sculptural style very different from Challuabamba's, described by Uhle as reflecting a relatively high culture. This contrasts with the massive, rounded naturalistic forms that the Challuabamba sculptors envisioned. Limited by the soft granular stone that was locally available, they were unable to produce large-scale compositions or sharply defined geometric shapes.

Figure 8.10. Stone sculpture found at Cerro Narrío, about 50 cm high (Uhle 1922:224, Figure 107).

Shell

Considering the location of Challuabamba near the headwaters of the Jubones River, which is one of the presumed trade routes for *Spondylus* shells from the Gulf of Guayaquil into the Peruvian highlands (Paulsen 1974; Marcos 1978:110) from at least late Valdivia times, it is surprising to find only four unworked fragments of *Spondylus* shell in our excavations, all in Cut 2.

Much more impressive was a local farmer's find at the site but some distance from our excavations, of what appears to be an offering of three complete *Spondylus* shells (both valves) containing beads of white shell and turquoise (Figure 8.11). It is now in possession of the National Patrimony office in Cuenca, along with all our excavated material. This offering is evidence of Challuabamba's participation in the *Spondylus* trade and of its retention of some shells for its own use. In Peru the *Spondylus* shell's symbolism of feminine fertility in nature was paired with the *Strombus* shell as a masculine symbol. In Ecuador the evidence suggests that the *Spondylus* was paired with turquoise or blue-green stones generally, with the shells symbolizing the feminine role of the natural world and the blue-green stones the fertilizing power of rain (Stothert 2003:362–364).

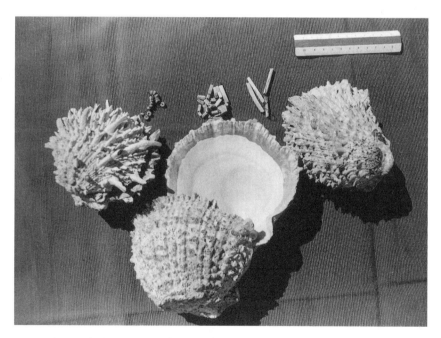

Figure 8.11. Three complete *Spondylus* shells containing shell and turquoise beads, found by a local farmer on the site.

If *Spondylus* shells were very rare in our excavations, snail shells were so numerous that it was not until we found one—an unusually large example—among the offerings in Burial 6 that we began to note and count them (Figure 8.12). Actually, the burial offering was the only place where the snail shell appeared to have been intentionally placed. All the other finds were isolated, without evidence of ancient use or curation.

A recent study (Heckenberger 2005:316) of the Arawakan communities in Brazil's Upper Xingu region provides a provocative, if distant, slant on snail shells:

> Virtually anything of value is traded, but there are recognized mediums of payment, most notable among which are ceramics and glass bead and shell ornaments (belts and necklaces), the latter having a somewhat unique exchange value as they are highly storable, displayable, and transportable wealth items: shell money. Shell necklaces are made with water snails, *oïke*, and shell belts are made from land snails, *iñu*. . . . they can be used to purchase virtually anything, a song, a cure, a favor, labor, and even food and constitute a rudimentary "currency."

Figure 8.12. Land snail shell, which was part of the offering with Burial 6 in Cut 3 Level 4.

Murra's (1963:800) description of Cañari burial offerings notes: "Weapons and ornaments of all kinds were included, along with land snails, which are found in the poorest graves." The isolated snail shells in Cuts 1, 2, and 3 may have been the last traces of early grave offerings which had been disrupted by building and decay.

Bibliography

Bruhns, Karen Olsen
2003   Social and Cultural Development in the Ecuadorian Highlands and Eastern Lowlands during the Formative. In *Archaeology of Formative Ecuador*, ed. J. S. Raymond and R. L. Burger, 125–174. Washington, D.C.: Dumbarton Oaks.
Bruhns, Karen Olsen, James H. Burton, and George R. Miller
1990   Excavations at Pirincay in the Paute Valley of Southern Ecuador, 1985–1988. *Antiquity* 64:221–233.
Burton, James H.
n.d.   Pirincay Postdata. *Miscelánea Antropológica Ecuatoriana*. In press.
Guffroy, Jean
1987   *Loja préhispanique*. Paris: Éditions Recherche sur les Civilisations.
Heckenberger, Michael
2005   *The Ecology of Power, Culture, Place and Personhood in the Southern Amazon, A.D. 1000–2000*. New York: Taylor and Francis Routledge.
Hocquenghem, Anne-Marie, Jaime Idrovo, Peter Kaulicke, and Dominique Gomis
1993   Bases de intercambio entre las sociedades norperuanas y surecuato-

rianas: una zona de transición entre 1500 A.C. y 600 D.C. *Bulletin de l'Institut Français d'Études Andines* 22(2):443–466.

Idrovo Urigüen, Jaime

1994   *Santuarios y conchales de la Provincia de El Oro.* Machala: Casa de Cultura Ecuatoriana, Núcleo de El Oro.

Marcos, Jorge

1978   Cruising to Acapulco and Back with the Thorny Oyster Set: Model for a Linear Exchange System. *Journal of the Steward Anthropological Society* 9(1/2):99–132.

Murra, John

1963   The Cañari. In *Handbook of South American Indians,* ed. J. H. Steward, vol. 2, 799–801. New York: Cooper Square.

Paulsen, Alison

1974   The Thorny Oyster and the Voice of God: *Spondylus* and *Strombus* in Andean Prehistory. *American Antiquity* 39:597–601.

Stothert, Karen E.

2003   Expression of Ideology in the Formative Period of Ecuador. In *Archaeology of Formative Ecuador,* ed. J. S. Raymond and R. L. Burger, 337–421.

Uhle, Max

1922   *Influencias mayas en el Alto Ecuador.* Boletín de la Academia Nacional de Historia 4, Nos. 10–12. Quito: Tipografía y Encuadernación Salesianas.

Villalba O., Marcelo

1988   *Cotocollao: una aldea Formativa del valle de Quito.* Quito: Museos del Banco Central del Ecuador.

The Burials and Their Offerings

JAMES D. FARMER

Seven undisturbed burials were discovered in Cuts 2 and 3, numbered in the order of their discovery. Despite the damp climate, these seven were sufficiently complete for study; and a few bones were solid enough to extract intact. Numerous other skeletal fragments were recovered from the two cuts but were too disturbed to assign specific burial contexts.

These seven appear to be undisturbed primary burials, damaged only by compression and moisture. They appear to have been laid in shallow graves, though the edges of the pits cannot be discerned. Accompanying the bodies in three cases were offerings of pottery, and in all cases the burial was covered by a cairn of river cobbles, which resulted ultimately in some crushing of the skeletons and offerings.

Table 9.1 lists the general characteristics of the seven burials. "Base depth" indicates the lowest level on which the body was placed. "Position" is flexed, seated, or extended. "Orientation" gives the general direction of the alignment of the torso. "Condition" refers to the preservation of the skeletal remains, ranging from "poor," in which the position and orientation are uncertain, to "excellent," in which the skeleton is relatively intact. Two categories of offerings are distinguished: "associated artifacts" (close to the body and probably in the burial and presumed to be part of the burial ritual) and "related artifacts" (in the soil around the burial but different in some respects from the sherds and debris in the surrounding strata levels). Related artifacts appear to have been cast into the burial before or during the building of the cairn by members of the burial party (cf. Grieder 1978:56–58, the "third offering"). This is particularly relevant to Burial 6.

Although seven burials represent a small sample, burial form, location, and associated artifacts have long been recognized as providing useful clues to burial practices as well as broader cultural practices and beliefs (Dillehay 1995). Following a model suggested

Table 9.1. Challuabamba Burials

Burial	1	2	3	4
Location	2/2.E	2/2.A–B	2/3.H-1	2/3.H
Base depth (cm)	60	60	80	80
Sex	?	?	?	?
Age	young adult?	young adult?	adult	young adult?
Position	tight flex on back	tight flex on back	tight flex, right side	tight flex, left side
Orientation	30°NNE	80°ENE	80°ENE	240°WSW
Length	42	42	58	40
Condition	fair	fair	good	good
Associated artifacts	red chert pebble	none	none	none
Related artifacts	pottery rim	mixed sherds	mixed sherds	earspool, 3 complete pots, 1 partial pot, 1 rim fragment, mixed sherds
Fill	soil	soil	soil	soil
River cobbles	17	11	10	12

Burial	5	6	7
Location	3/4.E	3/4.H	3/5.H
Base depth (cm)	80	110	120
Sex	?	male	?
Age	?	adult, 25–35	child, 6–7
Position	?	flexed, left side	flexed, left side
Orientation	?	295°WNW	280°WNW
Length (cm)	?	68	30
Condition	poor	good	good
Associated artifacts	?	7 pots (5 complete), 1 *Malea ringens* shell, 1 land snail shell, 1 carved bone wand	1 bowl
Related artifacts	mixed sherds	1 drilled incisor, 16 turquoise beads, 2 bone rings, 1 shark's tooth, 25 potter's tools	mixed sherds
Fill	soil	soil	soil
River cobbles	17	11	10

by John Rowe (1995), this chapter considers several specific aspects of Challuabamba burials as expressions of a cultural ideology. These aspects include the location and position of the body, contents of the offerings, evidence of associated rituals, and relationships to architecture.

Death, Status, and Tradition

A comparison of Burials 6 and 7 (Figure 9.1) with Burials 1–4 (Figure 9.2) shows important differences, which may be partly attributable to the lapse of a century or more between the two groups. (Burial 5, which belongs to the same period as 6, is too poorly preserved to provide a basis for discussion.) They show different attitudes toward the treatment of the dead, some perhaps dictated by the social standing of the deceased, and others probably dictated by changing traditions.

Both these sets of burials were in locations apparently set aside as cemeteries during different periods, to judge by the numerous bone fragments in the surrounding fill, with no trace of later burials above Burials 6 and 7 and only one possible burial (a very decayed skeleton identified as 4a) below the Cut 2 burials. There is no good evidence of a building associated with the earlier pair, and no evident connection between those two burials, but Burials 1–4 were clearly placed within the floors of an existing structure. Burials 6 and 7 are beneath the stone alignments marking later foundations, but there is no connection between the burials and the later building.

The isolation of Burials 6 and 7 and the offerings placed with each individual burial contrast with Burials 1–4 (Figure 9.3). The burials of the later group appear to have been laid sequentially, with 4 being the deepest and earliest, then 3, 2, and 1 in order over probably less than a century. Nothing suggests a significant difference in the status of these individuals, who appear to have been part of a group in life, perhaps genetically related.

While all the burials at Challuabamba were flexed, the young man in Burial 6 (Figure 9.1) was in a relaxed position, suggestive of the resting posture of a living individual rather than having been tightly bound into a bundle as were the other burials. Rowe (1995:27–28) notes this distinction in later Peruvian burials and suggests that this relaxed pose was a common trait in elite burials to indicate divine status, symbolizing both the ability to pass spiritually between this world and the supernatural world and continued existence in the afterlife. It is conceivable that this distinction had an earlier and wider currency. Such qualities might well be associated with a

Figure 9.1. Burial 6, Cut 3, base of Level 4. Burial 7 in lower right corner, in Level 5. (Photo by A. Carrillo B.)

Figure 9.2. Burials in Cut 2 (*from left*): 3, 4, 1, 2.

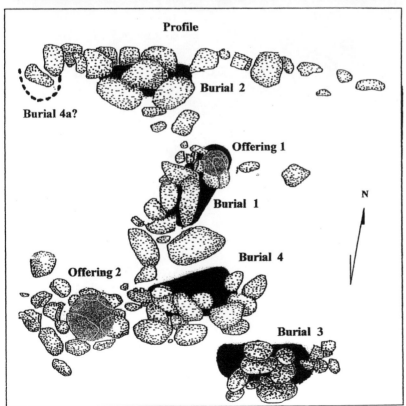

Figure 9.3. Cut 2 Levels 1 and 2, showing burials, offerings, and pattern of stones. (Drawing by B. Jones and J. Farmer)

powerful individual possessing shamanic powers, as the offerings in Burial 6 suggest.

Perhaps the most revealing part of these burials is the offerings deposited with them (see Table 9.1 for lists). Although the earliest burial was a child (Burial 7) who could not personally have attained power or prestige, one fine Red-on-Cream bowl (Figure 9.4) accompanied the burial. Probably a local product, it might have expressed the love of parents and relatives but also tells us about the status the child was expected to attain. A more impressive offering, and in fact one of the more remarkable Formative Period burial offerings yet reported, is found in Burial 6.

The seven fine serving vessels in Burial 6 are probably local products, but a few definite imports make the offering unique among the local examples. From the coast came a *Malea ringens* conch shell associated with the body, and in the related deposits was a shark's tooth (Figure 9.6c). The sixteen turquoise beads were probably not locally available; Bruhns et al. (1990:231) attributed turquoise found at Pirincay to the Ecuadorian south coast. The large shell of a land snail (Figure 8.12) may have been locally available; they were a common offering in Cañari graves in later times, "even in the poorest graves" (Murra 1963:800). The burial surely contained some perish-

Figure 9.4. Red-on-Cream bowls, Burials 6 and 7 offerings. (Photos by J. Farmer)

able materials—matting, textiles, perhaps baskets, and very likely coca leaf (the snail shell may have held lime, which the bone wand served to extract). The bone wand (Figure 9.5f), clearly a utensil, has a decorative knob on one end and signs of wear from scraping on the other, with microscopic gray residue. The bone spatulas and bone rings (Figure 9.6a, b) may have had some ritual use. Long-distance trade in such materials already had a very long history in Ecuador, dating back to the preceramic Las Vegas culture, in which similar shell receptacles and other drug paraphernalia were found in burials (Stothert 2003:371–373). These features of the burial offering appear to establish the individual in Burial 6 as a "beneficent ancestor," a link between his community and the cosmos.

One class of objects in the "related material" of Burial 6 is unique: 36 thin potsherds (Figure 9.7) carefully shaped as tools for scraping and shaping pottery vessels were scattered in the same level (Level 4) around the burial. The shark's tooth was also among this material and may also have been a potter's tool: something such as a shark's tooth or obsidian point was used to engrave the black catfish-effigy vase with jaguar features. This offering also contained a group of pottery disks (Figure 9.7b), the largest one pierced for use as a spindle whorl (Figure 9.7c), and a fragment of a small stone saw (Figure 9.7d). Deposited before the cairn was laid but on the opposite side of the body from the burial offering proper, this set of material might indicate that the man in the burial was a potter or perhaps that a person close to him deposited them as a personal offering. We have no knowledge whether men or women, or both, were potters in ancient Challuabamba, but modern preconceptions give no assistance. Weaving, for example, usually thought of now as something that women do, is a men's craft among modern Cañari and Shuar people (Murra 1963; Harner 1972:68–69). Ceramic art, especially of the quality of these items, might well have been a chiefly attainment, which could mean that some items in the offering might have been made by the deceased's own hands. If work in a craft was not incidental but an important identifier (which implies a level of specialization), then the offerings with Burial 6 suggest that pottery-making was compatible with elite rank.

Other artisan's tools (Figure 9.7c, d) were found among the material related to Burial 6: a ceramic disk, probably carved from a potsherd, about 7 cm diameter with a 1 cm hole in the center, and a fragment of a stone saw about 4 cm long, 3 cm high. The disk would have served as a spindle whorl, although a very light one, and the saw for working small objects in wood. It is hard to explain the in-

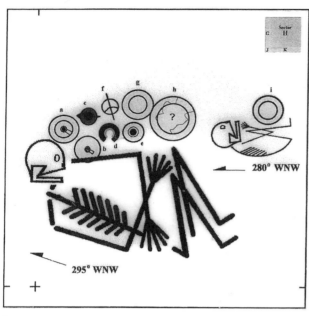

a

b

c

d

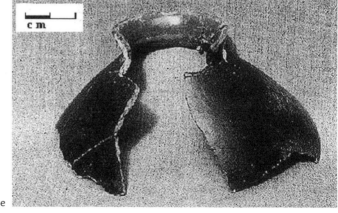

e

f

h

g

Facing page, above

Figure 9.5. Burial 6 offerings: *a*, plan; *b*, single-spout domed red bottle; *c*, single-spout Red-on-Cream bottle; *d*, Red-on-Cream jar; *e*, Red-and-Black rim fragment; *f*, bone wand and broken conch shell; *g*, bone wand (for coca lime); *h*, snail shell. (Photos by J. Farmer)

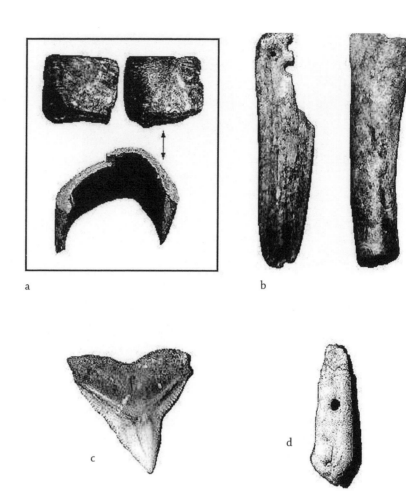

a

b

c

d

Figure 9.6. Bones and teeth in Burial 6 offering: *a*, bone ring fragments; *b*, bone "spatulas"; *c*, shark's tooth; *d*, drilled incisor. (Photos by J. Farmer)

Facing page

Figure 9.7. Artisan's tools related to Burial 6: *a*, group of potsherds reworked as potter's tools; *b*, potsherds reworked into disks; *c*, potsherd worked into spindle whorl; *d*, fragment of stone saw blade. (Photos by J. Farmer)

clusion of these objects in an offering but also hard to explain their presence among so many offering-like materials. Chiefly malocas (houses) were centers of production and trade in later periods (Salomon 1986:125–131), and we may be seeing early aspects of this at Challuabamba.

Two pots in this offering are especially noteworthy: the domed bottle (Figure 9.5b) and the Burnished Black vase (Figure 6.2). The former exemplifies the problem of defining pottery vessels as im-

a

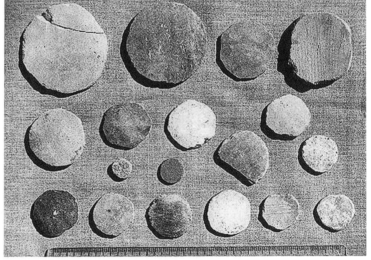

b

c

d

ported since the domed form is most common in the Chorrera style. There are other domed forms at Challuabamba (e.g., Form 1, Figure 2.4f; Form 4, Figure 2.7n, dd), which make a plausible case for the domed form being a local invention or a very early adoption. Challuabamba and Cotocollao are among the sites most identified with the sources of Chorrera style. The small Burnished Black vase (Figure 6.2), with its jaguar-spotted fish body, wide neck, and flaring rim, is unique but probably a local product, since it is more similar to other Burnished Black items than to the work of any other site. While the bottles (Figures 9.5b, c) and the jaguar-catfish effigy are likely local work, the two red and buff flaring bowls (Figure 9.4) may be imported, perhaps from Cerro Narrío, where pattern-burnish was applied to buff surfaces, as in the designs on the exterior walls. Pattern-burnish on buff, which is so subtle as to be nearly invisible, appears very rarely at Challuabamba, where areas of matte black were the preferred background.

In comparison with Burials 6 and 7, Burials 1–4 are more modest. Their location resembles a formal cemetery, similar to that described by Villalba (1988:75–101) at Cotocollao or the Osario at Real Alto (Marcos 1988:161–173), though on a much smaller scale. All the bodies appear to have been tightly bound into a fetal position and laid on their back or side. It is very likely they were wrapped in textiles or matting, but no trace remains. While neither the treatment of the body nor special individualized offerings indicate the social status of these individuals, their location under the floors of a single structure implies some group identity. The structure may have served as a type of ancestor house where periodic rituals were conducted and offerings placed. Tom Dillehay (1995:17) has summarized the importance of ancestor worship in establishing community cohesion and "political character." This group of burials seems to have been composed of revered ancestors. Stothert (2003:348–351) discusses modern Day of the Dead ceremonies in Santa Elena, on the Ecuadorian coast, which include feasting and food offerings to the deceased relatives, practices which may be evident in the later Challuabamba cemetery area. Placement of stones, such as the unworked cobbles around and over these burials, is a widespread custom found also at Santa Elena, apparently marking the grave and providing magico-religious protection (Stothert 2003:376–380). It is also a feature of modern Cañari burials, making it a very long tradition.

Only one item could be considered an associated offering in these four burials. It is the unworked red chert pebble beside the head of Burial 1, its red color perhaps symbolizing the soul. That burial was probably most closely identified with what we have called Offering 1: at the time of its deposit it was the complete rim of a Red-on-Cream tecomate (Figure 9.8), with the body of the vessel missing. The deposit of fragmentary pots is one of the few traits shared between Burial 6 (which had a large rim of a Red-and-Black jar, Figure 9.5e) and the later Burial 1. That is also a long tradition in the Andes. Ruth Shady Solís (1983) describes vessel rims and ceramic fragments in burials at Pacopampa as symbolic openings or portals for the spirit. Breaking, or more properly "sacrificing," pottery vessels was also a common ritual practice, found in the fill above burials at many sites (e.g., La Emerenciana; Staller 1994:356).

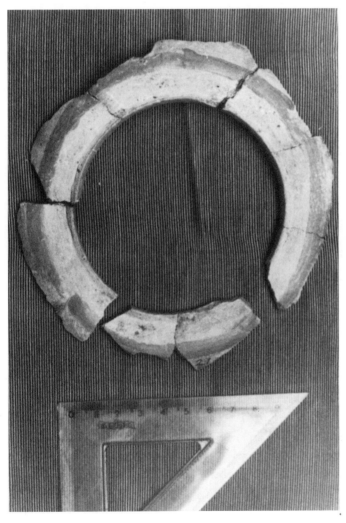

Figure 9.8. Cut 2, Burial 1 and Offering 1: rim fragment. (Photo by J. Farmer)

The initial assumption upon the discovery of Offering 2 in Cut 2 was that it marked a specific burial (No. 4), following the pattern of burials covered by unworked stones (Figure 9.9). It turned out to be a small chamber of rough stones which contained one complete rim sherd, four complete or restorable fineware jars (Figure 9.10), and a white ceramic earspool (Figure 9.11). Although the stones of the chamber's base intermingle with the stones over Burial 4, it is actually half a meter west of the burial and at a higher level. It appears

Figure 9.9. Cut 2, Burial 4 and Offering 2: *a*, drawing; *b*, view east across Level 2, showing stone chamber containing Offering 2. (Drawing by B. Jones, photo by J. Farmer)

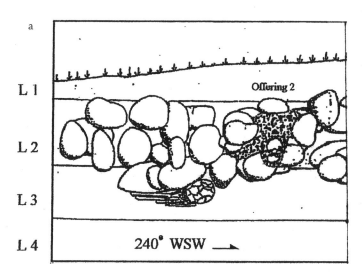

a

L 1

Offering 2

L 2

L 3

L 4

240° WSW ⟶

b

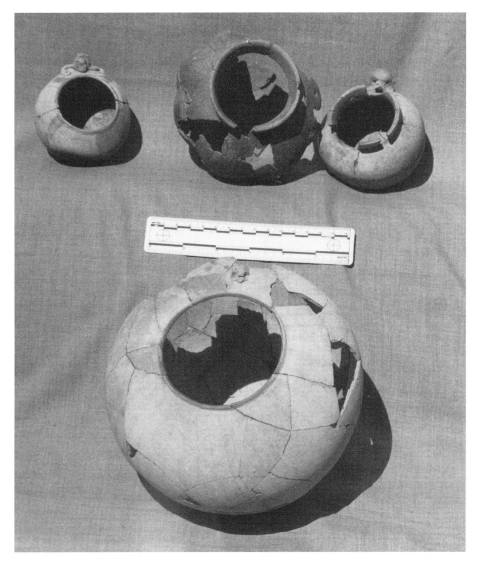

Figure 9.10. Cut 2, Offering 2: *top:* small Red-on-Cream jar with effigy; thin-walled brown jar; small jar with effigy head; *bottom:* large tecomate. (Photos by J. Farmer)

more likely that the chamber and its contents were intended to mark the area of the burials, rather than a single burial. The earspool, which is an attribute of elite status, and the very fine quality of the ceramics suggest a ceremony to sanctify the building as an ancestor shrine. The belief in burials as both shrines and points of communication with the dead was apparently widespread during the Formative Period and commonly associated with shamanic ritual.

Figure 9.11. Cut 2 Level 1: earspool of cream ceramic in Offering 2.

The ceramics in the Offering 2 chamber are significantly different from those with Burial 6 and exemplify the best work of the later phase. The largest vessel (Figure 9.10a), at the bottom of the chamber, is a polychrome tecomate 22 cm in diameter with very thin walls with a delicate brushed texture on the cream surface, a red rim, and blazes of orange and black on lower parts of the body, calculated to look accidental. A small animal in relief is attached just below the rim. Extremely light in weight, this jar was crushed but was temporarily restored and can be given a final restoration. Two small jars with animal heads overlooking the rim were next (Figure 9.10b, d).

Above those was a slightly larger jar (10 cm rim diam.) with very thin gadrooned walls, a low neck, and a reinforced rim (Figure 9.10c). Perhaps a squash effigy, it has a dark brown, unslipped, unpolished body, showing sparkling flakes of mica. The ware and finish are unique at Challuabamba, but its source cannot be specified. Its lobed form suggests a fruit or vegetal form, but the punched circle and grooved lines that remain on one side might be the eye and snout of an animal. This exceptional piece, along with the other effigy vessels, suggests that effigies may have been more common than the excavated material suggests and, along with the carved wares, were the highest level of art production of the site and its period.

The single earspool is of special interest, a hollow ring with a channel in the wall to be inserted in the perforation of the earlobe (Figure 9.11). The spool form is that known also in Mesoamerica. The Peruvian earplug of this period was a peg inserted through the ear, with an ornamental solid disk attached to the front (e.g., Grieder et al. 1988:92–95).

The isolation of Burials 6 and 7 and the offerings placed with each individual burial contrast with the later Burials 1–4. The burials of that later group appear to have been laid sequentially, with 4 being the deepest and earliest, then 3, 2, and 1 in order, over perhaps a century at most. Nothing suggests a significant difference in the status of these individuals, who appear to have been part of a group in life, perhaps genetically related. But the contents of Offering 2 are a strong indication that Burial 4, at least, and most likely all four of these burials involved individuals of rank.

Comparisons with other Formative Period burials provide some regional context for the Challuabamba burials. The Burial 6 offering has a cosmopolitan flavor, with the imported shell and turquoise beads. The Burnished Black effigy vase and the Red-on-Cream bottles especially suggest activities in ritual or ceremony and connections with shamanic ideals. In contrast, Offering 2 in Cut 2 contains two of the small jars with effigy heads so common that they appear to be employed in some ritual consumption (coca leaf perhaps) practiced by many people. While the pottery in Offering 2 is unsurpassed at the site in quality, Burnished Blackware and feline and cosmic themes are absent, suggesting a more egalitarian or at least popularly accessible cultural scene. The Burial 6 offering seems to anticipate Cupisnique-Chavín hieratic and symbolic styles, with its reduction-fired blackwares and feline and cosmic themes. While the gadrooned "squash" jar in Offering 2 is a likely import, it has more in common with Chorrera naturalism than with Chavín symbolism, and the earspool hints at a disconnection from Peruvian elite insignia.

The differences in preparation of the body, location relative to building, and the nature of the offerings between Burial 6 and the later Burials 1–4 argue for fairly rapid social and cultural developments throughout the middle phases of the site's history. While both the earlier and later burial types are consistent with local styles, and both contain anticipations of later Andean styles, the differences are indications of cleavages in the sociopolitical environment. Yet all the burials fall within the general pattern of Cañari burials of the fifteenth or sixteenth century AD described by Murra (1963:800). The set of burials in Cut 2 might be described with his phrase "collective interment of the dead was not unusual." The shells of land snails scattered in the levels with burials, found in "even the poorest graves," and the sealing of chiefly graves with "large boulders piled up at the mouth of the grave," like the cairns consistently found over Challuabamba burials, are noteworthy. Absent from the Challuabamba graves are any traces of individuals sacrificed to accompany the deceased, as described by Murra for sixteenth-century Cañari chiefly burials. The lapse of three millennia (more or less) between the excavated burials and those described by Murra is a sign of long-term cultural stability but also seems to suggest that much greater personal power was accumulated by high-ranking individuals in the more recent times described by Murra.

Bibliography

Bruhns, Karen Olsen, James H. Burton, and George R. Miller
1990   Excavations at Pirincay in the Paute Valley of Southern Ecuador, 1985–1988. *Antiquity* 64:221–233.
Dillehay, Tom D., editor
1995   *Tombs for the Living: Andean Mortuary Practices.* Washington, D.C.: Dumbarton Oaks.
Grieder, Terence
1978   *The Art and Archaeology of Pashash.* Austin: University of Texas Press.

Grieder, Terence, Alberto Bueno Mendoza, C. Earle Smith, Jr., and Robert M. Malina.

1988   *La Galgada: A Preceramic Culture in Transition.* Austin: University of Texas Press.

Harner, Michael J.

1972   *The Jívaro.* Garden City, N.Y.: Doubleday Anchor.

Marcos, Jorge G.

1988   *Real Alto: La historia de un centro ceremonial Valdivia.* Quito: Corporación Editora Nacional.

Murra, John

1963   The Cañari. In *Handbook of South American Indians,* ed. J. H. Steward, vol. 2, 799–801. New York: Cooper Square.

Rowe, John H.

1995   Behavior and Belief in Ancient Peruvian Mortuary Practice. In *Tombs for the Living: Andean Mortuary Practices,* ed. T. D. Dillehay, 27–41. Washington, D.C.: Dumbarton Oaks.

Salomon, Frank

1986   *Native Lords of Quito in the Age of the Incas: Political Economy of North Andean Chiefdoms.* New York: Cambridge University Press.

Shady Solís, Ruth

1983   *Una aproximación al mundo de las creencias andinas: la cultura Pacopampa.* Boletín No. 8. Lima: Museo Nacional de Antropología.

Staller, John Edward

1994   Late Valdivia Occupation in Southern Coastal El Oro Province, Ecuador: Excavations at the Early Formative Period Site of La Emerenciana. Ph.D. dissertation, Southern Methodist University.

Stothert, Karen E.

2003   Expression of Ideology in the Formative Period of Ecuador. In *Archaeology of Formative Ecuador,* ed. J. S. Raymond and R. L Burger, 337–421. Washington, D.C.: Dumbarton Oaks.

Villalba O., Marcelo

1988   *Cotocollao: una aldea Formativa del valle de Quito.* Quito: Museos del Banco Central del Ecuador.

Twelve of the fourteen cylinder seals are shown. *Top row:* No. 14, No. 7, No. 1 and No. 8; *second row:* No. 2, a flat stamp, No. 5, No. 9, No. 10; *third row:* No. 3, No. 11, a flat stamp, No. 4, No. 12. Photo by B. Jones. Cylinders Nos. 6 and 13 are shown in Figures 7.7 and 7.14.

Red-Banded Incised/Splashed sherds, Cut 3.H Level 2. These late versions of RBI/Splashed style add step-pyramids both inside and out, mixed with incised exteriors and splashed interiors.

Large stone revetment that supported a late period earth platform. Cut 3 is in the foreground, Cut 2 is in the background.

Cut 3. The most distant section is excavated to Level 3. The layer in the foreground is sterile base.

Neckless jar (tecomate) from Cut 2 Level 1, Burial Offering 2. Red-on-Cream, very thin walls. 13 cm high, 59 cm circumference, 8.8 cm rim diameter.

Neckless jar (tecomate) from Cut 2 Level 1, Burial Offering 2. Inverted to show painted pattern on base.

Bowls from Burial Offering 6, Cut 3.H Level 4.

Six exceptional ceramic vessels from burial offerings. The dark brown jar on the far right comes from Cut 2, Burial Offering #2; it is vessel #5. All the others were part of the large offering in Cut 3 Level 4, with Burial 6. *From left to right, front to back:* Red-and-Black small jar; Burnished Black jaguar-cat-fish effigy; Red domed, handled single-spout bottle; Red-on-Cream single-spout bottle with black fire-clouds; and one of two large Red flared bowls with nearly flat floors. A similar Red flared bowl accompanied the child in Burial 7, next to the adult male in Burial 6.

Seven Red-on-Cream painted and incised sherds and one modeled and carved Burnished Black sherd from Cut 3 Level 2. At the top is a straight-walled jar with a stepped design, then an incised crisscross design below a red rim. The third row has a red zigzag and broad red band on the interior of a wide bowl. The bottom three show late versions of "scroll and bars" on the interior of bowls.

Black and white ceramic forms from Cut 3.H Level 2: *top left:* rim with rocker-stamped border, incised designs; *top right:* Burnished Black hollow human torso and arms; *left:* white stamp of feline or dragon eye, snout, and tongue; *bottom:* large bowl with frog modeled at rim.

10

Human Remains   DOUGLAS H. UBELAKER

Excavations at the site of Challuabamba in the highlands of southern Ecuador produced human remains which appear to have originated from primary articulated burials in levels dated by radiocarbon between 1700 and 1400 BC. The remains have been in the custody of the National Patrimony offices in Cuenca. Those available for study were transported by Terence Grieder, who directed the excavation project, to Cautivo in coastal Ecuador to be analyzed in June 2003 by the author, assisted by Sally Graver of Ohio State University. All remains were examined and remained in the custody of Grieder. He returned all the specimens to the National Patrimony offices in Cuenca.

This chapter presents the results of that study (in order of archaeological feature number). Interpretations of age at death, sex, and pathological conditions follow standard procedures (Bass 1987; Buikstra and Ubelaker 1994; Ubelaker 1989).

All the remains analyzed were recovered from the excavation unit defined as Cut 3, which the excavators believe contained a cemetery used over several centuries.

Cut 3.C Level 1

The recognizable human remains recovered from this disturbed burial consist of only a fragment of the right parietal, including the area of the bregma. The bone is of adult size but with open sutures. The morphological indicators suggest an age between fifteen and thirty years, although an older age cannot be ruled out.

No reliable estimate of sex can be made from the morphological evidence.

The fragment reveals slight abnormal bone thickening and porosity on aspects of the periosteal surface suggestive of mild, remodeled porotic hyperostosis and/or infection. The area of abnormality measures approximately 8 mm in thickness, whereas the unaffected areas measure approximately 6 mm.

Disturbed Surface Collection from Cut 3.J Level 1

Fragments from adult-sized long bone diaphyses are present. Recognizable human bones consist of a left and right femur, left humerus, and the proximal area of a tibia. Several nonhuman animal bones are also present. The long bone fragments display extensive porosity on the endosteal border of the cortex, suggestive of advancing age. The diminished cortical thickness and porosity suggest a probable age at death of greater than sixty years.

Burial 6, Cut 3.H Level 4

The remains are fragmentary but all consistent with an origin from a single individual (Figure 9.1). Recognizable bones include the humeri, radii, ulnae, femora, tibiae, fibulae, scapulae, mandible, innominates, left patella, one proximal and one middle hand phalanx, left calcaneus, left cuboid, one foot navicular, right first cuneiform, four metatarsals, twelve foot phalanges, and the cranium. Male sex is suggested by the large mastoid processes, large supraorbital ridges, large femoral head diameters, and narrow sciatic notches on the innominates.

An age at death of approximately twenty-five to thirty-five years is suggested by the morphology of the innominates, cranial sutures, and other indicators.

All permanent teeth are present except the mandibular left canine.

Burial 7, Cut 3.H Level 4

Fragmentary remains of a child are present (Figure 9.1). Recognizable bones present consist of the right humerus, both temporals, left pubis, and seven vertebral centra. Numerous deciduous and permanent teeth are present. The extent of dental formation suggests an age at death between six and seven years.

Summary

The data presented above suggest the presence of three adults and one child. Ages at death are six to seven years, fifteen to thirty years, twenty-five to thirty-five years, and over sixty years. Of the three adults, at least one male is likely present. Bone pathology is limited to the periosteal alterations and thickening of the parietal fragment from Sector C, Level 1.

Although the size of this sample is very small, its antiquity and highland location merit some comparison with other data reported from ancient Ecuador (Buikstra and Ubelaker 1994; Ubelaker 1979, 1980a, 1980b, 1981, 1983a, 1983b, 1984, 1988a, 1988b, 1988c, 1988d, 1988e, 1988f, 1988g, 1990, 1992a, 1992b, 1992c, 1992d, 1994a, 1994b, 1995, 1997, 2000, 2003; Ubelaker and Jones 2002; Ubelaker, Katzenberg, and Doyon 1995; Ubelaker and Newson 2002; Ubelaker and Ripley 1999). The ratio of bones with periosteal lesions to adults in this sample is 0.33 and the ratio to total individuals is 0.25. Both these values are rather high in comparison with those reported from other sites (Ubelaker 2003). Periosteal lesions represent abnormalities thought to be produced by infection or similar morbidity that stimulates bone production.

Thirty-one fully formed and erupted permanent teeth were present in this small sample. Although no carious lesions were noted, four of these teeth (12.9 percent) displayed enamel hypoplasia, a condition of abnormal enamel formation thought to represent childhood morbidity (Goodman et al. 1984; Ubelaker 1992c). This frequency is very high in comparison with other reported values. Mean values for combined samples in various time periods range from 1.0 to 4.4 percent for precontact Ecuador and from 0.5 to 3.0 during the historic period. The hypoplastic lines in the Challuabamba sample were formed between the ages of four and five years.

No abscesses were noted in fifteen observations of the presence or absence of alveolar abscesses. Also, no permanent teeth had been lost antemortem (thirty-one observations).

Twelve deciduous teeth were present. No associated alveolar abscesses were observed, but five (41.7 percent) of these teeth displayed carious lesions.

Due to the fragmentary condition of the remains, it was not possible to record cranial or mandibular measurements. The following observations were recorded from the adult male from Burial 6. Mylohyoid bridge was present on the right mandible. Accessory mental foramen, auditory exostoses, and marginal foramen of the tympanic plate were all absent on the right side.

Discussion

Although the size of the sample reported here is extremely small, the data presented are noteworthy because of the early date and the highland location. The sample is too small to merit demographic discussion except to note that a considerable range of ages at death (from childhood to over sixty years) is represented.

Although trauma was not present, the periosteal lesion frequency suggests a high level of adult morbidity, likely due to infection. If this frequency was sustained in the analysis of larger samples from this period and location it would argue for a level of adult morbidity not recorded in other highland samples.

The recovered teeth lacked dental caries but presented elevated frequencies of dental hypoplasia. The dental hypoplasias were found in maxillary first premolars in Burial 7 and right canines in Burial 6. Examination of the locations of the defects within the crown of the teeth suggests that all formed between the ages of four and five years.

Although the sample is too small to support any broad conclusions about health, the data discussed above are suggestive of elevated morbidity in adults (periosteal lesions) and children (deciduous dental caries and enamel hypoplasias). These data may be augmented through study of other well-documented samples from this location and date.

Bibliography

Bass, William M.
1987   *Human Osteology: A Laboratory and Field Manual.* 3rd ed. Columbia: Missouri Archaeological Society.

Buikstra, Jane E., and Douglas H. Ubelaker, editors
1994   *Standards for Data Collection from Human Skeletal Remains.* Proceedings of a Seminar at the Field Museum of Natural History Organized by J. Haas. Arkansas Archeological Survey Research Series No. 44. Fayetteville: Arkansas Archeological Survey.

Goodman, Alan H., Debra L. Martin, George J. Armelagos, and George Clark
1984   Indications of Stress from Bone and Teeth. In *Paleopathology at the Origins of Agriculture,* ed. Mark N. Cohen and George J. Armelagos, 13–49. New York: Academic Press.

Ubelaker, Douglas H.
1979   Skeletal Evidence for Kneeling in Prehistoric Ecuador. *American Journal of Physical Anthropology* 51(4):679–685.

1980a   Human Skeletal Remains from Site OGSE-80: A Preceramic Site on the Sta. Elena Peninsula, Coastal Ecuador. *Journal of the Washington Academy of Sciences* 70(2):3–24.

1980b   Prehistoric Human Remains from the Cotocollao Site, Pichincha Province, Ecuador. *Journal of the Washington Academy of Sciences* 70(2):59–74.

1981   *The Ayalán Cemetery: A Late Integration Period Burial Site on the South Coast of Ecuador.* Smithsonian Contributions to Anthropology 29. Washington, D.C.: Smithsonian Institution Press.

1983a   Human Skeletal Remains from OGSE-MA-172: An Early Guangala Cemetery Site on the Coast of Ecuador. *Journal of the Washington Academy of Sciences* 73(1):16–27.

1983b   Prehistoric Demography of Coastal Ecuador. *National Geographic Society*

Research Reports 15:695–704. Washington, D.C.: National Geographic Society.

1984 Prehistoric Human Biology of Ecuador: Possible Temporal Trends and Cultural Correlations. In *Paleopathology at the Origins of Agriculture,* ed. Mark N. Cohen and George J. Armelagos, 491–513. New York: Academic Press.

1988a Human Remains from OGSE-46, La Libertad, Guayas Province, Ecuador. *Journal of the Washington Academy of Sciences* 78(1):3–16.

1988b Porotic Hyperostosis in Prehistoric Ecuador: Abstract. *Collegium Anthropologicum* 12 (supplement):34. Zagreb, 12th International Congress of Anthropological and Ethnological Sciences.

1988c Prehistoric Human Biology at La Tolita, Ecuador: A Preliminary Report. *Journal of the Washington Academy of Sciences* 78(1):23–37.

1988d A Preliminary Report of Analysis of Human Remains from Agua Blanca, a Prehistoric Late Integration Site from Coastal Ecuador. *Journal of the Washington Academy of Sciences* 78(1):17–22.

1988e Restos de esqueletos humanos del Sitio OGSE-80. In *La prehistoria temprana de la Península de Santa Elena, Ecuador: Cultura Las Vegas,* ed. Karen E. Stothert, 105–132. Guayaquil: Museos del Banco Central del Ecuador.

1988f Restos humanos prehistóricos del Sitio Cotocollao, Provincia de Pichincha, Ecuador. Appendix II in *Cotocollao: Una aldea Formativa del Valle de Quito,* ed. Marcelo Villalba O., 555–571. Quito: Museos del Banco Central del Ecuador.

1988g Skeletal Biology of Prehistoric Ecuador: An Ongoing Research Program. *Journal of the Washington Academy of Sciences* 78(1):1–2.

1989 *Human Skeletal Remains: Excavation, Analysis, Interpretation.* 2nd ed. Washington, D.C.: Taraxacum.

1990 Human Skeletal Remains from "Jardín del Este," Cumbayá, Pichincha, Ecuador. In *La preservación y promoción del patrimonio cultural del Ecuador,* 22–39. Cooperación Técnica Ecuatoriana—Belga No. 4. Quito: Instituto Nacional de Patrimonio Cultural.

1992a Enamel Hypoplasia in Ancient Ecuador. *Journal of Paleopathology, Monographic Publications* 2:207–217.

1992b Patterns of Demographic Change in the Americas. *Human Biology* 64(3):361–379.

1992c Porotic Hyperostosis in Prehistoric Ecuador. In *Diet, Demography, and Disease: Changing Perspectives on Anemia,* ed. Patricia Stuart-Macadam and Susan Kent, 201–217. New York: Aldine de Gruyter.

1992d Temporal Trends in Dental Disease in Ancient Ecuador. *Anthropologie* 30, no. 1:99–102.

1994a *Biología de los restos humanos hallados en el Convento de San Francisco de Quito (Ecuador).* Quito: Instituto Nacional de Patrimonio Cultural del Ecuador.

1994b The Biological Impact of European Contact in Ecuador. In *In the Wake of Contact: Biological Responses to Conquest,* ed. Clark S. Larsen and George R. Milner, 147–160. New York: Wiley-Liss.

1995 Biological Research with Archaeologically Recovered Human Remains from Ecuador: Methodological Issues. In *Archaeology in the Lowland American Tropics, Current Analytical Methods and Recent Applications,* ed. Peter W. Stahl, 181–197. Cambridge: Cambridge University Press.

1997 *Skeletal Biology of Human Remains from La Tolita, Esmeraldas Province, Ecuador.* Smithsonian Contributions to Anthropology 41. Washington, D.C.: Smithsonian Institution Press.

2000 *Human Skeletal Remains from La Florida, Quito, Ecuador.* Smithsonian Contributions to Anthropology 43. Washington, D.C.: Smithsonian Institution Press.

2003 *Health Issues in the Early Formative of Ecuador: Skeletal Biology of Real Alto,* ed. J. S. Raymond and R. L. Burger, 259–287. Washington, D.C.: Dumbarton Oaks.

Ubelaker, Douglas H., and Erica Bubniak Jones

2002 Formative Period Human Remains from Coastal Ecuador: La Emerenciana Site (OOSrSr-42). *Journal of the Washington Academy of Sciences* 88(2):59–72.

Ubelaker, D. H., M. A. Katzenberg, and L. G. Doyon

1995 Status and Diet in Precontact Highland Ecuador. *American Journal of Physical Anthropology* 97(4):403–411.

Ubelaker, Douglas H., and Linda A. Newson

2002 Patterns of Health and Nutrition in Prehistoric and Historic Ecuador. In *The Backbone of History, Health and Nutrition in the Western Hemisphere,* ed. R. H. Steckel and J. C. Rose, 343–374. Cambridge: Cambridge University Press.

Ubelaker, Douglas H., and Catherine E. Ripley

1999 *The Ossuary of San Francisco Church, Quito, Ecuador: Human Skeletal Biology.* Smithsonian Contributions to Anthropology 42. Washington, D.C.: Smithsonian Institution Press.

Zooarchaeology PETER W. STAHL

11

The collection of 6,060 archaeofaunal specimens recovered from Challuabamba between 1995 and 2000 is one of the largest recorded zooarchaeological assemblages from the highlands of southern Ecuador and extreme northern Peru. This is an area in which only a handful of early sites have yielded comparable data (Figure 1.1). These include mention of archaeofaunal material at Loma Pucara (Arellano 1994), Cerro Narrío (Collier and Murra 1943), and Pacopampa (Rosas and Shady 1975:22); small samples from Catamayo (NISP [number of identified specimens] = 250; Guffroy et al. 1987: 110) and Cueva Negra de Chobshi (NISP > 258; Lynch and Pollock 1981:98); and larger samples from Pirincay (NISP = 1,495; Miller and Gill 1990:52), Putushío (NISP = 6,110; A. M. Freire, pers. comm., 1993), and Cerro Ñañañique (NISP = 2,314; Guffroy 1994). Idrovo Urigüen (2000:118) gives passing mention to identified faunal specimens recovered from Challuabamba in earlier excavations by Dominique Gomis, including rabbit, opossum, deer, various birds, fish, turtle, and river crab (*pangora*). The current study expands on this list and draws inferences about zooarchaeological data for trade and selective faunal provisioning during the early appearance of Formative culture in the area, based on a detailed description and analysis of a larger archaeofaunal assemblage from the site.

Challuabamba is a particularly interesting venue for exploring early interregional connections. Elsewhere (Stahl 2005) I provide a summary of the zooarchaeological analyses from Challuabamba within the context of broader, regional Pre-Columbian interactions. Here I only briefly discuss the site's importance for elaborating these issues. Previous archaeological research in the southern highlands reveals close, likely intimate, contact between Pre-Columbian inhabitants in the northern highlands, western coastal lowlands, Amazon basin, and northern Peru from a relatively early date (Arellano 2002:168; Bennett 1946:19; Braun 1982:50; Bruhns 1989:63, 2003:167; Bruhns et al. 1990:229–230, 1994; Collier and Murra 1943:25, 84; Gomis

2000:149–150; Grieder et al. 2002:163; Guffroy 1989; Guffroy et al. 1987; Hocquenghem 1999; Hocquenghem et al. 1993:454, 456; Idrovo Urigüen 2000; Kaulicke 1991; Lanning 1963; Rostoker 1998; Shady 1987:480; Temme 2000). It has been suggested that Late Formative settlements were strategically located in areas from which trade routes could be controlled (Bruhns 2003:160; Idrovo Urigüen 2000:118; Shady 1987:460; Temme 2000:136), with speculation that at least some sites served as elite/ceremonial centers which housed the managers of an early trade network. These centers may have been characterized by site-specific specialization, including the trade of marine shells, various rocks, and semiprecious stones from the coast into the highlands and beyond as well as metal-working, particularly in gold (Arellano 1994:120; Bruhns 1989:63, 66, 2003:143, 158, 161; Bruhns et al. 1990:231; Collier and Murra 1943:69; Gomis 2000:146–147; Guffroy 1989:120; Guffroy et al. 1987:193; Hocquenghem 1999; Hocquenghem et al. 1993:454; Rehren and Temme 1992:269).

Scholars working in northern Peru and southern Ecuador suggest ˙that the earliest trade routes were initially terrestrial (e.g., Hocquenghem 1993, 1999; Hocquenghem and Peña Ruíz 1994; Hocquenghem et al. 1993). They characterize the area south of the Jubones River into northern Peru as intermediate between, and autonomous from, its neighbors to the north (independent agriculturalists of humid southern Ecuador) and to the south (irrigation-dependent, essentially Central Andean cultures of arid northern Peru). They downplay coastal exchange, suggesting that the prevailing winds and currents made maritime trade arduous; additionally, the incipient agriculture practiced by coastal Peruvians created little demand for *Spondylus* fertility symbolism. Instead, contemporaneous inland agricultural settlements in the dry upper portions of the Piura River were the more likely consumers of shell. Early trade connections in Ecuador were between coastal and highland agriculturalists. Coastal shell was exchanged through the Cordillera de Mullupungo (Quechuan for *Spondylus* door or port) via the Jubones River, after which southern highland groups in present-day Ecuador consumed and processed *Spondylus* for further overland trade to northern Peru. During the Late Formative other products like semiprecious stones, and eventually copper, were added to the list of traded items. Throughout prehistory, different Andean polities jockeyed for control of terrestrial trade routes and exchange termini that introduced goods between the southern highlands of Ecuador and northern Peru via this intermediate area. The zooarchaeological data from Challuabamba suggest that animal products were likely also a component of this early trade network.

The Challuabamba Archaeofaunas

Table 11.1 enumerates the archaeofaunal collection examined from the 1995 to 2000 excavation seasons, listing scientific and common names and number of identified specimens (NISP) for each taxonomic category. The following discussion includes notes on identification and systematics, recent geographical distributions, and brief synopses of characteristic natural histories for potentially analogous taxa currently known from the general area.

MOLLUSCA

The studied assemblage includes a total of 39 shell fragments, 4 of which are indeterminate molluscs. The majority are pulmonates or land snails, with a few marine gastropods and bivalves.

GASTROPODA

Stylommatophora
Megalobulimidae
On the basis of anatomical differences, Jose Leme (1973) created this new South American family of medium-sized to large (shells between 50 to 160 mm) primitive land snails, distinct from the small to medium-sized (shells 40 to 70 mm) Strophocheilidae. These snails are specific to the neotropics and currently include a number of Andean species that range from Colombia to Bolivia, especially *Megalobulimus oblongus, M. maximus,* and the giant *M. popelairianus.* All are strictly terrestrial, preferring well-watered areas with vegetation cover, in which they hide during the day. These nocturnal snails also bury themselves in soil for aestivation during dry periods. They tend to be common in anthropogenic settings, including cultivated clearings and secondary forest, and are used as human food (Bequaert 1948).

Neogastropoda
Conidae
This family of marine gastropods inhabits a range of deep and shallow water habitats and includes as many as 19 species of differently sized *Conus.* These gastropods characteristically use venom to capture live prey (Keen 1971:658).

Table 11.1. Archaeofaunal Representation

Scientific Name	Common Name	NISP
Mollusca	Indeterminate Mollusk	4
Gastropoda	Indeterminate Gastropod	13
Megalobulimidae	Megasnail	13
Megalobulimus	Megasnail	1
Conus	Cone/*Cono*	1
Bivalvia	Indeterminate Bivalve	5
Pecten	Scallop/*Venera*	1
Spondylus?	Spondylus/*Espondylus*	1
Osteichthyes	Indeterminate Bony Fish	32
Siluriformes	Catfish/*Bagre*	55
Ariidae	Ocean Catfish/*Bagre marino*	25
Reptilia	Indeterminate Reptile	1
Chelonia	Turtle/*Tortuga*	3
Crocodylidae	Crocodiles/*Cocodrilo*	1
Aves	Indeterminate Bird	8
Phalacrocorax	Cormorant/*Cormorán*	1
Vultur gryphus	Andean Condor/*Cóndor andino*	2
Accipitridae	Eagles, Hawks/*Águilas, Gavilanes*	2
Geranoaetus	Black-Chested Buzzard Eagle/*Águila pechinegra*	2
cf. *Geranoaetus*	Black-Chested Buzzard Eagle/*Águila pechinegra*	1
Columba	Pigeon/*Paloma*	2
Passeriformes	Perching Birds	1
Mammalia	Indeterminate Mammal	3,683
cf. *Chironectes*	Water Opossum/*Raposa de agua*	1
Didelphis	Opossum/*Zarigüeya*	1
Homo	Human/*Humano*	27
cf. *Homo*	Human/*Humano*	7
Sylvilagus	Rabbit/*Conejo*	317
cf. *Sylvilagus*	Rabbit/*Conejo*	3
Rodentia	Rodents/*Roedores*	12
Sciurus	Squirrel/*Ardilla*	1
Sigmodon cf. *inopinatus*	Cotton Rat/*Ratón de cola peluda*	1
Dasyprocta	Agouti/*Guatusa*	90
cf. *Dasyprocta*	Agouti/*Guatusa*	2

Table 11.1. Archaeofaunal Representation (*continued*)

Scientific Name	Common Name	NISP
Agouti	Paca/*Guanta*	3
Agouti cf. *paca*	Paca/*Guanta*	1
Agouti cf. *taczanowskii*	Mountain Paca/*Sacha cuy*	1
Carnivora	Carnivores/*Carnívoros*	2
Canis	Dog/*Perro*	2
cf. *Canis*	Dog/*Perro*	2
Tremarctos	Spectacled Bear/*Oso de anteojos*	3
cf. *Tremarctos*	Spectacled Bear/*Oso de anteojos*	2
Felis concolor	Puma	2
Felis cf. *concolor*	Puma	2
Tapirus	Tapir/*Danta*	1
Artiodactyla	Two-Toed Ungulates	291
Tayassu	Peccary/*Sajino*	10
Cervidae	Deer/*Venado*	163
Odocoileus	White-Tailed Deer/*Venado de cola blanca*	892
cf. *Odocoileus*	White-Tailed Deer/*Venado de cola blanca*	84
Indeterminate	Indeterminate Vertebrate	279
TOTAL		6,060

Note: "cf." denotes that the specimen looks like but is not confirmed to a taxonomic level.

BIVALVIA
Pterioida
Pectinidae
The scallops include variably sized marine bivalves that may attach temporarily to bottoms, but most are free swimmers in relatively deep waters. Species of *Pecten, Argopecten, Chlamys, Cyclopecten, Delectopecten, Leptopecten, Lyropecten,* and *Plicatula* currently inhabit coastal waters southward to Ecuador and the Galápagos Islands (Keen 1971:84).

Spondylidae
Two species of *Spondylus* inhabit the warm coastal waters of Ecuador, where they attach their shells to substrates at moderate depths. The large purple-rimmed giant rock oyster (*S. calcifer*) ranges from the

Gulf of California to Ecuador. The red-rimmed thorny oyster (*S. princeps princeps*) is found from Panama to the warm waters off southern Ecuador. Another form, *S. p. leucantha,* may be restricted to Ecuador. One small red shell bead was recovered but not recorded in this analysis; a large, weathered and purplish rim fragment may be a piece of the larger rock oyster.

Osteichthyes
A small but significant sample (NISP = 112; 2.7%) of bony fish specimens is included in the Challuabamba assemblage. The majority of these specimens appear to be catfish.

Siluriformes
Ariidae
As many as 80 cranial and postcranial specimens from all excavation areas and levels are identified as catfish, 25 of which compare well with representative examples of Ariidae at the American Museum of Natural History (AMNH). This identification was subsequently confirmed by Dr. John Lundberg of the Academy of Natural Sciences in Philadelphia. The Ariidae or ocean catfish are a primarily coastal family of medium to large catfish found in tropical and subtropical seas throughout the world. They are known to favor estuaries and coastal lagoons with muddy bottoms and may ascend rivers or streams beyond tidal influence, while a few can be permanently restricted to freshwater. Ariids are active, omnivorous bottom feeders that often school near surfaces. Recent Ecuadorian taxa include various species of *Bagre* and *Arius*. Members of either genus have strong bony, granular head shields (Burgess 1989).

Reptilia
Only 5 identifiably reptilian specimens were registered in the Challuabamba archaeofaunal assemblage, including 1 fragment that could be identified only to the level of class.

Chelonia
One plastron and two carapace specimens of an indeterminate turtle were identified in the assemblage.

Crocodylia
Alligatoridae/Crocodylidae
One complete centrum of a crocodilian caudal vertebra was recovered in Cut 3.H Level 3. A variety of alligators and crocodiles cur-

rently inhabit lowland contexts on either side of the Ecuadorian Andes (Ross 1998). The common caiman or *cocodrilo* (*Caiman crocodilus*) is a small to medium alligator, with adult males attaining maximum lengths under 3 m. It is the most widely distributed New World crocodilian, occurring in all wet habitats of both the western and eastern lowlands. This is a highly variable animal; one of potentially five subspecies (*C. c. chiapasius,* which may be the same as *C. c. fuscus*) currently ranges from Mexico to Pacific Colombia and possibly Ecuador. The largest American alligator is the black caiman or *caimán negro* (*Melanosuchus niger*), with males reaching over 4 m in length. The archaeological specimen conforms in size to caudal vertebrae of a smaller *M. niger* reference skeleton in the AMNH collection. The black caiman currently occupies a wide variety of habitats throughout Amazonia. Two smaller alligators, the dwarf caiman or *cocodrilo* (*Paleosuchus palpebrosus*) and the smooth-fronted caiman or *cachirre* (*P. trigonatus*), are found in the extreme eastern portion of Amazonian Ecuador, where they frequent a number of aquatic habitats. Males of the former species achieve a maximum length of only 1.6 m, while males of the latter are somewhat larger, at 2.3 m.

The large common caiman or *caimán de la costa* (*Crocodylus crocodilus*) can attain a maximum adult male length of 5 to 6 m or more and is the second most widely distributed neotropical crocodilian. It inhabits fresh or brackish waters, including coastal lagoons, mangroves, and saltwater sections of rivers along the Pacific coasts of Colombia, Ecuador, and extreme northern Peru. In particular, the Ecuadorian subspecies of common caiman *C. c. fuscus* ranges as far south as Machala, where it inhabits coastal waters and extends into low-lying alluvial pans below 500 meters above sea level (masl), preferring quiet waters, mangroves, swamps, lagoons, large river meanders, and small streams. In its adult stage, the common caiman may reach a maximum length under 1.5 m. Principally nocturnal and territorial, it subsists on aquatic invertebrates and vertebrates, with terrestrial vertebrate prey assuming greater importance with age (Gorzula and Seijas 1989). Another coastal form, the American crocodile (*Crocodylus acutus*), can achieve lengths over 4 m. It is a major predator of the common caiman and controls the latter's distribution and population size in areas of sympatric distribution. Its southern Pacific distribution has been traced to the Tumbes and Chira Rivers in northern Peru. Typically found in shoreline freshwater or brackish habitats, it is known to extend inland to considerable altitudes in Mexico, preferring access to shallow and deep waters, vegetation cover, and land for basking. A principally nocturnal predator, it displays ontogenic changes in diet similar to those described above (Thorbjarnarson 1989).

Aves

Very few bird bones were identified in the assemblage (NISP = 19; 0.3%), many of which remain indeterminate or only identifiable to the ordinal level, as in the case of a small perching bird. Nonetheless, some interesting taxa are included in the small subsample.

Pelecaniformes
Phalacrocoracidae

A proximal tibiotarsus was identified as likely that of a cormorant or shag. The neotropic cormorant or *cormorán neotropical* (*Phalacrocorax brasilianus*) is found near freshwater in lowland environments on either side of the Andes. It is most numerous in marine environments along the coast, especially the lower Guayas, and estuaries where large flocks are encountered. Although recorded from environments mainly below 800 masl, they are known to wander into higher elevational settings along rivers. An irregular visitor is the guanay shag or *cormorán guanero* (*P. bougainvillii*), whose sightings on the southern Ecuadorian coast are normally associated with El Niño (Ridgely and Greenfield 2001b:115). The more common neotropic cormorant is notably gregarious, markedly nomadic, appears anywhere that fish swim, and is often seen perched on snags or trees (Ridgely and Greenfield 2001a:49).

Ciconiformes
Cathartidae

Two fragments from the same humerus are unmistakably those of the Andean condor or *cóndor andino* (*Vultur gryphus*). Presently an endangered species in Ecuador, the condor is recorded from environments between 2,000 and over 4,000 masl, particularly in open and remote highlands, and especially páramo. Primarily a carrion eater, the condor nests and roosts in inaccessible cliffs (Ridgely and Greenfield 2001a: 73, 2001b:147).

Falconiformes
Accipitridae

The most numerous bird remains that are identified lower than class are of eagles, hawks, or kites (*águilas, gavilanes, elanios*), including specimens of black-chested buzzard eagle or *águila pechinegra* (*Geranoaetus melanoleucus*), the only member of its genus in Ecuador.

This bird can be locally fairly common in relatively open terrain and favors rocky cliffs, páramo, and arid temperate areas throughout the country. It can be seen in cleared areas in the montañas but is usually found above 2,000 masl, where it feeds on small mammals and perches on rocks or the ground (Ridgely and Greenfield 2001a:92, 2001b:167).

Columbiformes

Today the numerous and widespread band-tailed pigeon or *paloma collareja* (*Columba fasciata*) is the only member of the genus normally found in the Ecuadorian highlands (2 specimens of the genus are represented in Table 11.1). It frequents canopies and borders of subtropical, especially temperate, woodland mostly between 1,500 and 3,000 masl. Flocks of these gregarious and arboreal pigeons wander seasonally in response to food availability (Ridgely and Greenfield 2001a:171, 2001b:255).

Mammalia

The overwhelming bulk of the Challuabamba assemblage is composed of mammal bones, in both number (NISP = 5,606; 92.5%) and weight (26,889.36 g; 98.5%). Fragmentation, combined with the inability to identify less diagnostic skeletal materials only to the level of class, relegates most of the subsample to an indeterminate category (NISP = 3,683; 60.8%). However, nearly 2,000 specimens were identified to various lower-level taxonomic categories.

Marsupialia
Didelphidae
A complete femur compared well with that of a water opossum or *raposa de agua* (*Chironectes minimus*), which is today found on either side of the Andes. Living in tropical and subtropical habitats throughout northwestern South America, and possibly between 1,000 to 2,000 masl in the western montañas of Ecuador, it is confined to forest streams or rivers, where it feeds nocturnally on small aquatic animals (Marshall 1978; Tirira 1999). A complete dentary with no teeth compared favorably with a larger didelphid. At present the white-eared opossum or *zarigüeya de orejas blancas* (*Didelphis albiventris*) ranges widely from subtropical to high elevation contexts in Ecuador (Albuja 1991; Tirira 1999). A habitat generalist, it is highly omnivorous and, although capable of climbing, is mainly terrestrial (Eisenberg and Redford 1999:53). *D. albiventris* is also reported from deposits at Cueva Negra de Chobshi (Lynch and Pollock 1981:98) and

Pirincay (Miller and Gill 1990). *D. marsupialis* is identified at Putush-ío (A. M. Freire, pers. comm. 1993).

Primates
Hominidae
At least 34 human bones were identified in the archaeofaunal assemblage. Excavated burial remains are the subject of a separate study by Douglas Ubelaker of the Smithsonian Institution. It is likely that human specimens listed in this report are associated with interments and are not part of the midden sample.

Lagomorpha
Leporidae
A relatively large number (NISP = 320; 5.3%) of rabbit specimens constitute the second most abundant subsample of archaeofaunal materials. The Brazilian cottontail or *conejo silvestre* (*Sylvilagus brasiliensis*) is widely distributed as a crepuscular browser from sea level to páramo in Ecuador (Albuja 1991; Tirira 1999). *S. brasiliensis* is noted in recent studies of Sangay National Park (Downer 1996:47) and is recorded in páramo and cloud forest grasslands in the Cajas plateau (Barnett 1999:204). *S. brasiliensis* is also identified in deposits at Cueva Negra de Chobshi (Lynch and Pollock 1981:98), Putushío (Freire, pers. comm. 1993), Pirincay (Miller and Gill 1990), Catamayo (Guffroy et al. 1987: 110), Loma Pucara (Arellano 1994:118), and likely Cerro Narrío (Collier and Murra 1943:68).

Rodentia
Rodent specimens, overwhelmingly represented by large hystricomorphs, are the third most abundant identified archaeofaunal category in the assemblage (NISP = 111; 1.8%). A further 10 of 12 specimens that could not be identified lower than to the ordinal level are also from a large rodent. Otherwise, only 4 specimens derive from unidentified small rodents.

Sciuridae
The complete shaft of a medium-sized squirrel humerus was identified in the assemblage. At least four species of *Sciurus* currently range into Ecuador. The red-tailed squirrel or *ardilla colorada* (*S. granatensis*) exhibits a wide altitudinal tolerance and inhabits diverse habitats from sea level to 3,000 masl. Specimens are reported from the central Andean portion of the country. Only rarely feeding on animal material, it is an important seed disperser and is considered a

serious agricultural pest throughout its range, where it is pursued by humans as food (Nitikman 1985). The Guayaquil squirrel or *ardilla sabanera de Guayaquil* (*S. stramineus*) is reported from dry borders of the southwestern montaña, ranging into the southern Pacific lowlands (Albuja 1991; Eisenberg and Redford 1999:362; Tirira 1999).

Muridae

A right maxillary fragment with complete dentition was confirmed by Rob Voss of the AMNH as a cotton rat or *ratón de cola peluda* (*Sigmodon* cf. *inopinatus*). Differences in maxillary molar occlusal morphology are subtle among most of the revised species within the genus (Voss 1992:20). Two high-elevation localities are known for this large species of *Sigmodon,* at over 3,500 masl in Chimborazo (Voss 1992:36) and in the nearby Cajas plateau (Barnett 1999). Both collection locales lie within páramo grasslands. Tropical *S. hispidus* is associated with natural or anthropogenic nonforest vegetation, usually dominated by grass (Voss 1992:37). *S. hispidus* is reported from Putushío (Freire, pers. comm. 1993).

Dasyproctidae

A significant subsample of large rodent specimens (NISP = 97; 1.6%) includes at least two genera that overlap in size. All specimens were simultaneously compared at the AMNH with various reference skeletons of four separate taxa. The majority are identified as agouti or *guatusa,* which is today represented in Ecuador by Amazonian (*Dasyprocta fuliginosa*) and western (*D. punctata*) forms in a wide variety of tropical and subtropical habitats up to 2,000 masl (Albuja 1991; Tirira 1999). Usually diurnal and solitary, the agouti can forage terrestrially for a wide range of vegetable, and occasionally small animal, foods yet is mainly frugivorous and one of the most important neotropical seed dispersers. The agouti tends to be the most conspicuous cursorial forest animal during daylight hours. Heavily persecuted by humans, it is also prey for larger felids and raptors (Smythe 1978).

Agoutidae

Two species are currently found in Ecuador, a widely distributed lowland paca or *guanta* (*Agouti paca*), found up to 2,000 masl on either side of the Andes, and the mountain paca or *sacha cuy* (*A. taczanowskii*), found in temperate habitats above 1,800 masl (Albuja 1991). Lowland pacas feed opportunistically in a wide variety of forest habitats, preferably close to water. Mainly frugivorous, they are solitary nocturnal counterparts to the agouti and important in forests for seed dispersal. Pacas are heavily persecuted by humans and are also the prey of felids, dogs, crocodiles, and boas (Pérez 1992). Less is known of the somewhat smaller yet trophically similar mountain paca. Currently described from the páramo, it is endangered by heavy human persecution and habitat alteration (Patzelt 1989:60; Tirira 1999:78). Based upon a comparison of lower molar morphology, it is possible that at least one specimen of each species is represented in the assemblage. *A. taczanowskii* is also reported in deposits at Cueva Negra de Chobshi (Lynch and Pollock 1981:98) and Pirincay (Miller and Gill 1990).

Carnivora

A small sample of 15 carnivore specimens was identified, 2 of which are indeterminate, with the remainder identified to 3 separate families.

Canidae

Although 4 specimens are identified as, or compared well with, reference specimens from a domestic dog (*Canis familiaris*), a relatively large native canid is also recorded from the high Andes. The South American fox or *lobo de páramo* (*Pseudalopex [Dusicyon] culpaeus*) frequents a variety of habitats up to 4,500 masl and more. It prefers arid or semiarid conditions, where it nocturnally pursues rodents as well as lagomorphs, livestock, and carrion (Eisenberg and Redford 1999:282). Long-term residents in the Cajas plateau report that it was formerly plentiful but is now absent due to increased hunting pressure (Barnett 1999:204). *P. culpaeus* has been identified at Catamayo (Guffroy et al. 1987: 110). *Canis familiaris* is reported in deposits at Cueva Negra de Chobshi (Lynch and Pollock 1981:98) and Putushío (Freire, pers. comm. 1993). Desert fox (*Pseudalopex sechurae*) and *Canis familiaris* are reported from Cerro Ñañañique (Guffroy 1994:167).

Ursidae

Five specimens compare well with a medium-sized bear. The spectacled bear or *oso de anteojos* (*Tremarctos ornatus*) currently frequents a wide variety of habitats in either montaña, but generally in humid forests between 1,900 and 2,700 masl. A generalized omnivore, it feeds heavily on bromeliads, with additional inputs from cacti, fruits, palm leaf petioles, bark, and animals, and includes crop fields in its foraging range (Peyton 1980). The spectacled bear has been reported recently from the Cajas plateau (Barnett 1999:204) and is noted in all areas inhabited by tapirs in Sangay National Park (Downer 1996:52). *T. ornatus* is also identified in deposits at Cueva Negra de Chobshi (Lynch and Pollock 1981:98) and Pirincay (Miller and Gill 1990).

Felidae

Four appendicular specimens are identified as a large felid, likely a puma (*Felis concolor*), a cosmopolitan taxon found throughout the Ecuadorian mainland. Numerous subspecies of puma, a highly opportunistic carnivore, range throughout a marked variety of habitats from sea level to over 4,000 masl. Solitary pumas inhabit an extensive home range where various mammalian prey items, including domestic animals, are stalked. Diet can also include reptiles, birds, fish, insects, and berries (Currier 1983). Puma have been recorded recently in páramo and cloud forest of the Caja plateau (Barnett 1999:204) and are reported as common in Sangay National Park, particularly as a response to cattle invasion (Downer 1996:47). Puma specimens have been identified at Pirincay (Miller and Gill 1990).

Perissodactyla

Tapiridae

The upper right crown of a first molar is identified as tapir. The mountain tapir or *danta* (*Tapirus pinchaque*) is currently recorded from the Ecuadorian Andes between 1,400 and 4,700 masl, where it tends to frequent land between 2,000 and 4,300 masl. Solitary and crepuscular, it is an herbivorous browser that prefers moist habitats and requires forest cover. It has been recorded in the Cajas plateau and currently resides at higher elevations of Sangay National Park. Here it acts as an obligate symbiont in the germination of certain high Andean plants and is preyed upon by pumas and spectacled bears (Downer 1996:45). Mountain tapir is also identified in deposits at Cueva Negra de Chobshi (Lynch and Pollock 1981:98) and Pirincay (Miller and Gill 1990), and *T. terrestris* is identified at Catamayo (Guffroy et al. 1987: 110).

Artiodactyla

A considerable number of specimens (NISP = 291; 4.8%) were identified as indeterminate artiodactyl. The majority are vertebral fragments of large and medium-sized animals.

Tayassuidae

A small yet significant number (NISP = 10; 0.2%) of bones are identified as peccary. Two species currently range into Ecuador, the larger white-lipped peccary or *pecarí de labio blanco* (*Tayassu pecari*) and the smaller collared peccary or *pecarí de collar* (*T. tajacu*). These two peccaries are found in a variety of principally lowland habitats on both sides of the Andes from sea level to 1,900 masl (Bodmer and Sowls 1993; Mayer and Wetzel 1987), although collared peccaries have been reported from over 2,500 masl in lower Central America (Donkin 1985:19). A restricted subspecific population of white-lipped peccary (*T. p. aequatoris*) is confined to northwestern Ecuador near Gualeá in the western montañas of Pichincha Province (Mayer and Wetzel 1987:1); otherwise, collared peccary is the most cosmopolitan species within the country. A number of archaeological specimens compared favorably with larger *T. pecari;* however, one almost complete right dentary bearing intact postcanine dentition and associated with postcranial material fits well within the range of *T. tajacu*. Both taxa show essentially similar cranial proportions; however, measurements of the specimen's cheek tooth crown and condylar areas conform well to the smaller, nonoverlapping ranges of *T. tajacu* (Herring 1985:607). Highly adaptable collared peccaries are omnivorous and active by day or night in a wide variety of habitats from xeric savanna to moist tropical forest. Where food is particularly abundant, small bands occasionally aggregate into groups of as many as fifty individuals, but home ranges tend to be relatively small (Eisenberg and Redford 1999:335).

Cervidae

Much of the identified collection (NISP = 976; 16.1%) includes bones attributed to white-tailed deer (*Odocoileus virginianus*), which inhabits the southwestern lowlands below 1,000 m and the high Andes above 3,000 m (Albuja 1991). Misael Molina and Jesús Molinari (1999) have argued for taxonomic revision of South and Central American white-tailed deer. Ecuadorian forms have been considered to be conspecifics of *Odocoileus virginianus: O. v. tropicalis* in the Pacific regions of Colombia and Ecuador and *O. v. ustus* throughout the Andean region. They reinsert the oldest name available for South and Central American white-tailed deer: *O. cariacou*. As generalized diurnal browsers and grazers, white-tailed deer prefer edges, which can facilitate both feeding options, but graze in large groups where habitats are favorable. It is the only Ecuadorian cervid whose males possess highly developed, annually shed antlers (Eisenberg and Redford 1999:342; Patzelt 1989:323; Tirira 1999:22).

The rest of the unidentified cervid specimens consist of bones that were assigned arbitrary size categories: large (NISP = 9), medium (NISP = 147), and small (NISP = 7). Medium-sized deer may include the red brocket or *soche colorado* (*Mazama americana*). A widely distributed species of slightly smaller dimensions than its larger white-tailed counterpart, it is presently found up to 2,000 masl on either side of the Andes. The genus also includes the tiny dwarf red brocket (*M. rufina*), known locally as *yamala*, which frequents high-elevation forests from 1,500 to 3,500 masl and higher into the páramo. Dwarf red brocket and the even smaller pudu or *ciervo enano* (*Pudu mephistophiles*) could account for the few small cervid remains identified in the assemblage. The pudu is a high-elevation species that frequents the páramo (Albuja 1991; Eisenberg and Redford 1999; Tirira 1999). Recent studies have recorded *Odocoileus*, *Mazama rufina*, and *Pudu mephistophiles* in the Cajas plateau (Barnett 1999:204) and Sangay National Park (Downer 1996:47). Archaeologically, *Odocoileus* and *Pudu mephistophiles* are reported from Cueva Negra de Chobshi (Lynch and Pollock 1981:98). *Odocoileus* and *Mazama* specimens are mentioned for Cerro Narrío (Collier and Murra 1943:68) and at Catamayo (Guffroy et al. 1987: 110). *Odocoileus* is identified at Cerro Ñañañique (Guffroy 1994:167). All three genera are identified in deposits at Pirincay (Miller and Gill 1990) and Loma Pucara (Arellano 1994:118).

Zooarchaeological Analyses of the Challuabamba Archaeofaunas

Over 85% of the identified specimens (NISP = 5,190) in the Challuabamba collection were recovered in Cut 3, with the majority of specimens retrieved in Levels 1, 2, and 4, particularly from Sectors G and H.[1] These two units alone account for under one-half of the entire collection (43.7%; NISP = 2,647). Most of the remaining specimens (13.8%; NISP = 837) were recovered in Cut 4. In both areas, most of the identified specimens include artiodactyl bones, whereas virtually the entire sample of catfish, rabbit, and agouti bones was recovered in Cut 3. Most of the remaining taxa are relatively rare in the collection and are preserved as isolated specimens dispersed throughout the archaeological deposits. Table 11.2 includes data for each identified genus: NISP (number of identified specimens); total number of separate archaeological contexts (differentiated by unit and level) in which specimens were recovered; minimum MNI (mini-

Table 11.2. Numerical Representation of Identified Genera (Minimum MNI derived by site, Maximum MNI derived by archaeological context)

Genus	NISP	# of Contexts	Minimum MNI	Maximum MNI
Megalobulimus	1	1	1	1
Conus	1	1	1	1
Pecten	1	1	1	1
Spondylus	1	1	1	1
Phalacrocorax	1	1	1	1
Vultur gryphus	2	1	1	1
Geranoaetus	3	2	1	2
Columba	2	2	1	2
Chironectes	1	1	1	1
Didelphis	1	1	1	1
Homo	34	12	1	12
Sylvilagus	320	24	16	32
Sciurus	1	1	1	1
Sigmodon	1	1	1	1
Dasyprocta	92	18	6	16
Agouti	4	3	1	3
Agouti taczanowskii	1	1	1	1
Canis	4	4	1	4
Tremarctos	5	3	1	3
Felis	4	4	1	4
Tapirus	1	1	1	1
Tayassus	10	6	2	6
Odocoileus	976	45	47	105

mum number of individuals) on a sitewide basis; and maximum MNI differentiated by archaeological context. I next examine accumulation, preburial deposition, and postburial preservation by focusing on specimen representation of the two most abundant identified taxa.

Assemblage Preservation

Excavation in only a small area of the Challuabamba site recovered a large volume of bone specimens weighing over 27 kg. At first sight, the assemblage appears to be rather well preserved; nonetheless, indeterminate mammal fragments, many consisting of long bone shaft splinters, constitute over one-half of the assemblage. While washing specimens, it was immediately obvious that larger mammal long bone shafts were easily collapsed when rehydrated and freed of the compacted soil that filled their medullary cavities. These and other postrecovery fresh breaks were refitted with water-soluble glue wherever possible. Nevertheless, characteristic longitudinal and transverse fractures were regularly observed on limb bone shaft specimens, and I suspect that many of the small, longitudinally splintered diaphyseal fragments in the assemblage were originally fractured through postburial *in situ* collapse of limb shafts (Shipman et al. 1981; Villa and Mahieu 1991).

The excavation areas from which the assemblage was recovered are situated on the south bank of the Tomebamba River, within a few meters of its currently active channel. The deposits lie on the first terrace of an active alluvial floodplain, which is prone to periodic and catastrophic inundation (see Bruhns 2003:128). The river plain, at an elevation of approximately 2,300 m, is characterized by a temperate semihumid climate that supports a low montane dry forest. The area receives around 800 mm of annual precipitation, especially from March through May. Stable year-round temperatures vary slightly between highs of 18 to 21 degrees and lows of 7 to 10 degrees C, with a constant annual humidity between 73% and 76% (Blandín Landívar 1977; Cañadas Cruz 1983). Relatively high daily temperatures and constant humidity, along with a fluctuating water table, likely contribute to postburial *in situ* bone destruction.

Density-Mediated Preservation

As a first-order assessment of assemblage preservation, I examine the importance of relative bone mineral density for specimen survivorship. I begin by comparing bone mineral density values (g/cm^3) for *Odocoileus* (Lyman 1984) to the %survivorship of individual bone mineral density scan sites.

This assessment of specimen preservation yields a higher-resolution appraisal of assemblage survivorship by focusing on more specific anatomical portions rather than standard minimum number of elements (MNE) counts and avoids the need to average values between different scan sites. I combined metacarpal and metatarsal scan sites into a single metapodial category, because it is difficult to separate distal portions into fore and aft elements. The relationship, graphed as a scatterplot in Figure 11.1, is statistically insignificant (r_s = .18, p = .09, n = 89). The lack of a relationship could be due to the inherent difficulty of securely identifying rib and vertebral fragments as little more than "possible large mammal." However, adding all "large mammal" rib and vertebral specimens that were not identified to any lower zoological category does little to change the relationship. A closer look at Figure 11.1, however, suggests two relatively distinct subsamples: (1) scan sites correlated with bone mineral density; and (2) higher-density (> .30 g/cm³) scan sites with low survivorship (< 15%).

Removing the poorly represented scan sites with higher bone mineral density values (Figure 11.2) clearly results in a highly significant correlation (r_s = .77, p ≤ .001, n = 60). I suspect that this correlation represents a more accurate depiction of survivorship at Challuabamba: namely, that higher-density portions of cervid bone elements are being preserved in statistically greater proportions.

The 29 underrepresented higher-density scan sites are presented

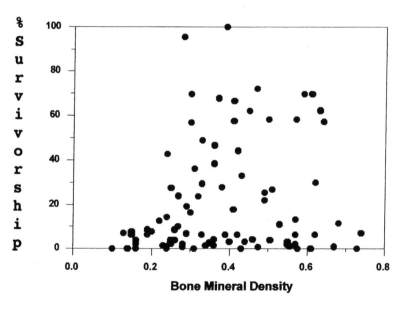

Figure 11.1. Scatterplot of %survivorship of deer skeletal scan sites against bone mineral density values for deer.

Art and Archaeology of Challuabamba, Ecuador

CHB Large Cervids

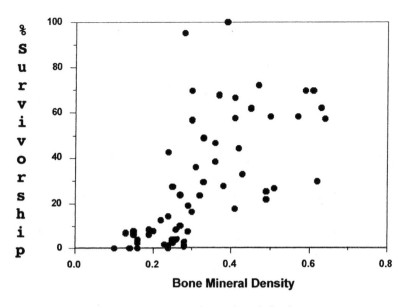

Figure 11.2. Scatterplot of %survivorship of deer skeletal scan sites against bone mineral density values for deer, with underrepresented high-density specimens removed.

as a scatterplot in Figure 11.3. These scan sites can be grouped into three major anatomical units: (1) 44.8% (13/29 scan sites in the sample) are from the lower leg, including complete naviculo-cuboid (NC1-3), metapodia (MET1-6) and proximal phalanges (P11-3), and the distal second phalanx (P23); (2) 27.6% (8/29) represent the complete dentary (DN1-8); and (3) 13.8% (4/29) are limb bone mid-shaft scan sites of the humerus (HU3), radius (RA3), tibia (TI3), and femur (FE4). These anatomical units include over 86% of the scan sites graphed in Figure 11.3; the remaining 13.8% (4/29) consists of scan sites that are difficult to identify, particularly when preserved as fragments (scapular blade, rib shaft, distal ulna, pubis).

An almost identical pattern of survivorship can be demonstrated for smaller cervid specimens, which could include the red brocket or *soche colorado* (*Mazama americana*). Figure 11.4 plots the relationship between %survivorship of medium-sized deer against bone mineral density values for white-tailed deer. It is also statistically insignificant (r_s = .11, p = .31, n = 89). The relationship is statistically significant (r_s = .59, p ≤ .001, n = 54) when 35 scan sites of over 30 gm/cm³ with less than 15% survivorship are removed (Figure 11.5).

CHB Large Cervids

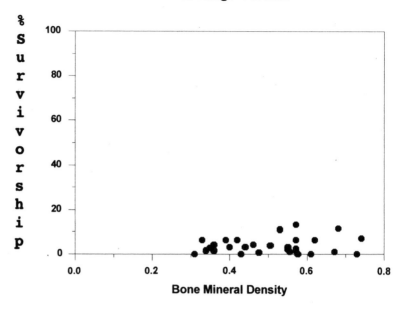

Figure 11.3. Scatterplot of %survivorship of deer skeletal scan sites against bone mineral density values for deer, illustrating underrepresented high-density specimens.

CHB Small Cervids

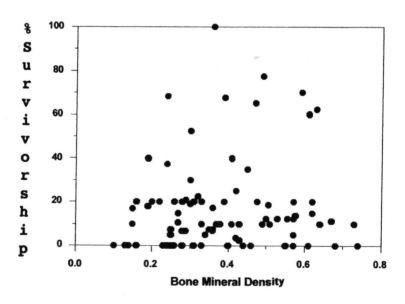

Figure 11.4. Scatterplot of %survivorship of smaller deer skeletal scan sites against bone mineral density values for deer.

CHB Small Cervids

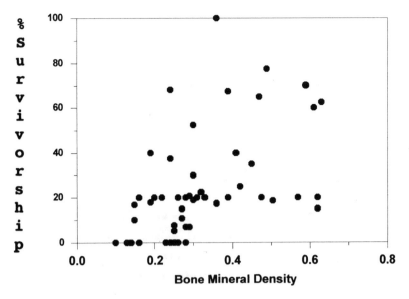

Figure 11.5. Scatterplot of %survivorship of smaller deer skeletal scan sites against bone mineral density values for deer, with underrepresented high-density specimens removed.

The underrepresented higher-density specimens (Figure 11.6) are not identical to, yet highly similar to, the same sets of scan sites identified for specimens of larger cervids. These include (1) 20% (7/35 of the sample) from the lower leg, comprising metapodia (MET1-2, 4), complete proximal phalanges (P11-3), and the distal second phalanx (P23); (2) 22.9% (8/35) consisting of the entire dentary (DN1-8); and (3) 8.6% (3/35) from limb bone mid-shaft scan sites of the humerus (HU3), radius (RA3), and femur (FE4). The remaining specimens in this groups include similarly hard-to-identify fragments, with the addition of scan sites representing the distal radius (RA 4-5), distal femur (FE4-5), distal tibia (TI 4-5), and calcaneum (CA1-2,4). Moreover, this pattern of density-mediated survivorship for all large and medium-sized cervid skeletons, when lower limbs, dentary, and limb bone mid-shafts are excluded, is vertically consistent throughout the depositional strata at Challuabamba. This pattern is important for understanding postburial preservation and possibly assemblage deposition of cervid skeletons, particularly in Levels 1, 2, and 4 at the site.

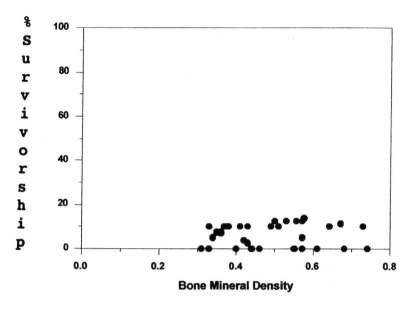

CHB Small Cervids

%Survivorship

Bone Mineral Density

Figure 11.6. Scatterplot of %survivorship of smaller deer skeletal scan sites against bone mineral density values for deer, illustrating underrepresented high-density specimens.

Figure 11.7 is a scatterplot graph of the relationship between %survivorship of lagomorph (likely *Sylvilagus brasiliensis*) bone scan sites and bone mineral density figures for *S. floridanus* (Pavao and Stahl 1999). The South American cottontails are relatively small rabbits that usually do not exceed 1 kg in live weight and 400 mm in total length (Eisenberg and Redford 1999:519), so humans likely brought entire carcasses to the site. Density mediation of rabbit skeletons at Challuabamba is suggested by a statistically significant correlation ($r_s = .69, p \leq .001, n = 58$) between %survivorship and bone structural density. Rabbit specimens were primarily preserved in two levels, Level 2 and a major concentration in Level 4. The statistically significant correlation is consistent in each of the major bone-bearing strata. If four higher-density (> .30 gm/cm³) underrepresented (< 15% survivorship) bone scan sites are removed from consideration, the relationship is strengthened ($r_s = .83, p \leq .001, n = 54$).

The four sites (AT1, AX1, LU1, SC1) are all vertebral, representing the most craniad region of the neck and caudad region of the lower back. Although this may be of significance for behavioral inferences, I suspect that it is more likely due to fragmentation and the subsequently poor preservation of individual scan sites. For example,

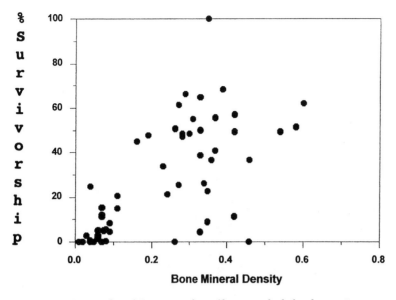

Figure 11.7. Scatterplot of %survivorship of lagomorph skeletal scan sites against bone mineral density values for *Sylvilagus floridanus*.

although vertebral elements are uniformly underrepresented, there are relatively numerous lumbar fragments that do not pertain to the specific scan site area. Nonetheless, the survivorship of lagomorph elements at Challuabamba clearly implicates density-mediated preservation of skeletons which were most likely accumulated at the site as relatively complete carcasses. Coupled with the cervid data, density-mediated preservation of the entire assemblage is likely. Very little carnivore-related damage was observed in the assemblage. Significant numbers of specimens (*n* = 220) are visibly weathered. The majority are from superficial contexts (surface and Level 1, *n* = 105, 47.7%; Level 2, *n* = 112, 50.9%) and implicate a degree of possible preburial exposure and/or postburial erosion and subsequent reexposure. However, I suspect that postburial *in situ* destruction largely resulted from a combination of high annual temperature and humidity and a fluctuating water table within the context of riverine alluvium.

The patterning of cervid skeletal preservation requires explanation. The underrepresented higher-density skeletal elements illustrated in Figures 11.3 and 11.6 should be relatively abundant in density-mediated contexts. They are precisely the most underrepresented, and there is a shared anatomical specificity among these sites, which leads me to question whether they were (1) originally deposited and buried but subsequently not identified; (2) originally introduced but never buried; or (3) never originally introduced into site contexts.

Underrepresented Higher-Density Cervid Specimens

Underrepresented cervid specimens that would otherwise be expected to survive density-mediated preservation because of their high bone mineral density fall into three distinct anatomical groups: (1) limb bone mid-shafts; (2) heads, especially the dentary and possibly the cranium; and (3) lower legs. This underrepresentation is illustrated in bar charts for scan sites of larger cervids, likely *Odocoileus* and possibly the smaller *Mazama*. Figure 11.8 illustrates hypothetical density-mediated survivorship of individual scan sites on a site-wide basis.

The scan site density value (g/cm^3) is multiplied by its frequency in the skeleton and is then multiplied by the minimum number of individual large cervid skeletons (MNI = 47) and normed as a percentage. Figure 11.9 illustrates the observed survivorship of individual

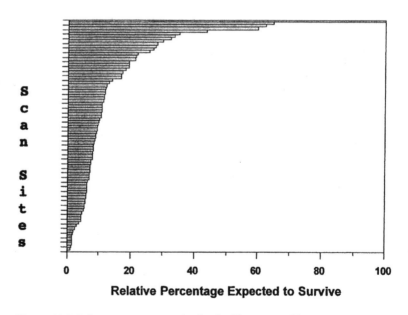

Expected Large Cervid Survivorship (MNI=47)

Relative Percentage Expected to Survive

Figure 11.8. Relative percentage of individual large cervid bone scan sites expected to survive density-mediated preservation.

Art and Archaeology of Challuabamba, Ecuador

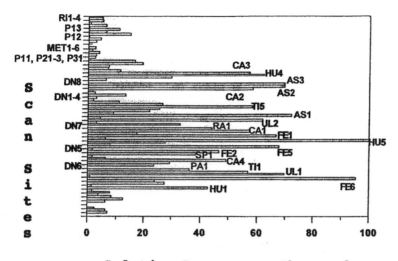

Figure 11.9. Relative percentage of individual large cervid bone scan sites observed in the Challuabamba assemblage.

scan sites (also normed as a percentage) and highlights some of the major disparities between expected and observed samples.

It is apparent that the larger cervids at Challuabamba are dominated by upper limb elements. Nonetheless, limb bone mid-shaft scan sites of the humerus (HU3), radius (RA3), tibia (TI3), and femur (FE4) are underrepresented, despite their high mineral density. Clearly, as both proximal and distal long-bone portions are preserved in the assemblage in a greater than expected frequency, there is no compelling reason to believe that mid-shafts were originally absent. Considering the context of preservation, the prevalence of longitudinal and transverse fracturing along the diaphysis, and the observed collapse of rehydrated limb cylinders, I strongly suspect that long bone mid-shafts were preserved as fragments that were not identified. The relative absence of these mid-shaft portions is most likely a methodological artifact, which if corrected would simultaneously augment evidence of density-mediated preservation and increase the predominance of limb bone specimens (e.g., Bartram and Marean 1999; Marean 1998; Marean and Frey 1997; Marean and Kim 1998). I return to the dominance of upper limb portions below.

Very few dentary and cranial specimens or teeth were identified in the Challuabamba assemblage. Cervid dentary scan sites are characterized by relatively high bone mineral density (Lyman 1984) that is certainly high enough to expect their increased visibility in density-mediated contexts. Unfortunately, we have no comparable bone mineral density values for cranial elements. Were cranial and dental elements originally deposited and subsequently buried at the site, only to be preserved in a highly fragmented and subsequently unidentifiable state? Taking into account all identified artiodactyl bones (excluding identified peccary), antler (NISP = 6), cranial (NISP = 18), dentary (NISP = 13), and tooth (NISP = 29) specimens amount to a little over 4.6% of the 1,430 specimens. Particularly durable teeth are relatively rare at Challuabamba. Each adult cervid has 30 to 32 teeth; thus as many as 1,590 to 1,696 complete teeth are potentially deposited by a minimum of 53 deer heads (MNI value for all cervids, both large and small). The mastoideus, a durable element of the cranium that survives heavy fragmentation, is represented by only one specimen. Dense antler fragments, often used in tool production, are very rare. There is no compelling evidence to suggest that deer heads were deposited, subsequently buried, and destroyed *in situ*. However, it is possible that heads were either originally introduced to the site but deposited and subsequently buried elsewhere or never introduced at all.

A third, and very noticeable, pattern involves a marked underrepresentation of lower limb elements. Table 11.3 summarizes the following points for large cervids considered separately and for all cervids combined. Figure 11.10 illustrates lower limb representation at Challuabamba for the combined sample of larger and smaller cervids. In the hind limb, the astragalus and calcaneum articulate tightly with the distal tibia; all are comparably well preserved in the Challuabamba assemblage (around 50% survivorship). However, elements immediately distal to the kinetic articulation are rare, beginning proximally with the large and dense naviculo-cuboid and proceeding distally along the leg. For purposes of identification, lower hind limb and fore limb elements were not considered separately, yet specimens of these durable and abundant elements are consistently underrepresented: metapodia, first phalanges, second phalanges, and third phalanges. A similar pattern is apparent in the distal fore limb. The durable distal articular surface of the radius is relatively abundant, whereas the smaller elements of the front ankle joint (cuneiform, lunate, scaphoid, pisiform, unciform, magnum) are less so. This patterning suggests possible detachment of lower fore and hind limbs through the kinetic portion of the joint. I doubt that durable elements of the lower leg were abundant yet became difficult to iden-

Table 11.3. Cervid Lower Limb Representation

Element	Large Cervids (MNI = 47)			All Cervids (MNI = 53)		
	NISP	# Expected	%	NISP	# Expected	%
Fore Limb						
Distal Radius	23	94	24.5	23	106	21.7
Lunate	10	94	10.6	10	106	9.4
Magnum	2	94	2.1	2	106	1.9
Unciform	8	94	8.5	9	106	8.5
Pisiform	3	94	3.2	3	106	2.8
Scaphoid	12	94	12.8	14	106	13.2
Cuneiform	8	94	8.5	8	106	7.5
Total Carpal	43	564	7.6	46	636	7.2
Hind Limb						
Distal Tibia	47	94	50.0	49	106	46.2
Astragalus	46	94	48.9	54	106	50.9
Calcaneum	48	94	51.1	52	106	49.1
Lateral Malleolus	9	94	9.6	9	106	8.5
Naviculo-Cuboid	4	94	4.3	6	106	5.7
Internal Cuneiform	0	94	0	0	106	0
External & Middle	0	94	0	0	106	0
Fore Limb & Hind Limb						
Metapodium	9	108	8.3	18	212	8.5
First Phalanx	18	376	4.8	22	424	5.2
Second Phalanx	7	376	1.9	10	424	2.4
Third Phalanx	7	376	1.9	7	424	1.7

Note: MNI values are based on the right distal femur for large cervids (likely *Odocoileus*) and all cervids (large and small forms combined) for the entire site. NISP values are observed frequencies. Expected values are computed by multiplying MNI by the number of times each element is found in the skeleton. Percentage values calculate the percentage of observed specimens (NISP) compared to the number expected (# Expected). Note that metapodia and phalanges are not separated into hind limbs and fore limbs.

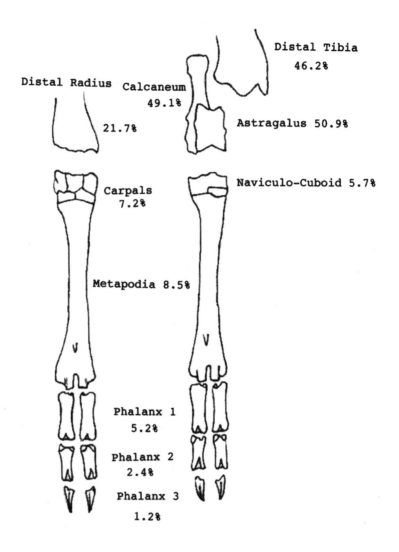

Figure 11.10. Cervid lower limb representation at Challuabamba.

Distal Radius

Calcaneum 49.1%

Distal Tibia 46.2%

21.7%

Astragalus 50.9%

Carpals 7.2%

Naviculo-Cuboid 5.7%

Metapodia 8.5%

Phalanx 1 5.2%

Phalanx 2 2.4%

Phalanx 3 1.2%

tify because of heavy fragmentation. I suspect that they were never originally buried in the excavated portions of Challuabamba.

Following Curtis Marean (1991), I consider fragmentation of durable carpal and tarsal bones that are rarely broken by humans or carnivores for nutritional reasons. At Challuabamba, high proportions of these elements are preserved as relatively complete specimens: astragalus (96%); calcaneum (58%); lateral malleolus (100%); naviculo-cuboid (100%); cuneiform (100%); lunate (90%); scaphoid (100%); pisiform (100%); unciform (100%); and magnum (100%). Some obvious cases of postburial breakage involving the astragalus and calcaneum were refitted. Most of these elements are roughly spherical in shape, which mitigates the extent of postburial fragmentation; however, phalanges are rodlike in shape, with a higher, albeit slim, nutritional value for humans and carnivores (Darwent and Lyman 2002). Nevertheless, considering their relatively high bone mineral density, overall marginal nutritional value, high frequency in the artiodactyl skeleton, and easy identification even when heavily fragmented, postburial attrition cannot explain their obvious absence in the assemblage. There remains the possibility that lower limbs were originally introduced to the site but deposited and subsequently buried elsewhere. Carnivores may have completely removed smaller compact bones that can be swallowed whole (Marean et al. 1992); however, evidence of carnivore attrition is rare in the assemblage and would not account for the near absence of dense and highly identifiable metapodial articulations and shafts. I suspect that limb bones were not originally introduced to Challuabamba. In the following discussion I consider some possible reasons for the higher representation of some cervid body portions and the potential absence of others.

Selective Provisioning at Challuabamba

Upper limb portions dominate large cervid skeletal representation in the Challuabamba assemblage. Figure 11.11 plots the relative distribution of selected large cervid body portions by the percentage of their MAU (minimum animal units) preserved in the assemblage. %MAU is based upon the highest minimum number of elements (MNE) for each element, divided by the number of times that element appears in the cervid skeleton, and normed to a scale of 100. Large cervid skeletons are dominated by the upper fore (scapula, humerus, radius, and ulna) and upper hind (hip, femur, tibia) limbs. In contrast, vertebrae and ribs are poorly represented. Ribs, in particular, are dramatically underrepresented when their relative bone mineral density values and frequency in the skeleton are considered (Figure 11.9). It is possible that vertebral, and especially rib, fragments were deposited and subsequently buried at the site, only to preserve in a fragmented and poorly identifiable state. Mammalian rib fragments (n = 253) are preserved as shaft splinters (33.6%) or unspecified fragments (43%) in the assemblage. Similarly, a considerable portion of the overall mammalian specimens includes vertebral fragments (n = 691), many of which survive as unspecified fragments (15%).

Nonetheless, cervid head and distal limb representation is very low and cannot be attributed to density-mediated survivorship. Figure 11.12 illustrates average meat yield according to body parts in Figure 11.11. Heads and lower limbs contribute insignificant amounts

Representation of Large Cervid Body Portions

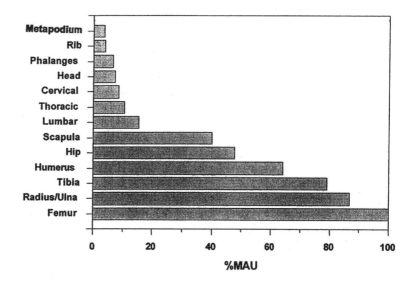

Figure 11.11. Large cervid body parts at Challuabamba.

Large Cervid Meat Weight Yields

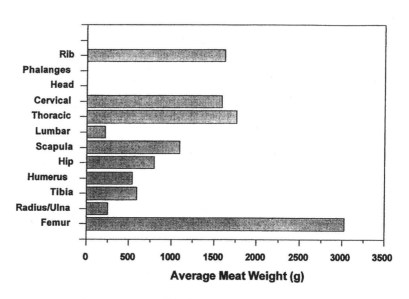

Figure 11.12. Average meat yield by large cervid body part.

of meat (Madrigal and Holt 2002:748), although brains or tongues were not taken into consideration. It is probably significant that all helical and V-shaped fractures, associated with relatively fresh bone breakage, are restricted to the four limb bones (tibia, femur, humerus, radius) that provide the greatest amount of usable marrow in the cervid body (Madrigal and Holt 2002:751).

High-yield items dominate the assemblage. Low-yield body portions were probably not buried at Challuabamba, yet it remains open to question whether or not low-yield items were originally introduced into the site. It is possible that only select, easily transportable, cervid skeletal portions bearing larger quantities of meat were brought to the site. These may have been provisioned fresh or preserved. In the latter case, the pattern of preserved cervid body portions at Challuabamba conforms well to expectations for discard contexts of Andean *chalona* consumption, in which the preserved meat product is desiccated by splitting and flattening the body with bones left in, after the head and feet are removed (Stahl 1999). It is still possible that entire carcasses were introduced to Challuabamba, with heads and lower limbs removed and subsequently discarded elsewhere. It is also possible that selected elements were removed either before or after their introduction to the site for subsequent modification.

Bone Modification

Examples of modified bone are quite rare in the Challuabamba assemblage; however, the few preserved specimens illustrate how osseous material, particularly from underrepresented mammalian elements, was manipulated for tool use. Figure 11.13a shows a rare, complete cervid first phalanx that is circumferentially scored toward its distal end. Figure 11.13b illustrates a cervid distal tibia that was similarly scored and apparently snapped. Elsewhere in the Ecuadorian Andes, the same kind of bone modification has been recorded for the removal of shafts (Stahl and Athens 2001). Other examples of worked long bone shafts are preserved at Challuabamba. These include an apparently drilled tubular shaft (Figure 11.13d); similar examples from the northern Ecuadorian Andes are described as flutes (Villalba 1988: Plate 55a; see also Stahl and Athens 2001: Figure 14). Figure 11.13e illustrates a cut and ground bone ring, fashioned from a mammalian long bone shaft. Figure 11.13f is a possibly heat-treated tibial shaft fragment of a large mammal, probably a cervid, which has been polished and modified to a point. Figures 11.13g and 11.13h illustrate worked mammalian long bone shafts with blunted and pointed ends.

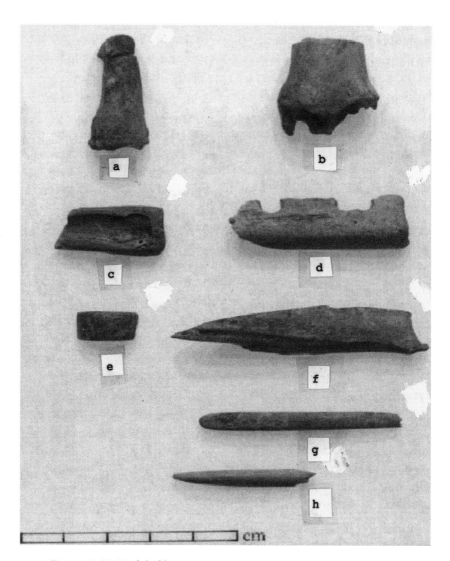

Figure 11.13. Modified bone specimens: *a*, cervid 1 phalanx (3.H Level 4b); *b*, cervid distal tibia (3.D–F Level 2); *c*, cervid proximal metatarsus (3.F Level 1); *d*, mammal long bone (4.A, 30–40 cm); *e*, mammal long bone (3.G Level 2); *f*, possible cervid tibia shaft (4.A, 30–40 cm); *g*, mammal long bone (3.C Level 1); *h*, mammal long bone (3.G Level 3).

Figure 11.13c is the proximal articulation and shaft of a cervid metatarsus. The modified specimen is split longitudinally, ground, and smoothed. Elsewhere in the Andes of Ecuador (Villalba 1988: Plate 54) and Peru (Izumi and Terada 1972:261), similar artifacts have been referred to as spatulas. Many examples of comparable metapodial tools have holes opposite a blunted shaft (MacNeish and Nelken-Turner 1980:318), especially in the northern and southern highlands of Formative Ecuador (Collier and Murra 1943: Plate 48; Stahl and Athens 2001: Figure 13). These may be analogous to the archaeological *wichuñas* (*huichuñas*) of the Bolivian highlands (Bermann 1994:22) that are used by contemporary Andean weavers to separate warp yarns (Ravines 1978:260). Items such as these and the modified deer phalanx (Figure 11.13a) suggest the utilization of lower leg elements in bone tool manufacture at this time and place, a point corroborated by Formative assemblages in the northern Andes of Ecuador (Stahl and Athens 2001; Villalba 1988). However, evidence for intensive utilization of cervid (mainly *Odocoileus*) antlers in tool production, which is so prevalent at high elevations to the north (Stahl and Athens 2001), is not apparent at the lower-elevation context of Challuabamba in the southern highlands.

Extralocal Animals at Challuabamba

In addition to a suite of animals that is fairly typical of the southern Andean highlands, the Challuabamba assemblage also includes a number of exotic taxa that were introduced from lowland contexts, likely to the west. Principal among these are ocean catfish (Ariidae), which frequent coastal waters and are known to ascend larger rivers of the western lowlands. These medium-to-large fish are represented in an archaeological context by cranial and vertebral elements in all depositional contexts at the site. Their presence at Challuabamba is supported by the identification of marine shells, especially *Spondylus,* in the form of a worked bead and a possible shell rim. Although it is difficult to provide more detailed identification, a caudal vertebral centrum of a large crocodilian clearly indicates prehistoric connections with lowlands either directly to the west or eastward into the Amazon basin. In the case of a patterned movement of animals or animal parts from the western lowlands, the specimen could be of a larger reptile like the common caiman (*Crocodylus crocodilus*) or American crocodile (*C. acutus*), whose southern ranges extend to coastal Machala and extreme northern Peru. Three lowland mammals might be added to this list, as they appear today in contexts below 2,000 masl. Agouti (*Dasyprocta* sp.), paca (*Agouti paca*), and some form of peccary (*Tayassu* sp.) are all found in primarily lowland contexts on either side of the Andes. Their presence in an archaeological context at Challuabamba may suggest the introduction of exotic specimens from lowland contexts, perhaps in the west, or even a potentially expanded altitudinal range in prehispanic times.

Extralocal trade connections are a hallmark of the Late Formative occupations in the southern highlands. Including durable items of pottery, shells, metals, and lithics, we might add the exchange of animal products. Elsewhere I have traced the association of *Spondylus* with animal domesticates introduced from the south (Stahl 2003). Although the Challuabamba deposits appear to contain no trace of foreign animal domesticates, we can certainly add trade in exotic wild animals or animal products as a compelling corroboration of the selective provisioning in cervid body portions outlined above.

Summary

Analyses of 6,060 bone specimens recovered from the 1995 to 2000 excavations at Challuabamba provide data for one of the largest Formative zooarchaeological collections yet recorded in the southern highlands of Ecuador. Most of the specimens were recovered from two excavation units (3.G and 3.H), with five depositional layers in stratigraphic sequence beginning approximately 2.5 m below the present ground surface. Sample radiocarbon determinations from analyzed bone material suggest initial calibrated dates no earlier than 1400 BC, with subsequent deposition clustering around 900 BC (cf. Table 1.1).

The assemblage is composed of many taxa currently typical of the southern highlands, including animals often associated with anthropogenic settings. A significant component of the collection includes extralocal animals, some of which were introduced from distant areas. Notable examples include marine gastropods and bivalves, particularly *Spondylus,* which is preserved in both worked and unworked forms. Ocean catfish is relatively abundant within the excavated contexts at the site and was undoubtedly introduced from coastal lowlands to the west. A crocodylid vertebral centrum also originates from a lowland context and, if part of a western exchange focus, could be similar to contemporary species of caiman or crocodile with southward ranges into El Oro province and northern Peru. A number of popular food taxa found today below 2,000 m on either side of the Andes are relatively abundant in the collection. The identification of agouti, lowland paca, and peccary could also indicate the introduction of extralocal animals or animal parts to Challuabamba.

Most identified taxa are relatively rare in the collection, preserving as isolated specimens that are dispersed throughout the archaeological deposits. Deer and rabbit specimens numerically dominate the identified fraction. Their skeletal representation in the assemblage is instructive for assessing aspects of accumulation, preburial deposition, and postburial preservation. Complete carcasses of small-bodied rabbits were likely introduced to the site. Lagomorph skeletons exhibit consistent density-mediated preservation throughout the deposits. Cervids show density-mediated preservation only when underrepresented, higher-density elements are removed from consideration. These elements include long bone mid-shafts, the entire dentary, and lower limbs. In all likelihood, dense mid-shafts were originally deposited at the site yet preserved in unidentifiable form due to fragmentation. High mean temperature and humidity and the fluctuating water table of riverine alluvium likely contributed to specimen fragmentation and density-mediated attrition. Heads and lower limbs were not destroyed *in situ* and were likely never originally deposited at the site. Preserved skeletons of large cervids are dominated by choice meat-bearing limb bones, the inferior utility lower leg portions having been detached through the kinetic articulation of the ankle joint prior to deposition. Major cervid limb bones may also have been modified for marrow extraction. Whether Challuabamba was provisioned with fresh high-meat-yielding body portions or as a desiccated product akin to Andean *chalona,* limited artifactual specimens illustrate that certain underrepresented mammalian skeletal elements were modified for tool manufacture.

Zooarchaeological analysis of preserved archaeofaunal remains from Challuabamba suggests that the identification of select animal products provides additional clues for inferring the likelihood of prehispanic provisioning and long-distance exchange within the northern Andean Formative. Preserved zooarchaeological correlates that indicate the special prehistoric status once afforded Challuabamba include indirect evidence for the selective provisioning of nutritionally prized deer carcass portions and the identification of extralocal animal taxa obtained from lowland areas, probably to the west.

Long-distance exchange is a hallmark of the Late Formative occupations in the southern highlands. Preserved archaeological correlates include durable items like pottery, shells, metals, and lithics, and to this list we can add the exchange of animal products. Marine shells at Challuabamba clearly implicate the easily accessed western lowlands. In later times, *Spondylus* in particular is associated in archaeological contexts with domesticated animal specimens introduced from the south (Stahl 2003). Although the excavated deposits contained no trace of foreign animal domesticates, the identification of ocean catfish, crocodile, agouti, paca, and peccary offers compelling evidence for prehistoric contacts between far-flung areas at an early date. Fish, deer, and peccary meat are mentioned in colonial period chronicles as exchange items that were often transported over long distances between lowland and highland areas within the Northern Andes (e.g., Salomon 1986; Villamarín and Villamarín 1999). Their discovery at Challuabamba offers durable evidence of a similar exchange in the southern highlands, some three thousand years before the arrival of Europeans.

Note

1. The Challuabamba collection was temporarily housed in the *bodega* of the Instituto de Patrimonio Cultural, Dirección Regional del Austro, in Cuenca. In May 2002 I removed all bone sample bags from the larger collection and inventoried each field specimen bag while screening the bones through fine mesh in order to remove adhering soil. In early June we shipped the collection to an open and secure patio area across town for washing. Two students from the Escuela de Restauración de Bienes Muebles and I cleaned the collection in water with toothbrushes and picks. All provenience data were checked against the original inventory and recorded onto new plastic bags, into which all specimens were repacked after complete drying. The collection was shipped by air express in July 2002 to the Archaeological Analytical Research Facility of the Department of Anthropology, Binghamton University, where it was unpacked and shelved for subsequent analysis.

Analysis was undertaken by provenience, using the facility's reference collection. Identifications were simultaneously recorded in a computerized database (Paradox), along with area, unit, and level data. Each identification was entered into a hierarchically ordered template to accommodate different levels of taxonomic designation (class, order, family, genus). Each zoological identification also included a separate field for recording arbitrary size (small, medium, large) where appropriate. Skeletal element, anatomical portion, and body side were also registered. The presence/absence of all teeth was noted for tooth-bearing bones. Weights of separate and grouped items were recorded to one-hundredth of a gram. Additional attributes were noted where appropriate, including epiphyseal fusion and dental eruption stages; codified heat alteration and anatomical position; breakage and location; articulation; abrasion; carnivore alteration; rodent gnawing; intrusive appearance; polishing; root etching; weathering; carbonate accretion; and human modifications involving butchery and tool production. A specific coding system was employed to monitor density-mediated survivorship in assemblage preservation. The survivorship of individual bone mineral density scan sites for cervid (Lyman 1984) and lagomorph (Pavao and Stahl 1999) specimens was estimated in quartile increments and recorded along with qualitative notation of element, position, and side.

Difficult identifications were placed in separate bags and labeled by provenience for further consultation with reference collections in the departments of Herpetology, Ichthyology, Mammalogy, Ornithology, and Invertebrate Paleontology at the American Museum of Natural History. Representative catfish specimens were sent to, and eventually returned by, Dr. John Lundberg of the National Academy of Sciences, Philadelphia. A stratigraphic series of faunal specimens from Cut 3, Sector G, was submitted to the National Science Foundation–Arizona Accelerator Mass Spectrometry Facility of the University of Arizona for carbon dating. These were returned after small portions were removed for dating purposes. The entire collection was repacked into museum-quality boxes and shipped to Cuenca in August 2003, where it is currently stored on permanent shelves constructed in the *bodega* of the Instituto de Patrimonio Cultural, Dirección Regional del Austro, in Cuenca with funds from the National Science Foundation.

Bibliography

Albuja, Luis
1991 Lista de vertebrados del Ecuador: Mamíferos. *Revista Politécnica* 16(3):163–203.

Arellano, A. Jorge
1994 Loma Pucara: A Formative Site in the Cebadas Valley, Ecuador. *Research and Exploration* 10:118–120.
2002 Primeras evidencias del Formativo Tardío en la Sierra Central del Ecuador. In *Formativo sudamericano: una revaluación*, ed. P. Ledergerber-Crespo, 160–175. Quito: Abya-Yala.

Barnett, Adrian A.
1999 Small Mammals of the Cajas Plateau, Southern Ecuador: Ecology and Natural History. *Bulletin of the Florida Museum of Natural History* 42:161–217.

Bartram, Laurence E., Jr., and Curtis W. Marean
1999 Explaining the "Klasies Pattern": Kua Ethnoarchaeology, the Die Kelders Middle Stone Age Archaeofauna, Long Bone Fragmentation and Carnivore Ravaging. *Journal of Archaeological Science* 26:9–29.

Bennett, Wendell C.
1946 *Excavations in the Cuenca Region, Ecuador.* Yale University Publications in Anthropology 35. New Haven: Yale University Press.

Bequaert, Joseph C.
1948 Monograph of the Strophocheilidae, a Neotropical Family of Terrestrial Mollusks. *Bulletin of the Museum of Comparative Zoology* 100:1–210.

Bermann, Marc
1994 *Lukumarta: Household Archaeology in Prehispanic Bolivia.* Princeton: Princeton University Press.

Blandín Landívar, Carlos
1977 *El clima y sus características en el Ecuador.* Quito: XI Asamblea General y Reuniones Panamericanas de Consulta Conexas.

Bodmer, Richard E., and Lyle K. Sowls
1993 The Collared Peccary (*Tayassu tajacu*). In *Pigs, Peccaries, and Hippos*, ed. William L. R. Oliver, 13–22. Gland, Switzerland: International Union for Conservation of Nature and Natural Resources.

Braun, Robert
1982 The Formative as Seen from the Southern Ecuadorian Highlands. In *Primer simposio de correlaciones antropológicas andino-mesoamericano*, ed. Jorge G. Marcos and Presley Norton, 41–119. Guayaquil: Escuela Superior Politécnica del Litoral.

Bruhns, Karen O.
1989 Intercambio entre la costa y la sierra en el Formativo Tardío: nuevas

evidencias del Azuay. In *Relaciones interculturales en el área ecuatorial del Pacífico durante la época precolombina,* ed. J.-F. Bouchard and M. Guinea, 57–74. British Archaeological Reports, International Series 503. Oxford: BAR.

2003 Social and Cultural Development in the Ecuadorian Highlands and Eastern Lowlands during the Formative. In *Archaeology of Formative Ecuador,* ed. J. Scott Raymond and Richard L. Burger, 125–174. Washington, D.C.: Dumbarton Oaks Research Library and Collection.

Bruhns, Karen O., James H. Burton, and George R. Miller

1990 Excavations at Pirincay in the Paute Valley of Southern Ecuador, 1985–1988. *Antiquity* 64:221–233.

Bruhns, Karen O., James H. Burton, and Arthur Rostoker

1994 La cerámica "incisa en franjas rojas": evidencia de intercambio entre la sierra y el oriente en el Formativo Tardío del Ecuador. In *Tecnología y organización de la producción cerámica prehispánica en los Andes,* 53–66. Lima: Pontificia Universidad Católica del Perú.

Burgess, Warren E.

1989 *An Atlas of Freshwater and Marine Catfishes: A Preliminary Survey of the Siluriformes.* Neptune City, N.J.: T. F. H. Publications.

Cañadas Cruz, L.

1983 *El mapa bioclimático y ecológico del Ecuador.* Quito: Banco Central del Ecuador.

Collier, Donald, and John V. Murra

1943 *Survey and Excavations in Southern Ecuador.* Anthropological Series 35. Chicago: Field Museum of Natural History.

Currier, Mary Jean P.

1983 *Felis concolor. Mammalian Species* 200:1–7.

Darwent, Christyann M., and R. Lee Lyman

2002 Detecting the Postburial Fragmentation of Carpals, Tarsals, and Phalanges. In *Advances in Forensic Taphonomy: Method, Theory, and Archaeological Perspectives,* ed. W. D. Haglund and M. H. Sorg, 355–377. Boca Raton: CRC Press.

Donkin, R. A.

1985 The Peccary—With Observations on the Introduction of Pigs to the New World. *Transactions of the American Philosophical Society* 75(5):1–152.

Downer, Craig C.

1996 The Mountain Tapir, Endangered "Flagship" Species of the High Andes. *Oryx* 30:45–58.

Eisenberg, John F., and Kent H. Redford

1999 *Mammals of the Neotropics.* Vol. 3. Chicago: University of Chicago Press.

Gomis, Dominique

2000 La cerámica Formativa Tardía de la sierra austral del Ecuador. In *Formativo sudamericano: una revaluación,* ed. P. Ledergerber-Crespo, 139–153. Quito: Abya-Yala.

Gorzula, Stefan, and Andrés Eloy Seijas

1989 The Common Caiman. In *Crocodiles: Their Ecology, Management and Con-*

servation, 44–61. Gland, Switzerland: International Union for Conservation of Nature and Natural Resources.

Grieder, Terence, James D. Farmer, Antonio Carrillo, and Bradford M. Jones

2002 Art and Prestige among Noble Houses of the Equatorial Andes. In *Andean Archaeology II: Landscape and Society*, ed. H. Silverman and W. H. Isbell, 157–177. New York: Kluwer Academic.

Guffroy, Jean

1989 Las tradiciones culturales de Catamayo en el ámbito Formativo Andino. In *Antropología del Ecuador: memorias del Primer Simposio Europeo sobre Antropología del Ecuador,* ed. S. Moreno Yañez, 113–133. Quito: Abya-Yala.

1994 *Cerro Nañañique: un établissement monumental de la période formative, en limite de désert (Haut Piura, Pérou).* Paris: Orstom.

Guffroy, J., N. Almeida, P. LeCoq, C. Caillavet, F. Duverneuil, L. Emperaire, and B. Arnaud

1987 *Loja préhispanique: recherches archéologiques dans les Andes méridionales de l'équateur.* Institut Français d'Études Andines. Paris: Éditions Recherche sur le Civilisations Synthèse 27.

Herring, Susan W.

1985 Morphological Correlates of Masticatory Patterns in Peccaries and Pigs. *Journal of Mammalogy* 66:603–617.

Hocquenghem, Anne-Marie

1993 Rutas de entrada del mullu en el extremo norte del Perú. *Bulletin de l'Institut Français d'Études Andines* 22:701–719.

1999 En torno al mullu: manjar predilecto de los poderosos inmortales. In *Spondylus: ofrenda sagrada y símbolo de paz,* 57–102. Arequipa: Fundación Telefónica del Perú.

Hocquenghem, Anne-Marie, Jaime Idrovo, Peter Kaulicke, and Dominique Gomis

1993 Bases del intercambio entre las sociedades norperuanas y surecuatorianas: una zona de transición entre 1500 A.C. y 600 D.C. *Bulletin de l'Institut Français d'Études Andines* 22:443–466.

Hocquenghem, Anne-Marie, and Manuel Peña Ruiz

1994 La talla del material malacológico en Tumbes. *Bulletin de l'Institut Français d'Études Andines* 23:209–229.

Idrovo Urigüen, Jaime

2000 El Formativo en la sierra ecuatoriana. In *Formativo sudamericano: una revaluación,* ed. P. Ledergerber-Crespo, 114–123. Quito: Abya-Yala.

Izumi, Seiichi, and Kauo Terada, editors

1972 *Excavations at Kotosh, Peru: A Report on the Third and Fourth Expeditions.* Tokyo: Tokyo University Press.

Kaulicke, Peter

1991 El Período Intermedio Temprano en el Alto Piura: avances del proyecto arqueológico "Alto Piura" (1987–1990). *Bulletin de l'Institut Française d'Études Andines* 20:381–422.

Keen, A. Myra

1971 *Sea Shells of Tropical West America: Marine Mollusks from Baja California to Peru.* Palo Alto: Stanford University Press.

Lanning, Edward P.

1963   *A Ceramic Sequence for the Piura and Chira Coast, North Peru.* University of California Publications in American Archaeology and Ethnology 46(2). Berkeley: University of California Press.

Leme, Jose Luiz M.

1973   Anatomy and Systematics of the Neotropical Strophocheiloidea (Gastropoda, Pulmonata) with the Description of a New Family. *Arquivos de Zoologia* 23:295–337.

Lyman, R. Lee

1984   Bone Density and Differential Survivorship of Fossil Classes. *Journal of Anthropological Archaeology* 3:259–299.

1994   *Vertebrate Taphonomy.* Cambridge: Cambridge University Press.

Lynch, Thomas F., and Susan Pollock

1981   La arqueología de la Cueva Negra de Chobsi. *Miscelánea Antropológica Ecuatoriana* 1:92–119.

MacNeish, Richard S., and Antoinette Nelken-Turner

1980   Bone Tools. In *Prehistory of the Ayacucho Basin, Vol. 4: Non-Ceramic Artifacts,* ed. R. S. MacNeish, R. K. Vierra, A. Nelken-Turner, and C. J. Phagan, 309–321. Ann Arbor: University of Michigan Press.

Madrigal, T. Cregg, and Julie Zimmerman Holt

2002   White-Tailed Deer Meat and Marrow Return Rates and Their Application to Eastern Woodland Archaeology. *American Antiquity* 67:745–759.

Marean, Curtis W.

1991   Measuring Post-depositional Destruction of Bone in Archaeological Assemblages. *Journal of Archaeological Science* 18:677–694.

1998   A Critique of the Evidence for Scavenging by Neanderthals and Early Modern Humans: New Data from Kobeh Cave (Zagros Mountains, Iran) and Die Kelders Cave 1 Layer 10 (South Africa). *Journal of Human Evolution* 35:11–136.

Marean, Curtis W., and Carol J. Frey

1997   Animal Bones from Cave Sites to Cities: Reverse Utility Curves as Methodological Artifacts. *American Antiquity* 62:698–711.

Marean, Curtis W., and Soo Yeun Kim

1998   Mousterian Large-Mammal Remains from Kobeh Cave. *Current Anthropology* 39 (supplement):S79–S113.

Marean, Curtis W., Lillian M. Spencer, Robert J. Blumenschine, and Salvatore D. Capaldo

1992   Captive Hyena Bone Choice and Destruction, the Schlepp effect and Olduvai Archaeofaunas. *Journal of Archaeological Science* 19:101–121.

Marshall, Larry G.

1978   *Chironectes minimus. Mammalian Species* 109:1–6.

Mayer, John J., and Ralph M. Wetzel

1987   *Tayassu pecari. Mammalian Species* 293:1–7.

Miller, George R., and Anne L. Gill

1990   Zooarchaeology at Pirincay, a Formative Period Site in Highland Ecuador. *Journal of Field Archaeology* 17:49–68.

Molina, Misael, and Jesús Molinari

1999   Taxonomy of Venezuelan White-Tailed Deer (*Odocoileus,* Cervidae,

Mammalia), Based on Cranial and Mandibular Traits. *Canadian Journal of Zoology* 77:632–645.

Nitikman, Leslie Z.

1985   *Sciurus granatensis. Mammalian Species* 1, no. 246:1–8.

Patzelt, Erwin

1989   *Fauna del Ecuador.* Quito: Banco Central del Ecuador.

Pavao, Barnet, and Peter W. Stahl

1999   Structural Density Assays of Leporid Skeletal Elements with Implications for Taphonomic, Actualistic and Archaeological Research. *Journal of Archaeological Science* 26:53–66.

Pérez, Elizabeth M.

1992   *Agouti paca. Mammalian Species* 404:1–7.

Peyton, Bernard

1980   Ecology, Distribution and Food Habits of Spectacled Bears, *Tremarctos ornatus,* in Peru. *Journal of Mammalogy* 61:639–652.

Ravines, Rogger, editor

1978   *Tecnología andina.* Lima: Instituto de Estudios Peruanos.

Rehren, Thilo, and Mathilde Temme

1992   Pre-Columbian Gold Processing at Putushío, South Ecuador: The Archaeometallurgical Evidence. In *Archaeometry of Pre-Columbian Sites and Artifacts,* ed. D. A. Scott and P. Meyers, 267–284. Los Angeles: Getty Conservation Institute.

Ridgely, Robert S., and Paul J. Greenfield

2001a   *The Birds of Ecuador: Field Guide.* Ithaca: Cornell University Press.

2001b   *The Birds of Ecuador: Status, Distribution, and Taxonomy.* Ithaca: Cornell University Press.

Rosas, Hermilio, and Ruth Shady

1975   Sobre el Período Formativo en la sierra del extremo norte del Perú. *Arqueológicas* 15:6–35.

Ross, James P.

1998   *Crocodiles: Status Survey and Conservation Action Plan.* 2nd ed. Gland, Switzerland: International Union for Conservation of Nature and Natural Resources.

Rostoker, Arthur

1998   Recuerdos de la montaña mágica, revisitados. In *Intercambio y comercio entre sierra, selva, y costa,* ed. Felipe Cárdenas-Arroyo and Tamara L. Bray, 154–162. Bogotá: Universidad de los Andes.

Salomon, Frank

1986   *Native Lords of Quito in the Age of the Incas: The Political Economy of North Andean Chiefdoms.* Cambridge: Cambridge University Press.

Shady, Ruth

1987   Tradición y cambio en las sociedades Formativas de Bagua. *Revista Andina* 5:457–487.

Shipman, Pat, Wendy Bosler, and Karen Lee Davis

1981   Butchering of Giant Geladas at an Acheulian Site. *Current Anthropology* 22:257–268.

Smythe, Nicholas

1978   *The Natural History of the Central American Agouti* (Dasyprocta punctata). Smithsonian Contributions to Zoology 257. Washington, D.C.: Smithsonian Institution.

Stahl, Peter W.

1999 Structural Density of Domesticated South American Camelid Skeletal Elements and the Archaeological Investigation of Prehistoric Andean Ch'arki. *Journal of Archaeological Science* 26:1347–1368.

2003 Pre-Columbian Andean Animal Domesticates at the Edge of Empire. *World Archaeology* 34:470–483.

2005 Selective Faunal Provisioning in the Southern Highlands of Formative Ecuador. *Latin American Antiquity* 16:313–328.

Stahl, Peter W., and J. Stephen Athens

2001 A High Elevation Zooarchaeological Assemblage from the Northern Andes of Ecuador. *Journal of Field Archaeology* 28:161–176.

Temme, Mathilde

2000 El Formativo en Putushío—sierra sur del Ecuador. In *Formativo sudamericano: una revaluación,* ed. P. Ledergerber-Crespo, 124–138. Quito: Abya-Yala.

Thorbjarnarson, John B.

1989 Ecology of the American Crocodile, *Crocodylus acutus.* In *Crocodiles: Their Ecology, Management and Conservation,* 228–258. Gland, Switzerland: International Union for Conservation of Nature and Natural Resources.

Tirira, Diego

1999 *Mamíferos del Ecuador.* Museo de Zoología Publicación Especial 2. Quito: Pontificia Universidad Católica del Ecuador.

Villa, Paola, and Eric Mahieu

1991 Breakage Patterns of Human Long Bones. *Journal of Human Evolution* 21:27–48.

Villalba, Marcelo

1988 *Cotocollao: una aldea Formativa de Valle de Quito.* Serie Monográfica 2. Quito: Museos del Banco Central.

Villamarín, Juan, and Judith Villamarín

1999 Chiefdoms: The Prevalence and Persistence of "Señoríos Naturales" 1400 to European Conquest. In *The Cambridge History of the Native Peoples of the Americas,* vol. 3 (1), ed. F. Salomon and B. Schwartz, 577–667. Cambridge: Cambridge University Press.

Voss, Robert S.

1992 A Revision of the South American Species of *Sigmodon* (Mammalia: Muridae) with Notes on Their Natural History and Biogeography. *American Museum Novitates* 3050:1–56.

Reconstructing Challuabamba's History

12

Despite having no trace of ruins on the surface, the site named for the village of Challuabamba has been a focus of study for many years and the subject of various theories on its cultural connections. This chapter considers our findings as they provide clues to the lives of its ancient population.

Sometime before the period bracketed by our two earliest radiocarbon dates (2300–1700 BC from Cut 1 Level 4 and Cut 3 Level 4) small groups of people living in the lowlands of western Ecuador began to wander eastward into the Andean highlands. We have little direct knowledge of these people, but some pieces of the puzzle in combination give us a picture of the way of life that they developed in their new home.

The radiocarbon dates from Challuabamba and the style of the early pottery there suggest that the settlers were familiar with Valdivia pottery of Phase 6, dated 2100–1950 BC, and also had a knowledge of maize agriculture that could be adapted to the new environment. Pottery and maize were two of the principal cultural attributes spreading through the Americas at that time. The place they chose to settle must have been carefully selected: a major river valley with numerous tributary streams, with low passes through the mountains to the north and south, and relatively easy access to the Amazon forest lands to the east. While a small Archaic population had occupied this region for centuries, our study found no evidence of their presence.

Our excavations were located where alignments of large stones were eroding out of the riverbanks. Those were the only traces of ancient construction; whatever surface mounds, platforms, or walls had once existed had been obliterated long ago. The alignments of stone appear to have supported the edges of platforms on which perishable buildings were erected. A few postholes were found that hint at the stockade-style walls, along with chunks of mud plaster shaped by poles and cords. Thatched roofs would have been required by the frequent rains. The remaining stone alignments suggest that this area was a center of the ancient settlement.

Agriculture and Health

Two of the defining features of the Formative are pottery and agriculture, which in the Americas included domesticated maize. The cultivation of maize already had a history on the Ecuadorian coastal lowlands: a "primitive maize" was probably grown by the preceramic Las Vegas people (Stothert 1985:634), and intensive maize agriculture was found in the coastal river valleys by late Valdivia times. Maize was the basic carbohydrate in the diet of the new settlers. Among the indications of a diet rich in maize are pathological conditions produced by an iron deficiency, which maize tends to produce. Ubelaker's analysis of the human skeletons finds evidence of iron-deficiency anemias, particularly affecting young children that produced dental caries, and a pathological thickening of the vault of the skull called porotic hyperostosis. The data, according to Ubelaker, suggest "a level of adult morbidity not recorded in other highland samples."

This disturbing description of Challuabamba's health is by no means unique in the Pre-Columbian world. A recent paper by Andrew Scherer, Lori Wright, and Cassady Yoder (2007:100) on the diet of the Maya site of Piedras Negras concludes: "The data presented in this paper demonstrate that maize was a primary staple food of the ancient Maya at Piedras Negras. We documented high levels of dental caries, porotic hyperostosis, and high carbon isotope ratios that together point toward a diet rich in maize."

The two largest collections at Challuabamba are ceramics and animal bones, which tell us some similar things about life in that community, among them that local tastes depended for their satisfaction in part on external connections. Imported meat and fish products seem to have provided some segments of the site's population with an unusually good diet, but apparently everyone suffered from ailments attributable to a diet whose basic carbohydrate was maize.

Some features of the food supply (as described by Stahl) are particularly noteworthy. The clustering of animal bones in the upper levels of Cuts 3 and 4, with almost all the artiodactyl bones (mainly deer and peccary) as well as catfish, rabbit, and agouti in that small area, implies a group of inhabitants who received especially high-quality imported cuts of meat and fish. Stahl makes a convincing case for the selective import of the best cuts of the deer and, more surprising, the presence of the bones of ocean catfish (presumably from the Gulf of Guayaquil), probably imported dried and salted. The colonial sources cited by Stahl describing fish, deer, and peccary meat as items in long-distance exchange support the picture of Challuabamba as an important center of a trade network some three thousand years earlier. Stahl's analysis provides important new evidence of Formative Period interregional contacts.

This brief account of the resources available to sustain life in the highlands gives an impression of relative abundance. That may be a true impression if we compare Challuabamba with its contemporaries in the Peruvian highlands. While the Peruvian coast was growing maize before 2000 BC, at La Galgada in a highland valley the first sign of maize was a single small cob imported from elsewhere about 1500 BC (Smith 1988:126, 147–148, 151). La Galgada was one of several contemporary sites, of which "none has a clearly defined primary carbohydrate resource," according to Earle Smith (1988:145).

As Ubelaker notes, the four individuals whose remains he examined died at the ages of six to seven years, fifteen to thirty years, twenty-five to thirty-five years, and over sixty years. By modern standards all but the oldest are early deaths, but we must take into account that it is virtually certain that these were survivors in a community in which half the infants born died before the age of five, as was true worldwide before the advent of modern medicine. In spite of these conditions, it appears that by about 1600 BC the valleys of the Tomebamba and its tributaries were one of the most populous regions in the southern highlands of Ecuador.

Interregional Contacts and Exchange

Although we can identify a few items that were imported at Challuabamba, it is hard to identify what might have been exchanged. Coca was imported from lower elevations on the eastern slopes, to judge by a well-used bone wand in Burial 6 used for dipping lime, and coca may have been traded on to other sites in the highlands or western lowlands. Pottery was surely a trade item, to judge by the influence of Challuabamba's style on its neighbors.

E. Jean Langdon (1981:101) describes "trade items" as including "magical knowledge" and "hallucinogenic visions and songs as well as associated material objects" that are part of shamans' rituals employing *yagé* (*Banisteriopsis*). It is quite likely that a large site such as Challuabamba may have had famous shamans who attracted apprentices, given the prevalence of shamanism in the region. It has been proposed, with particular reference to Valdivia, that ceramic

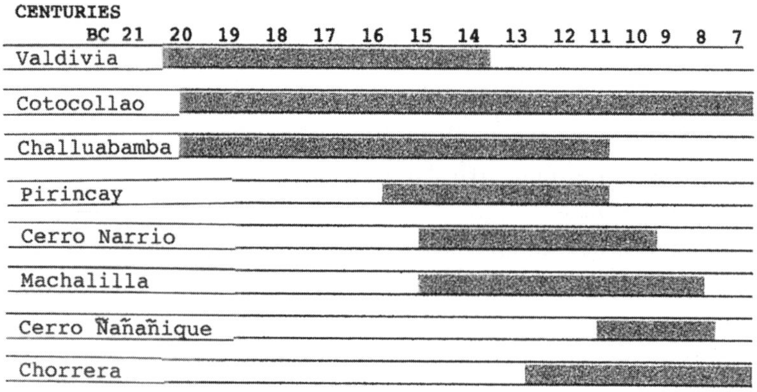

Figure 12.1. Proposed relative ceramic chronology for selected Formative sites.

figurines functioned as visual aids in shamanic ritual (Stahl 1986), which might also apply to Challuabamba, especially in its earliest period.

The historical significance that we attribute to Challuabamba's ceramics depends in some measure on the period it represents and particularly on how it is related to the great Chorrera style (as described in Chapter 5). The comparisons noted there leave no doubt that Challuabamba precedes Chorrera, which derives some features from the late phases of Challuabamba ceramics, after about 1300 BC. This places Challuabamba in the direct line of descent from the Early Formative Valdivia style to the Late Formative Chorrera style, which makes the somewhat controversial designation Middle Formative seem appropriate (Figure 12.1).

The Red-Banded Incised Style

Evidence is accumulating that suggests a wider and much longer influence of Challuabamba's ceramic style in a region along the eastern slope of the Andes and into the northern highlands of Peru as far south as Ancash. The style of ceramic decoration called Red-Banded Incised (RBI) provides the best evidence currently available for an area of interaction (Figure 4.6).

This beautiful and distinctive style of decoration was first described at Cerro Narrío (and Alausí and Macas) by Collier and Murra (1943:61–62). It is only partly described by its initials (RBI), since at Challuabamba, where currently available evidence suggests that it was invented before c. 1800 BC (Cut 3 Level 5), the red bands with incised borders on the exterior were always accompanied by an interior decoration of splashed red paint (see Figure 4.6). While the interior red splash and exterior red bands with incision were never separated at Challuabamba, at Pirincay (about 20 km east of Challuabamba) the splashed interior appears alone early ("mid-2nd millennium BC"; Bruhns et al. 1990:224) and the red-banded incised (RBI) exterior appears alone in the later period, c. 400 BC–AD 100 (Bruhns et al. 1994:58).

As defined at Pirincay the RBI type has a cream paste with moderately thick walls and decoration only on the exterior. Red bands formed geometric designs with fine incised outlines (Bruhns et al. 1994:53). Since the splashed interior appears early at Pirincay and the RBI exterior is found many centuries later, it appears that the interior and exterior decorative styles diffused separately. A petrographic study of the Pirincay RBI sherds suggests that they were imports to Pirincay and were produced at an unknown site close to the Sangay volcano on the eastern margin of the highlands north of Macas (Bruhns et al. 1990, 1994). A petrographic analysis of one RBI sherd from Challuabamba (see Chapter 3) is very similar to that reported for the Pirincay samples, with the exception of the inclusion of eutaxitic tuff and the conclusion that the minerals were believed to be natural inclusions in the clay source rather than added as temper.

The history of RBI at Challuabamba tends to support the implication that at least most of the RBI pottery found there was produced there. Fifteen individual RBI bowls have been identified: two from the deep Level 5 (3.A, 3.G), three from Level 4a and 4b (3.H), three (twelve sherds) from Level 3 (3.H), five from Level 2 (3.H, 3.J, 3.I), and two from surface collections (X-1-2). All appear to be part of wide bowls (18–31 cm diameter, 5 to 8 cm high). The earlier bowls have straight walls slightly slanted inward, with a fairly sharp angle to a flat base. Some of the later examples are smaller (18–20 cm diameter) and have walls that curve slightly inward. The surface finds are larger and have straight walls slanted outward but are hard to place chronologically. All these vessels seem alike in their design: on the exterior a very light cream slip highly burnished, having a red band at the rim and usually at the base, with wide red vertical bands dividing the exterior panels, which may contain an angular or circular motif; all the painted areas were bordered with incision, which was usually applied after the paint. Interiors were a burnished cream slip splashed with red paint. All these were notably fine pieces.

Of the various identifiable types of vessels produced at Challuabamba, the Red-Banded Incised with a Splashed interior is among the most enduring and consistent: neither the exterior nor the interior decoration ever appears alone or in a different context. That implies that the vessels and their design had an important use and symbolism, although it is no longer interpretable.

Mapping the finds of RBI and Splashed pottery shows only Pirincay briefly experimenting with the splashed interior but the exterior red geometric shapes bordered with incision spreading widely to the north (Cañar, Alausí) and from Pirincay northeast to Macas and the Upano Valley, with just one find south at Villa Jubones. At Challuabamba the interior and exterior were inseparable, so the transfer of the design in separate parts means that the design had lost its symbolism and become merely fashionable. The exterior design at Challuabamba was limited to red circles, wide bands (vertical, slanted, or horizontal), and stepped pyramids, with one angular volute. The RBI sherds from Cerro Narrío, Shillu, Alausí, Macas (Collier and Murra 1943: Plates 6, 7, 34), and Pirincay (Hammond and Bruhns 1987: Figure 6; Bruhns et al. 1990: Figure 10) show denser and more varied designs combining circles, steps, triangles, and pointed shapes— surely a later development of the style. Whatever trade there may have been in RBI pottery (and it may have been considerable), it did not emanate from Challuabamba. None of the outlying examples show the style as it appears there; they represent the later elaboration found at Pirincay and Macas.

The most recent development in this history of Red-Banded Incised greatly expands its range in time and space. Warren DeBoer (2003:295–297) describes Red-Banded Incised as "an apparent import" at Pirincay "between 400 BC and AD 1" and later as a local adoption in the eastern lowlands around Macas and Sangay and ultimately, about AD 900, at Cumancaya on the upper Ucayali. According to DeBoer (2003:297), "similarities between Cumancaya designs and the Ecuadorian materials generally glossed as Red Banded Incised (RBI) are sufficiently specific to argue for a historical relationship between the two." This is an unusually long chain of historical connections and one based on reasonably well dated material.

Some of Challuabamba's most direct trade connections seem to have been southward into Cajamarca and Ancash, where oxidized cream and white wares were popular. In the Recuay style at Pashash (AD 300–600) oxidized and reduced wares retained the relationship they had at Challuabamba: a majority being cream or orange with red-painted decorations, a minority being reduction-fired burnished blackware. Also, small effigy heads, very similar to those attached to Challuabamba jars, were attached to some Pashash Recuay pots

(Grieder 1978:62, 139). The enduring influence of popular additions to the inventory of designs is noteworthy. Although a very small percentage of ceramic products appear to have been exported from their source, they were still so widely traded that they contributed to a shared cultural language of form and style.

Ceramic Production

David Hill's petrographic analysis of the sherds from Challuabamba, along with two sherds from the Chorrera region chosen for comparison, shows consistent contrasts between the clays of those two regions (see Chapter 3). Compared with Chorrera, Cerro Narrío's clay sources had a much closer relationship to those in use at Challuabamba. As analyzed by Sharat K. Roy (1943:91), the clays used in the three wares at Cerro Narrío are similar in their volcanic sources. Roy believed that the masses of tuff, pumice, or calcic plagioclase were added as temper by the potters, but Hill considers all the minerals and rock fragments natural inclusions, not added by the potter as temper, since the weathering and range of particle sizes are similar to those of the other constituents. The main difference between Cerro Narrío clays and Challuabamba's is the greater weathering endured by all the volcanic materials as they were carried by streams down the valley. The eight specimens from Challuabamba have many features in common but show the exploitation of at least three separate clay sources, not surprising for a site with a long history of intense pottery production.

Considering the amount of pottery that has come to light, it might seem surprising that a potter's production area has not been found. In the Pre-Columbian world the arts and crafts were generally practiced in domestic settings, often with the collaboration of family members. A recent study of craft production at the Classic Maya center of Aguateca, in its last days and under threat of attack, shows "a significant portion of Maya elites, both men and women, engaged in artistic creation and craft production. . . . Artistic and craft production appears to have been a common pursuit among Classic Maya elites at Aguateca, including courtiers of the highest rank and even members of the royal family" (Aoyama 2007:24). James Farmer's suggestion that the set of potter's tools placed in the fill of Burial 6 might belong to the elite male (see Chapter 9) in that burial gains credibility in the light of Aoyama's analysis. Although widely separated in time and space, Challuabamba and Classic Maya Aguateca appear to have shared some fundamental traits of social structure and technical practice. According to Aoyama (2007:24), "Classic

Maya elite men and women participated collaboratively in many aspects of artistic and craft production. . . . Artistic creation by noble men and women as well as the garnering of ideological, religious, and esoteric production knowledge were important in exclusionary tactics and elite identity at Late Classic period Aguateca."

The art and craft production of individuals in these ancient communities was usually part of a multiple social identity (as warrior, potter or stonecarver, ritual specialist, etc.), as was the Maya case. Both utilitarian and luxury items were produced for local use but also for interregional exchange. Aguateca, a small and relatively short-lived center, is hard to compare with Challuabamba, which was larger, longer-lived, and formed part of a much larger and more interactive region. Nevertheless, both these centers were part of a preindustrial world in which full-time industrial production in the modern sense was unknown.

As we handle the remaining fragments of Challuabamba's pottery, it is hard to imagine them as the work of laborers producing under the lash of clock and quota. The contrasting qualities of participation in a shared esthetic and commitment to a personal expression—which I have felt to be basic qualities of Challuabamba's ceramic work, evident in the careful formation and ornament of the clay bodies in a strong local style—are easiest to imagine as the work of independent artist-artisans.

That description helps us imagine the community that made and used Challuabamba's ceramics. The ritual and offerings that accompanied burial of the dead must surely have been one of the focal ceremonial activities. The variety of vessel forms and their development toward more complex forms with more decoration tell us that their presentation and use on ceremonious occasions were part of their function. Ownership of the most prestigious vessels, such as Burnished Black bottles and service vessels, would enhance the reputation of a chief.

The offerings that accompanied burials were principally pottery vessels, and many of them unusually fine examples. The two intact burials in Cut 3 most likely involved people of some standing: one a young child, the other a mature male with valuable offerings. The four intact burials in Cut 2 likewise appear to have been individuals of some importance, as fine pottery offerings and an earspool suggest. As Farmer makes clear, the burials conform to traditions still followed by Cañari people in the modern period (since the fifteenth century, when colonial observers began to describe their culture). The long-term stability of life in the valleys of Azuay, despite Inca and Spanish conquests, suggests a core of cultural values that have retained their validity despite the impacts of historic changes.

The quality that comes to mind in working with the piles of pot-sherds coming out of the excavations is the potter's sensitive attention to every feature of the emerging pot. The thousands of sherds inevitably include a majority of thick basal sherds and inexpressive body sherds but also a sufficient minority that catch the eye or the fingers as somehow expressive. When it is possible to reassemble some sherds into a fragment that expresses some of the original content, it is not merely the pleasure of that achievement that gives satisfaction but also the sudden sharing of a vision or intention with the potter. While that intention may have been to boil dinner, there is almost always an intention to gain the pleasure of a contrast, an unexpected difference in texture or color, weight, or shape. Those are the fundamentals of ceramic expression, and the ancient potters were well aware of them. Two pots are good examples of the esthetic of contrast that was basic to Challuabamba's distinctive style.

The Burnished Black effigy vase from Burial 6, despite being made of the serious ritual ware, seems to strike all observers as amusing. The basic contrast is between the large and elegant neck and rim and the small, bulging form of the jaguar-catfish which carries it. The awkward incised spots appear to be later additions, but they enhance the contrast between the body and the spout: the spout making the effigy appear still more awkward, the effigy making the spout appear even more excessively elegant.

The Burial 6 offering contained so many special items (including imported seashells and the jaguar-catfish vase) that it was clearly considered valuable but probably amusing as well. If the deceased was a potter, as seems likely, there is also the possibility that he made the vase himself and knew its value.

The standard color scheme at Challuabamba was cream, red, and black, usually applied as a slip, a paint, and a smudge from a smoky fire. A late example is the large tecomate from Cut 2.B Level 1 (see Figure 4.14). The standard color scheme is a minor part of its appeal. The shape and size of a pumpkin, it achieves contrast mainly by texture, weight, and shape. In picking up the large globular vessel, the first sensation is that it weighs nothing, like holding a balloon. Inspection reveals walls about 2 to 3 mm thick, with its light weight enhanced by its light color. Then one notices the texture of the body: a very slight roughness produced by long, shallow burnish lines running from the narrow red rim to the widest part of the body. The long vertical lines are nearly invisible, since the only contrast is the burnish of the line against the matte cream surface of the wall. Then one observes the delicate red rim, the tiny effigy figure just below the rim, and a light orange wash from the rim beside the tiny figure as well as a spatter of tiny orange dots over the exterior.

When the vessel is turned upside down, the main areas of paint are found on the lower part of one side: a wide irregular splash of orange paint appears, with a small area of black inside it, perhaps applied with a smoky burning stick. All these effects appear accidental but are obviously intentional and controlled. The appealing contrast in this vessel is the extreme expertise of its techniques, with the appearance of casual ease in their application.

Shamanism and Cosmology

Shamanism appears to have been the dominant form of spiritual expression in South America from earliest times. Even late in the twentieth century Michael Harner (1972:122) could report that among the neighboring Jívaro "about one out of every four adult men is a shaman." Successful shamans attracted apprentices and younger shamans desirous of advanced training (Langdon 1981) and were an economic as well as spiritual asset to their local communities. The highlands of Ecuador and Colombia are still occupied by indigenous groups in which shamans are believed to have the power to transform into jaguars and in which *yagé*-inspired visions verify "their world view of a multilayered universe inhabited by spirits" (Langdon 1981:112).

Most of what we have learned about Challuabamba concerns the practical aspects of life and was not an intentional expression of ideology. It is in the symbols inscribed on stamps and seals that we can find intentional messages about fundamental concerns and beliefs. The most elaborate of these compositions are on the fragmentary cylinder seals. If, as seems probable, they were all originally complete circles, we have recovered less than half of every example. This very likely means that they were intentionally broken and the parts dispersed—perhaps in several separate burials or ritual offerings. Yet even these fragmentary messages are worth examining.

Cylinder seals Nos. 3 and 8 have the most complex designs. No. 3 centers on a quincunx from which wide diagonal bands emerge, a design appropriate to the galaxy: the Milky Way moves across the sky at changing angles during the year, which would have been very clear in the brilliant night sky at Challuabamba. With these bands are a birdlike eye and winglike designs to assure us that the reference is to the sky. No. 8 centers on a square flanked by wings, with a broad volute below. If the volute is always connected with the feline, and the wings are connected with the sky, then we have a square in the sky—either the area covered during the year by the sun's path or a constellation. The sun rules the celestial region; the feline, who is the shaman in jaguar form, rules the terrestrial region. This describes the cosmos visited by shamans and their followers in visions induced by consumption of *yagé* in which they travel through the multilayered universe and encounter powerful spirits (Langdon 1981). The esthetic of contrasts in their ceramic art conforms to the contrast experienced in shamanic rituals between the natural world and the visionary world, which for the ritualist has become the real world. The artists and artisans of Challuabamba witnessed every day the transformation of the mundane clay into the idea, which is to say the ideal: the visionary world of the imagination took form under the artist's hands, to be given near-eternal solidity by passing through the flames of the kiln.

Bibliography

Aoyama, Kazuo
2007   Elite Artists and Craft Producers in Classic Maya Society: Lithic Evidence from Aguateca, Guatemala. *Latin American Antiquity* 18(1):3–26.
Bruhns, Karen Olsen, James H. Burton, and George R. Miller
1990   Excavations at Pirincay in the Paute Valley of Southern Ecuador, 1985–1988. *Antiquity* 64:221–233.
Bruhns, Karen Olsen, James Burton, and Arthur Rostoker
1994   La cerámica "incisa en franjas rojas": evidencia de intercambio entre la sierra y el oriente en el Formativo Tardío del Ecuador. In *Tecnología y organización de la producción de cerámica prehispánica en los Andes,* ed. Izumi Shimada, 53–66. Lima: Pontificia Universidad Católica del Perú, Fondo Editorial.
Collier, Donald, and John Murra
1943   *Survey and Excavations in Southern Ecuador.* Anthropology Series No. 62. Chicago: Field Museum of Natural History.
DeBoer, Warren R.
2003   Ceramic Assemblage Variability in the Formative of Ecuador and Peru. In *Archaeology of Formative Ecuador,* ed. J. S. Raymond and R. L. Burger, 289–336. Washington, D.C.: Dumbarton Oaks.
Grieder, Terence
1978   *The Art and Archaeology of Pashash.* Austin: University of Texs Press.
Hammond, Norman, and Karen Olsen Bruhns
1987   The Paute Valley Project in Ecuador, 1984. *Antiquity* 61:50–56.
Harner, Michael J.
1972   *The Jívaro.* New York: Doubleday Anchor.
Inomata, Takeshi, Daniela Triadan, Erick Ponciano, Estela Pinto, Richard E. Terry, and Markus Eberl
2002   Domestic and Political Lives of Classic Maya Elites: The Excavation of

Rapidly Abandoned Structures at Aguateca, Guatemala. *Latin American Antiquity* 13(3):305–330.

Langdon, E. Jean

1981   Cultural Bases for Trading of Visions and Spiritual Knowledge in the Colombian and Ecuadorian Montaña. In *Networks of the Past: Regional Interaction in Archaeology,* ed. Peter D. Francis, F. J. Kense, and P. G. Duke, 101–116. Calgary: Dept. of Archaeology, University of Calgary.

Roy, Sharat K.

1943   Appendix A: Paste Analysis of Cerro Narrío Wares. In *Survey and Excavations in Southern Ecuador,* by Donald Collier and John Murra, 91. Anthropology Series No. 62. Chicago: Field Museum of Natural History.

Scherer, Andrew K., Lori E. Wright, and Cassady J. Yoder

2007   Bioarchaeological Evidence for Social and Temporal Differences in Diet at Piedras Negras, Guatemala. *Latin American Antiquity* 18(1):85–104.

Smith, C. Earle, Jr.

1988   Floral Remains. In *La Galgada, Peru,* ed. Terence Grieder, Alberto Bueno Mendoza, C. Earle Smith, Jr., and Robert M. Malina, 125–151. Austin: University of Texas Press.

Stahl, Peter W.

1986   Hallucinatory Imagery and the Origin of Early South American Figurine Art. *World Archaeology* 18(1):134–150.

Stothert, Karen E.

1985   The Preceramic Las Vegas Culture of Coastal Ecuador. *American Antiquity* 50(3):613–637.

DeBoer, Warren R., 49: on diffusion of Red-Banded Incised to eastern lowland sites, 212
Dillehay, Tom, on ancestor worship, 152
domed forms, 88–89, 91
domestic setting of art and craft production, 213
dragon subjects, 90

Earspool, 93, 107, 156–157
earth ovens, 28
Ecuador, early technical advances, 8
effigy vessels and figurines, 97; hollow effigy attachments, 103; jaguar-catfish effigy vessel, 100; solid effigy attachments, 101
El Descanso bottle, Duran Collection, 49, 90, 92
Erickson, John, 5
excavation permits, 8: rationale for, 9–10; sample of, 7

faces modeled on bowl exterior, 109
feline theme in designs, 121–124
figurines: hollow, 107–109; solid, 97–99
fillets, 78

Gastropoda (land snails), 167
Gomis, Dominique, 5, 19, 82, 165
Guffroy, Jean, 20, 30, 89

Hammond, Norman, 5
Harner, Michael, 216
Heckenberger, Michael, on shell ornaments, 139
Helms, Mary, on colors, 33
Hill, Betsy D., on Valdivia, 43, 63
Hocquenghem, Anne-Marie, 5
Huancarcuchu, 36, 50
Huayna Capac (Inca emperor), 7

Idrovo Urigüen, Jaime, 5

Jama Coaque cylinder seals, 117
Jaramillo, Juan Pablo, 9

Jubones River, 4

Kotosh, 84

La Emerenciana, pottery decoration at, 62, 63
La Galgada, 1, 3
Langdon, E. Jean, 209
Lanning, Edward, 1, 29
Lathrap, Donald, 30, 111
La Vega, Catamayo, 20
life expectancy, 209
Lippi, Ronald D., 108
Loma Pucara site, 5, 165
Lumbreras, Luis, 90

Machalilla site: carinated pottery from, 43; culture of, 29; figurines from, 108; incised designs on pottery from, 64
maize agriculture, 207; as cause of iron deficiency (porotic hyperostosis), 208
Mammalia (agouti, cotton rat, dog, human, oppossum, paca, peccary, rabbit, rodent, spectacled bear, squirrel, tapir, water puma, white-tailed deer), 173–179
matte orange ware, 76
metallurgy, 27
Mollusca (land snails, marine gastropods, and bivalves), 167
monster designs, 90
Murra, John V., 4

Ñañañique. See Cerro Ñañañique
Naula, Maria, 103

obsidian, 129
Osteichthyes (catfish), 170

Pacopampa, faunal remains at, 165
Pashash, 1, 3
pawsa lliklla, as fertility symbol, 66
Pectinidae (scallops), 169
phases of pottery decoration, 66
Pirincay: faunal remains at, 165;